FIRST
IMPRESSIONS

Twirp,
It is so great to finally
get to know you!

God Bless
Libby

BY JOHN PAUL RIGER

To Our Friend Twirp,
Thanks for all you do for
so many but most of all thanks
for your friendship!

John L

ACKNOWLEDGEMENTS

*This book could not have been written
without the loving and inspired help
of my betrothed.
Wherever you may find words
of wit or optimism within these pages
they most likely came from her.*

~

CONTENTS

PREFACE

My earliest first impression is embedded in my very first memory. At a young age, I recall being startled by our dachshund that jolted from the extreme rear of our station wagon, past my right shoulder, and started snarling and gnashing at the police officer that was asking my mom some questions. That's when I realized that it was hot. I mean we were in sunny terrain somewhere, maybe in the desert southwest. I must have been asleep and was startled by our dog's vicious attempt to protect my mom and our family. What does it all mean? I don't know but police and dogs were integral fixtures of my very first memory. What do they have to do with first impressions? A whole lot when you consider the primal clash between authority and rebellion. It was that very experience that sparked me into the conscious world.

We all have those obscure, faint memories that seem more like figments than fact. Many of them are real, though, and some so impress us as to forever contour our behavior. I have learned to yield to my first impressions and allow them to guide my life. We all have first impressions and rarely are they wrong. We can be fooled on occasion, and that is the subject of this book. God has blessed me with a great memory just as He has blessed us all with remarkable memories. I hope you enjoy the recounting of our true story. Some names have been changed to protect the guilty.

"Be not forgetful to entertain strangers: for thereby some have entertained angels unawares."
HEBREWS 13:2

BACK HOME

I took one last look around, not that I had any more room in my backpack. It was stuffed full, every pocket and pouch. But I had to take just one last look around my room. When we moved to the old farm in Centre County, Pennsylvania, we each got our own room. My eldest sister had already married so there were only four of us kids left. I loved my room. The wallpaper had columns of stock price quotes and article headers from the business section of the newspaper. I used to stare endlessly at the columns of positive and negative numbers not knowing what they meant except that they all had something to do with money.

I painted the ceiling of my room black to kind of match the paper. I felt really bad about it afterwards and painted all the wood trim black so that it would hopefully match. It only got worse and my attempt to refurbish my portion of the dying, dairy farmhouse was a mess. My brothers and sisters tried to help me fix it and between us all we'd painted the ceiling in fluorescent figures. It was supposed to come out like the Sistine Chapel, but it kind of went on its own. At the one end sister Bets had painted a great sunrise with the hand and finger of God outstretched to almost touch that of Adam, or was it Abraham or maybe just man. At the other end brother Charlie had painted a massive mushroom cloud complete with mass destruction and holocaust. I guess in a way my ceiling had a beginning and an end. Among other figures were the Zig Zag man, Puff the magic dragon, peace signs, dogfight biplanes, and Lord only knows what else. Over my door was an old Colorado license plate and the antlers of a six-point, white tail buck.

I put my hand to the American flag that hung on a door covered with squirrel tails and pheasant feathers, the fallen quarry of boyhood taken with my first-ever twenty-gauge, single-shot shotgun. Yeah, it was a boy's room for sure. I'd miss that old room though I knew it was time to leave, to move on, to grow up and become a man.

I shouldered the hefty pack and walked down the hall, then down the stairs to join my bride, mother, and younger brother all waiting for me under the mulberry tree. I gave my mom a hug. She had a curiously happy look about her.

"So where are you guys going?" she asked, almost knowing our answer. I had learned long ago that I couldn't lie to her, but this time I didn't want her to worry.

"Well, we're going to head up to Milesburg and then west to do some camping," I replied unconvincingly. After all, we were a day late getting on our way. We had stuck around an extra day to help clean things up, get them back to normal, and help kick the keg of beer left over from our wedding.

"Now you look here, John," my mother said with a direct and confident smile. "If things get a little rough out there, you two just come right on home. I mean it. There will always be a room for the two of you here." She had profound, maternal instincts and knew damn well we wouldn't be coming home. I played it down, though, and told her that we'd keep in touch and that there was no need to worry at all.

With that, Libby and I threw our backpacks into the trunk of the car and piled into the old '54 Chevy and headed north for the interstate highway that ran through Milesburg. Little brother Hugh, who until my wedding day was my very best friend, hopped into the back seat. We'd grown up together and had already been through thick and thin. We even got into trouble a time or two, but truthfully it was always just good, clean fun. Hugh was fifteen years old and wanted to come with us, but there was no longer any room for him in my life. Our reverend had set us straight on a few things the day before we got married; one of those being that my wife and I were forever best friends and that no one would ever come between us. He also made us promise that we'd never, ever go to sleep mad at each other. We adopted his advice without question, as you were supposed to honor any man of holy order. I knew that meant Libby and I would go on to live our own life and that day was to be a fresh start for us.

We sat for lunch at a McDonald's restaurant near the mall in State College on our way to Milesburg. Libby and I weren't really hungry and didn't care much for fast food, but Hugh always ate like a bulldog and McDonald's was a special treat for him. I was hoping to see one last, familiar face before leaving town to maybe show off my beautiful bride. Ironically though, the main entrance to the restaurant was locked and said, "No Entry Use Other Door." It kind of struck us all funny and seemed, well...right in that moment.

After Hugh had his fill of a filet of fish sandwich with a cola and French fries we headed out for the interstate, of course not having seen anyone we knew. I pulled the sturdy old car to a stop on the jug-handle ramp of Interstate 80. We got out, pulled our heavy packs from the trunk and gave little brother Hugh the keys to the car.

"The car's yours, bud. You take good care of her now," I told him.

He gave us both a grand smile. He didn't have a driver's license yet but his learner's permit allowed him to drive unsupervised. The long drive back to the farm would be his first solo cruise and we knew that he was ready. We all shared a three-way hug and Hugh drove off in the wet wink of an eye.

Libby led the way as we started to walk up the rounding curve of the on ramp. Neither of us was certain of our choice to head west and we didn't really know where to go or how to get there other than hitchhike. I had heard that the interstate went the whole way to the West, maybe even to the Pacific coast and the farthest I had ever been on Interstate 80 was Ohio. We were both very curious about life out west.

We arrived at the merge of traffic to see the fast race of other travelers also headed west. Our very first ride was a black conversion van with an unmarried couple just a few years older than us. They were headed for Colorado. They called them conversion vans because they had a bed in the back and were shag carpeted from the dashboard to the license plates. They were also searching for a fresh start on life and he, being a carpenter, had already lined up some work out west. We struggled to make small talk as they were strangers but managed to hold a reasonable conversation. Soon night fell on us and we camped just outside their van in our sleeping bags in a wooded field somewhere in eastern Ohio.

We woke early the next morning and piled back into the van. We hadn't gotten back to the interstate before the girlfriend explained some ground rules to us. We could tell they had talked at length about us overnight and she spoke for them both as he drove. She said that we could ride with them part of the way, but that we'd have to go on our own sometime before reaching Colorado.

Libby and I immediately sensed that at some point along the way to Colorado we would, sooner or later, wear out our welcome with them. We never really spoke to each other about it but thanked them for the ride and asked to be let out as soon as we reached the on ramp to the interstate just minutes away. In another wink of an eye, we stood alone roadside and they were happily on their way to Colorado without us.

Around midday, we'd made it all the way to Toledo, where we got terribly spun around in heavy urban traffic. We fought hard to get out of the city, but all road signs seemed to either return on an eastern course, which was out of the question, or to Detroit, an even worse choice. We felt suddenly like not only had we dropped out of school but that we had dropped into real America by mistake. We'd left home without a map and by moving about on instinct and dead reckoning, somehow we ended up traveling north. Only after a myriad of rides and countless exits it appeared like Saginaw was our route for the day.

Late that afternoon Libby asked one of our rides if he'd mind stopping briefly along the way to patronize one of the roadside cheese shops. He needed a break from driving too so we made a quick potty stop. After Libby had bought a loaf of bread, a couple of bricks of cheese, and two bottles of wine, we continued on our way to parts north.

A GREAT LAKE

It was a relief to see the countryside open up a bit and we felt as though we'd put in a hard day's work. Just passing through eastern Michigan by thumb was a test of nerves and patience. We eventually found ourselves rumbling down a wooded backcountry road with an elderly fellow in his old green pickup truck. We explained that we were married just days before and that we were traveling through the area. It was he who offered that we were kind of like on a honeymoon and truthfully, up to that point, we hadn't really given it much of a thought.

The old fellow opened right up and revealed a lot to us about the local area. "You guys must go out to Beaver Island," he said emphatically as he described it in captivating detail. He laid out such a confident travel plan to Beaver Island and beyond that we agreed to go check it out. At least his plan gave us a temporary objective and time was definitely on our side.

We thanked him for his help and asked to be let out in a wooded forest on a little-traveled asphalt road. As Libby slammed the heavy truck door, we waved him off with smiles then stepped off into the woods to set up camp for the night.

Now the spectacular northern woods of Michigan in early June can only be described in a word: "mosquitoes." We'd never set up our brand new, two-man polyester tent before and within seconds of stepping off the road to an open flat the mosquitoes were upon us. They were absolutely ferocious. We threw down our packs and fumbled with the tent and for a brief moment we seriously thought about scrapping the whole idea to just hop straight into our bags, but we stayed with the tent up tough.

Forget the directions, we thought. Just snap poles together, shove them through here and there and, just like that, in minutes, we had a little home of our own. We threw all our gear in, climbed inside then zipped the flap closed. We prayed aloud that they couldn't get through the polyester tent as Libby methodically hunted down and killed every single mosquito that had already gotten inside. We literally felt like the only thing saving us from certain death was that thin little polyester tent.

It got a little stuffy inside because we had worked up a sweat so we zipped open the two window flaps to get some fresh air. There were hundreds of mosquitoes staging on the netting of the windows with their piercing jabbers poking through the tiny mesh, but they couldn't get inside. We yelled back at them through the mesh window and laughed at their futility. We started scratching the bites we had already gotten as we talked on. Within minutes we realized that though the mosquitoes couldn't pass through the mesh, the little, iddy biddy no-see-ums could. They were worse! We did our best to smash as many of them as we could and rather than be eaten alive, we opted to put up with being a little stuffy and zipped up the window flaps. At that point we were safe but feared any notion of having to make a perilous, quick trip outside to go to the bathroom during the night. Libby began referring to our insect enemies as "saber-toothed skeeters."

Though the little tent was barely big enough for us and our few things it was actually perfect. Having outsmarted the skeeters we celebrated on wine, bread, and some fantastic Michigan cheese inside our new little home. It was totally the right supper for the day. After wining and dining we rolled out my bag to provide bedding beneath us while over us we shared Libby's down-filled bag. Both our feet and legs entwined in the bottom of her bag because it wouldn't unzip completely. We used our packs as pillows and finally draped a hand-crocheted afghan over her down bag. The afghan was made by the loving hands of Libby's beloved Granny and provided a loving comfort and sense of security for us both.

I removed a brass chain and crucifix from around my neck and draped it through the small finger hole at the very peak of the tent just an arm's reach away. The crucifix and necklace were a wedding gift made for me by an old family friend. We agreed to drape it from the peak of our tent every night thereafter to protect us from evil, which on that evening were the skeeters. Soon night came over us and we fell peacefully asleep to the cool silence and serenity of the great, wooded north.

I don't think that either of us had ever slept so deeply. While stirring to wake and admiring the design, construction, and portability of our little home, we agreed to take very good care of the tent. It had already saved our lives once. Not nary a skeeter had gotten through its paper-thin fabric. It had been a long time since either of us had slept in, so we did. We rustled about and eventually rolled up our throws to head out into a cloudy day. The skeeters were knocked back by the chill of night and morning air. We enjoyed the temporary reprieve.

We gave Beaver Island another thought but agreed to pursue whatever venture and direction would come our way. Admittedly, we were excited to check out Beaver Island. Its name was so appropriately suggestive for honeymooners and, as newlyweds, our fledgling marriage was in a state of perpetual consummation.

Our traveling progress slowed because there was so little traffic, but ride-by-ride we found our way to the rolling, grassy hills of Michigan's western shore. As luck and perhaps fate would have it, the last ride of our short day was given to us by a gentlemen from Charlevoix, the port town from which the Beaver Island ferry departed. He was a teacher, a married man with children, and because his entire family was off visiting the in-laws, he offered us a shower and warm bed for the night at his home. He assured us that getting to Beaver Island was a full day's work and a good night's rest he offered would give us a fresh start in the morning.

We gratefully accepted his kindness in what had become a threatening night of storms though we weren't accustomed to such open friendliness from a stranger. His was a small, quaint home within walking distance of the ferry. The view from his hilltop house was spectacular having the advantage of the entire western horizon of Lake Michigan through a residential stand of deciduous and needled trees.

Our host pretty much left us to ourselves for the night and said that he probably wouldn't see us in the morning as he had early commitments. We again thanked him and turned into the cozy double bed in the dainty room that was likely his daughter's. I lay awake wondering of many things and particularly about the person behind the house's feminine touch. *Is she as kind as he?* I thought she had to be. The flash of lightening and the rumble of thunder against the house occasionally broke our sleep.

The storms had cleared the following morning and we stepped out into a gloriously moist and sunny day. The ferry was scheduled to leave at two o'clock so the day was all ours. There was a delightful restaurant right on the water within a skipped stone's throw of the ferry already docked at the pier. We ordered a full breakfast of ham and eggs with coffee and juice for just a few bucks. In as much as we were her only patrons, we started to make improvised small talk with the waitress who was glad to have our company. She filled us in on a lot of details about Beaver Island. She said that it was still early in the season so there would be little excitement on the island. She admitted that there was always little excitement on the island. She said that there was only one bar/grocery store that comprised all of an unnamed town and its commerce. She also said that most of the island's residents, all one hundred or so, only lived there for the summer months. According to her there were only about a dozen people and a few dogs that lived there year round. She thought that they were descendants of Native Americans.

"Other than that, the island's deserted," she said with a smile. The more she spoke, the more enthralled we became with our choices of late. She said that the ferry only ran once each day, but later in the summer it would make two trips. The ferry would shut down for the year right after Labor Day because there was no interest in the island after the summer vacation season. She also made it clear that the waters of Lake Michigan were often treacherous in the fall. Somehow, those words struck the memory of chords from a familiar song by Gordon Lightfoot in my mind's ear.

We had our fill of breakfast and coffee so we just sat and visited for the longest time with our waitress, then with each other. It was a pleasant morning on the waterfront of Lake Michigan. We had some sketch paper and pencils in our packs and just for yucks I scratched out a drawing of the harbor view from our table. Aside from the largely unfinished fluorescent drafts on the ceiling of my room back home, I had never really tried my hand at drawing. My siblings were much better artists, but I'd never really given it much of a try before. As always, my impatience overtook my hand and I finished a scribbled go at it.

The waitress was astonished by my craft and thought I was an accomplished artist. She offered to buy the sketch but I scoffed. She all but demanded that I hand over the finished sketch to her as a genuine possession, a piece, if you will. Until that moment I could not recall the last time anyone had acknowledged the work of my hand, let alone with such praise and want. She lit the spark of self-esteem in me that had been snuffed by the boredom and hopelessness of a failed attempt at higher education. I wondered what other potential skills, if not gifts, we were given that needed a means and time to express.

The morning turned into afternoon and before long we heard our call to board as the ferry sounded its great foghorn in a couple of short bursts. We were surprised how few other ferry travelers there were for the size of the boat; it was the largest boat either of us had ever boarded. In addition to a half-dozen passengers, the ferry was loaded with one car and one pickup truck. Nonetheless, and with one last, long blast of its horn, we were floating out of the harbor and headed due west into the great lake.

Within minutes the chill of the wind was too much for us so we pulled our sweaters and weather gear from our packs. The great ferry pushed to the western horizon in white-capped water on what was apparently a calm day for Lake Michigan. We sensed how furious the lake could become as the waitress had warned. On the ferry we met an older woman who ran the bar/general store on the island. She filled us in with more detail of what lay ahead and chuckled when she cautioned us to not expect much. She told us that neither the bar nor the general store was yet open for business.

"Beaver Island's a pretty quiet place. You'll see," she said. It would be another week before all that opened up, but she said that we could go in the bar to check it out if we wanted. Our eyes were fixed on the emerald green water as she spoke. "You'd only last a few minutes in that water this time of year," she said with a haunting tone. We both shifted our attention to her. "Many mariners have been lost to these waters," she said as she turned to seek the shelter of the passenger's cabin.

The thought of danger brought us closer together as we snuggled nose-to-neck on the deck of the ferry. My wet nose could smell Libby through her woolen turtleneck sweater. Her rosy cheeks and unforgettable smile told me that she was in heaven and that our choices had been right. She was a brave woman and our love fostered a shared courage of heart. In the distance we could see the island rising on the horizon.

We arrived at the island late that afternoon and sure enough the place was dead quiet. We stepped up to the Shamrock Bar to see that it was closed, as was the general store. We walked down a dirt road that led south from the harbor passing a few cottages that seemed deserted.

Suddenly, out of nowhere, an old, beat-up pickup pulled up as we had thumbed him to stop. The cab had two riders who appeared to be locals. We thought that maybe they were Native Americans by their coal-black hair. Without saying a word we hopped into the bed of the old truck and just as quickly as they had appeared we sped away, rambling south on that old gravel road.

They were definitely headed somewhere fast, although we weren't. I had a sudden apprehension so in the middle of a small opening in the woods I thumped on the cab and asked them to pull over.

As we slowed Libby asked, "What's wrong, John?"

"Nothing. I just want to get out here," I explained.

We said nothing further to our escorts nor they to us. We raised our open palms, strapped on our packs, and headed off into the woods surefooted, as though we knew exactly what we were doing. They must have been scratching their heads in laughter as we stepped off into the evening wilderness.

Within seconds, the skeeters were upon us and they were ravenous.

"Where are we going?" Libby asked, frantically slapping at her face, arms, and neck.

"I dunno but we gotta keep movin'," I said in an equally frantic voice.

They were horrible. They bit right through our clothes. Nothing could stop them and the further into the woods we went, the worse they got. We could hear a swirling breeze in the treetops far above and the sky was darkening from overcast clouds. We were in panicked misery from their onslaught while seeking a clearing of any sort to pitch our tent as there was no escaping them.

We couldn't even find a trail as we plowed our way through the woods on a course west. I recalled the island to be only a few miles wide and thought that if we pushed west sooner or later we'd have to come out of the woods on some type of shore. We had no choice but to trek through the wilds, lush with briars clawing at our flesh and voracious skeeters nipping at our heels. Our trek turned into a jog and then an all-out run through the woods.

Just as we'd hoped, we could see daylight ahead and literally ran the last quarter mile out onto a vast, cobblestone shore. The brisk breeze of day had turned into a windy evening. The skeeters couldn't venture far from the windbreak of the woods so we were safe for the moment. While splash bathing in the lake's icy waters to take down the swelling of the countless welts that covered us, we appreciated just how impossible it would be for any warm-blooded beast to survive those woods.

The cobblestone shore turned out to be our destination for the day. We could see with the approach of night would come a round of electrical storms that were building off to the northwest. In a few hours they were going to be right on top of us. We braved a venture back into the breaks of the dune-like woods just yards inland from the shore and found a soft, sandy flat just perfect for our tent. There was enough of a breeze to keep the skeeters at bay, but any thought of taking even another twenty steps back into the woods was unthinkable.

We had lots of time to pitch our tent and did a much better job of it even using its optional rain slicker for the stormy night ahead. There was still enough daylight to enjoy the setting sky over our wild and private Lake Michigan, which had a horizon as expansive as that of any ocean. We headed back out to the cobblestone shore to enjoy the evening and our supper, sharing our other bottle of wine, a small piece of stale bread, and our last clump of scrumptious, lip-smacking, melt-in-your-mouth Michigan muenster cheese. We had our own wine and cheese party right then and there, just we two. It was all of our food but it was quite ample.

After supper we rummaged around on the shore, but there was no trash, litter or any other thing man-made. The shore was covered with large, round cobblestones, which were a little tricky to walk over and impossible to sit on comfortably. Every here and there was driftwood and Libby was fully entertaining in pointing out the various animal likenesses of their shapes. One piece of driftwood, she pointed out, looked like a pair of dolphins. Another had the spitting image of an alligator. She then had me turn my focus to the enormous clouds building in the sky. In their bright, white-silver lining she could point out dogs, horses, and even Abraham Lincoln. We watched with child-like fascination; the shapes would appear then fade in the time it took to take only a few, slow breaths.

We sat and talked long about the day and the days. We so loved the day with all its ups and downs. Just facing the unexpected with courage was liberating. We knew that our venture to Beaver Island was a dead-end excursion. Or was it? In a way, the beauty and serenity of that evening was divine. We felt a rush of love, the connectedness to all that is, all that was, and all that will ever be. How we found ourselves on that western shore of Lake Michigan was truly unbelievable and we sensed a true Greatness among, between, and within us.

Libby said that she felt released having successfully left so many rough things behind. She then came out with profound words that I'd never forget. "I guess freedom isn't just for the rich anymore," she said while standing tall and staring west into an ominous sunset, her hair blowing back in a full breeze.

The setting of that day was unlike any we had ever seen before. The sunset gave way to an awesome electrical storm raging across the night sky. We could see the lights of two barges way off on the horizon, steaming to get out of harms way. Cloud-to-cloud, then cloud-to-water, lightening cracked the night sky in all directions. Some bolts seemed to cover twenty, perhaps thirty miles of erupting cumulus clouds. We counted seconds between the crack of lightening and the clasp of thunder to gauge the storm's distance and could tell the storms were rapidly moving our way. We knew that we were about to experience a night like none other and the roar of the approaching storm warned us to find the shelter of our tent. Although the tent rustled and shook into the wee hours, that night we enjoyed the most impressive thunderstorm of our lives from the safety and comfort provided by polyester, down, and each other.

There may have been a seasonal weather cycle working on the lake because we woke again to perfectly clear skies and once again the night air had checked the skeeters. There was definitely a rhythm about such things. We rose early to get a jump on the bugs and hoped we could find an alternate and easier route back to the harbor.

Heading north on the cobblestone shore rather than take our chances of getting lost and eaten alive in the woods, we hopped from stone to stone with our hefty packs on our backs. Eventually, we could see a cabin on the shore a mile or so ahead. We figured there we might find a road that would lead to "town" and lumbered our way to the cabin in no time at all. The cabin appeared to be deserted and sure enough, we found a good dirt road which was a relief from hiking over cobblestone. The road cut straight through a thick patch of woods and passed a peaceful, quiet pond.

Libby dropped her pack, stripped down to her birthday suit on the spot then approached the water's edge. After testing the icy water with my hand, I figured I'd let her give it a go first. I was a little concerned that such cold water might cause irreversible shrinkage of the honeymoon equipment. I dropped my pack and reclined on a huge, flat rock to take in her exquisite nakedness. There were lily pads on the lake and its ripples sparkled from the climbing morning sun. She gently held her long, brunette hair back with both hands as she waded deeper into the water. I could see that she was an experienced skinny dipper.

"Is it cold?" I asked, hoping to hear different.

"Yeah, it's cold alright, but remember I'm from New Hampshire. I used to do this all the time as a kid," she proclaimed with pride and a smile.

I sat in quiet and full admiration of her beauty as she slightly bent over and cautiously looked for frogs, fish, or snapping turtles though there were none. When she got waist deep I got a little worried because that is usually the point of no return, when a jump and kick plunges one headfirst in a fully immersed swim. I knew that I'd have to do the same if she made a full swim of it. I knew that if she couldn't stand the cold water, I wouldn't have a chance of it. Luckily for me, she just splash-bathed her upper body from there then skedaddled back to shore with a great, laughing grin. She put on only her hiking boots, barefooted and unlaced, and joined me on the warming rock to sun out. Reclining with both our heads on my pack, we talked for the longest time. It was an unforgettable morning on Beaver Island in the heart of Lake Michigan.

The warming calm was broken by the bite of the day's first skeeter and so we decided to gather up and head for "town." We got to the harbor after noon and had time to burn before the ferry's four o'clock departure. The doors of the Shamrock Bar/general store were open so we went inside to check it out. We called out to see if anyone was near, but the place was eerily quiet, like a "Twilight Zone" episode or something.

We decided to wait for the ferry outside the bar and dropped our packs on a log near the water. As Libby played her flute and I sketched the harbor scene in pencil we noticed once again the sky starting to build a grey overcast. The ferry arrived and departed on time and in the course of just a few hours we were back on the mainland headed to nowhere particular.

After Beaver Island, mainland Michigan had little to offer us in adventure and our sights were peering toward a distant, unknown course. At dusk we pulled up at an off road clearing somewhere and set up the tent. That time it took only minutes.

The night passed with little trouble, some rain and thunder, but we stayed dry and woke again to clear skies. We wrapped up camp early wanting to burst out of Michigan and lay down some miles. It's not that we didn't love Michigan, but from all the locals we gathered there was no work or future for us there. In a few days we could make the Rocky Mountains, our next goal in mind.

Our first ride of the day was with an older fellow in a flatbed truck with short, wooden-stake side-rails. The bed of his truck was covered with a couple dozen spent car batteries that he was hauling to the local dump. We threw our packs over the side-rails onto the bed and climbed into the cab. He was headed north for what he called, "The U.P." which meant "The Upper Peninsula" of Michigan. He took us over the Mackinac Bridge and tried to encourage us to venture out to Mackinac Island where horses and carts were the only means of transportation.

It sounded intriguing but we couldn't imagine it better than Beaver Island so we passed on his suggestion and opted to continue on instead.

Our second ride of the day came from two silly middle-aged women who seemed really excited about giving us a lift. They were locals and we traveled down the north shore of Lake Michigan on the U.P. with them. It was a spectacularly beautiful ride with the sun glistening off the lake to the south. The two ladies really wanted us to see their town, which was a short excursion off the main route. They were really happy and proud of their town, which sat right on the shore of a small lake.

We arrived in their little town just before lunch and thanked them for the ride. We set our packs down just outside the town bar and went inside to have some lunch. The bar was barely open and so we settled for a couple of drafts, a handful or two of beer nuts and a quick game of pool. In many ways the quiet town reflected the untouched nature of the entire U.P.

With adventure waiting, we marched back out to the main route and pushed across the Upper Peninsula. That afternoon we found ourselves riding in the back of a pickup truck on some back roads in northern Wisconsin. It had started to rain lightly and we got a little wet waiting for the ride so we huddled together closely near the cab as the air had a chill to it. We noticed something very distinct about northern Wisconsin. It appeared that if you staked out a one hundred-foot square on any patch of forest, in it you would likely find every pine and deciduous tree of North America. The health and diversity of continuous forest was stunning, even in a steady rain.

The chill set in a bit harder so I raised my collar and pulled down my hat. As we huddled together, I looked down to see that there was something very wrong with my backpack. It looked like it was melting in places. The rain slicker and my pack had inadvertently touched some battery acid from our first ride of the day and were slowly being eaten away. I pushed them farther out on the truck bed hoping that enough rainwater might neutralize the acid.

Oh well, we figured. *Not much we can do about them now.* Libby sighed as she attempted to run her fingers through her back-of-the-pickup wet, snarled hair.

The driver took us right to his trailer out in the forest just off the route because he kind of wanted us to visit a spell, which we did briefly. He had some baking soda, which we sprinkled over the burns on our packs and camp gear though it looked like the damage was already done. The rain had stopped and the sun was peeking through in patches so we thanked him for the ride and headed on out. We didn't want to reach St. Paul in the dark so we held up for another quick camp set just off the road somewhere between Wausau and Eau Claire.

THE GRASSLANDS

Afraid to hitchhike through Minneapolis and St. Paul greater metropolitan rush hour traffic, we started the next day early and a little anxious. We hoped to melt right into the flow of the morning commute. With little effort we passed right through the twin cities without a moment's trouble. By midmorning we were on a direct course across Minnesota, which was far more populated than either of us had imagined.

Our day's travel was fairly unremarkable from then on as we struggled to get only short rides, exit to exit, many times over. Finally very late in the day, a semi stopped to give us a ride at the interstate on ramp. The trucker spoke very little and it was difficult to talk over the roar of his diesel engine. Well after dark west of Fargo, North Dakota, we asked him to stop between exits so that we could pitch up for the night. We jumped the highway fence into a thicket of brush then thrashed and spun about until finally stumbling into a small opening. We rolled out our bags right on the dirt and soon fell asleep in the dim light of a waxing moon to the Doppler whine of cars and semis rolling past at interstate speed.

The traveling slowed way down the next day. We struggled to make just a few hundred miles. *Never no mind,* we figured. Time was on our side and the prairie was so vast and new to us. At one point we watched a convoy of enormous earth scrapers roll past on their way no doubt to do some type of road construction. We wondered what it would take to get a couple of jobs running those, how fun that would be. Surely along the way any heavy equipment operator would have to get a lucky break from someone passing the baton of experience to an apprentice or two. *If only we could meet up with a guy like that, maybe he'd hire us both,* we wondered. Enough for the day were its own sunny joys though and the beauty of an unfolding West was most exciting.

That afternoon an older gentleman named "Howard" gave us a ride in his older white van. By then our small talk had become straightforward, even interesting, and putting our honeymoon to the front of our conversation seemed to be most enjoyable.

As we traveled I felt something on my shin. I reached inside my jean pant leg and plucked from my flesh a small, brown tick. Apparently it had gotten aboard the night before as we blundered through the brush in the dark.

Howard was a well-to-do tire salesman who shared countless tidbits of elderly advice. The day was getting late and he asked what our plans were for the night.

"We'd like to find a meal then hit the sack. Is there a place we might be able to grab some fast food up ahead?" I asked.

"Tell you what," he said. "I'm going to spend the night and a couple days in Bismark on business. I could get you a job changing tires in town. It doesn't pay much but at least it's a start," he added as a caring, almost fatherly gesture.

I wasn't quite sure what he meant by "changing tires in town." I envisioned going around town with a tire iron and a jack putting spare tires on cars that had flats. I didn't really get it at all but I was curious about his offer. We were curious about having gotten an offer, any offer. After all, we had only known him a few hours and in that short time we sensed that he was a really good man. Apparently, he saw enough good in us to extend a generous offer so I suppose we had established a mutual trust. We agreed to head into town to check it out and if nothing else we'd grab some food as we were both hungry.

As we pulled into Bismark, I felt another itch against my skin inside my right sock. With my thumb and forefinger I reached in about the ankle and pinched another tick from my skin. I never really gave it much thought.

Howard pulled his van into a gas station where we all got out and walked right into the mechanic's garage. He carried himself with established authority and the attendant knew well who he was. It seemed he was a regular salesman or perhaps even the owner of the garage. The attendant was greasy and grubby up to his biceps. He took us over to the tire changing machine and tried to explain how to operate it. It was somewhat pneumatic with a lot of handwork involved and I knew well that the first day on the job I would smash a thumb or worse. There was a lot of clutter around the machine and it looked like they probably had trouble keeping an employee to do that kind of work.

I had come to a point of decision. *If I accept his offer then the honeymoon is over. But, hey, is this the guy who could get us both jobs running those huge earth scrapers?* I thought for a moment then looked to Libby who was all smiles.

Howard could see in my face that I was infinitely more interested in chasing my new bride around the continent than changing tires at a service station in Bismark, North Dakota, for the rest of my life. Without having to make many excuses I declined his offer and thanked him repeatedly for the ride and his open generosity. I could see in Libby's face that she was even more cheerful that I had chosen our time together over what could have led to a career. It was clearly a chance at opportunity and a life-changing, or for that matter a "tire changing," direction.

We returned to the van to get our packs and start on the long slug back to the interstate when Howard stopped us.

"So you guys are just going to head on down the road?" he asked.

"Sure enough, Howard, it's no problem," I replied.

"Hey, I got a better idea. It's your honeymoon, right? When was the last time you guys slept in a bed?" We actually had to give it some thought but before we could answer he said, "Let me buy you guys a room at the hotel for the night."

We simultaneously looked to each other with raised eyebrows and mouths wide open, feeling as though we'd already imposed on him far too much. He had a very happy and giving smile on his face. We stumbled over some words to decline but couldn't. The thought of the long hike back to the interstate at dusk was a little painful and it had been a hot, dusty, North Dakota summer day.

"Please," he said. "That way you can get a good night's rest and a fresh start in the morning."

Libby had come to a decision. "Howard, that is so kind of you. We would love to take you up on that! I would absolutely love a hot bath and some clean sheets for the night."

"Fine, it's settled. Let's head over to the hotel and check you guys in. You're gonna love our hotel," he said.

It was a lovely old hotel in the heart of town with old-fashioned fixtures and hand-carved wood pillars, doors, and moulding. Howard walked us right up to the hotel desk and paid cash for our room. He explained to the receptionist that we were from out of town, on our honeymoon, and asked her to check us in.

"Now you guys don't want to spend the rest of your night with me so why don't you head on upstairs? Here's my business card if you decide to change your mind about that job. You never know, maybe down the road a ways or in a couple of weeks, you might change your mind," he said. "Give me a call if you need anything."

We were overwhelmed. I shook his hand and arm as Libby patted his back. He was absolutely gratuitous, yet for him we hadn't done a thing whatsoever.

Minutes later we were in our room cleaning up and unwinding. Funny though, just as Howard had said, it was nice to be alone again. Libby took a long, hot bath after which I showered. When I came out of the bathroom she stood wrapped in a towel before a large, ornate dressing mirror. She would tilt her head one way, then the other, from side to side, untangling and brushing out her lovely, wet hair. We were both still in disbelief of our good fortune for the day.

She joined me on the king-size bed still wrapped only in a towel. With her head resting on my chest and her arm folded across my torso, we felt such tremendous relief. A long sensual kiss then led us into full-blown passion and time was again on our side. Being so clean gave us a rare opportunity to fully explore each other. But in the heat of passion we froze in our lovemaking to hear someone fumbling with keys at our door.

Surely they won't come inside, I thought as I heard the door fly open! Libby looked straight at me as I struggled to get a look at whoever had entered our room without knocking. I never got a look at the intruder because they shut the door and left the room quicker than they had entered.

"It must have been the maid," Libby said.

"This time of day, what the hell's with that?" I barked loud enough that they could probably hear me if still outside the door.

Whoever it was, imagine their surprise. The door was centered on a wall about five feet directly from the foot of our bed. They certainly had a very interesting perspective. A minute or so passed and we heard absolutely nothing outside our door. Rather than let the interruption steal the moment we resumed and completed our lovemaking in its usual and explosive grand finale.

We couldn't get a ride the next morning and figured that folks in those parts hadn't seen many hitchhikers. By noon we knew that we had to change our luck somehow and found a discount store within walking distance of the interstate. Something about our look wasn't working for us so we bought Libby a brand-spanking-new cowgirl hat. Libby needed a hat anyway because the sun was bearing down. She had never owned a cowgirl hat before and we found a sharp, black felt one that was so her. Who could resist such a western beauty? I certainly couldn't. And somehow gazing at her with that hat and her beautiful, long hair blowing in the Montana prairie afternoon breeze, well...it was right. She was born for it. We were born for it. In no time at all it would be ride after ride, without any waiting.

Wouldn't you know it? A brand new, three-quarter-ton pickup truck with a brand new, cab-over camper pulled up to give us a ride. The driver was a western cowboy with his own black felt hat. I suppose Libby's hat was like honey to the bee.

He worked for Burlington Northern out of Great Falls and was on vacation, just he and his adorable little boxer mutt named Wendi. Wendi had her name branded into her leather collar. The driver admitted that he never picked up hitchhikers but couldn't resist stopping to help out somebody in a black cowgirl hat.

His was a workingman's life and he was doing well. We could tell that he virtually lived for his vacations with his devoted little dog. He had never married and we could tell that his load had shifted somewhere along his life's way. He had a slow quality about him. His speech was slow, his words were deliberate, and he lagged to respond to our conversation. Some things he missed entirely and I don't think he ever got that we were on our honeymoon. He rubbed off on us and so we slowed down as well. *Never no mind us,* we figured. We four rambled across the prairie, plains, grasslands, and some butte country he called, "the badlands." We rode with him and little Wendi all day.

When he learned that we had never seen the West, he convinced us that we must see the Little Bighorn on our tour and offered to detour his route so that we could take it in. He liked to camp at KOAs and said many times through that day, "You can't beat these KOAs."

We figured that KOAs were AOK too and pulled into one just north of the Crow Indian Reservation for the night. They charged us a couple of bucks to pitch our tent, which seemed like a rip-off in such wide-open country. A shower was another dollar.

The driver kept insisting that Libby save the dollar and use the shower in his camper. He never offered me one and his repeated, insistent pressure to get her in his shower kind of got a little weird. Libby was uncomfortable about it and we both realized that we needed some separation from him. We saw a sad look come over him as I let him know that we'd be moving on our own again in the morning. We thanked him for the ride but we could clearly see a slump in his attitude that Libby was not a fixture in his life. He distanced himself from us immediately and turned into his camper for the night. It was a melancholy close to the day for everyone except little Wendi who eagerly wagged her cropped tail waiting for him to come snuggle up in the camper's bed.

We rose early the next morning to avoid our friend from Great Falls, and a quick ride took us straight to the Little Bighorn Battlefield National Monument, the site of General George Armstrong Custer's last stand. We didn't realize until we arrived that it was located in the heart of the Crow Indian Reservation. The reservation had a different feel to it altogether, almost Third World in a way. The buildings of the monument were modern, almost governmental in design, and very unlike most other structures on the reservation. They housed artifacts and displays about the events of the battle. Ironically, members of the Crow Nation worked at the site giving tours and keeping grounds. There was one handsome and obviously Native American man selling jewelry and crafts right inside the museum entrance.

Right from the get-go we felt out of place approaching the monument. We knew little about the "Monument" which seemed at first like a poor choice of words for what we thought had occurred. *Righteous massacre might have been a better choice,* we thought. After all, the Lakota and Cheyenne basically kicked hell out of three battalions of horse soldiers that desperately had it coming. As we walked about looking at interpretive panels, we were overwhelmed with a sense of intrusion. One panel had a push button audio narration describing the battle in detail.

The closing remark of the narrative resounded throughout the museum in finality. "The battle of the Little Bighorn may have been the Indians' greatest victory, but it was their last," it blurted out every five minutes or so. I wondered how many times each day those Native American employees and jewelers had to listen to that insulting commentary, over and over again, though they seemed numb to it all.

We stayed at the monument no more than ten minutes and were soon overcome by an odd, macabre feeling. We left in a hurry heading for Interstate 90, which put us back on a fast track northwest.

THE WILD WEST

Libby's jet black cowgirl hat was already showing some wear, and getting rides was difficult as we headed further west. We'd been on a roll until that afternoon. It was impossible to keep the crisp, sharp look of a felt cowgirl hat when rolling up and down the road like a couple of tumbleweeds. Crumpled and dusty, it more resembled the road rash we were beginning to feel. The acid burns on our gear had slowed but had made holes that were already fraying. We could see that they'd continue to unravel, but at least all the zippers still worked.

A long, two-door hardtop pulled up after what seemed like an entire afternoon of waiting. The driver and passenger looked pretty rough and both smelled of alcohol, but without asking, we hopped right into the back seat. The car started immediately racing up a very long, steep hill. As it turned out, our two would-be good Samaritans were in trouble with the law, something about robbery and assault, or so they said. We could tell they were sauced, weaving and wandering all over the road and we wanted out of the car, but then again and what the heck, we were going somewhere.

I recalled Dood on Christmas morning telling me, "Patience is a virtue, my son." I never really quite understood what he meant until that moment in the back seat of the sedan. I had let my boredom overcome my better judgment and gotten into a car that I knowingly shouldn't have. At the same time I was consciously trying to be less judgmental and more like Libby. *What a mouthful. How can a person be judgmental when they themselves are worthless road trash?* I thought as I began to own our predicament.

When we finally topped out on the crest of a mountain I asked the driver, "Hey, man, what say you slow down a bit?"

The driver turned fully around with reckless, laughing abandon and said, "You think we're going fast now? Wait till we get to the bottom of this hill. This is hill thirteen."

"What the hell is hill thirteen?" I asked, noticing that the speedometer was vibrating near one hundred miles per hour.

His pal in the front seat said, "Shit, man, this is the Continental Divide."

That was the first time I'd ever heard the words "continental divide." I didn't know exactly what that meant but it didn't sound good.

They were thrilled. We were repentant. Well, on the down slope, the front end started to shimmy and then the right front tire blew out. We heard the tire blow and the driver instantly lost control of the speeding vehicle. We were all over the interstate weaving right, then left, then right as he tried to get it back.

I grabbed Libby by the back of her head and pushed her down between the seats. She told me, "I love you, John!" I folded my body over hers and hung on tight to the front seat.

We skidded and screeched to a roll against a guardrail that kept us from going over a steep cliff. The car never came to a complete stop, but as it slowed to a roll, Libby hopped out. I threw out our packs and bailed out right behind her. The drunks were still laughing and both got out of the car on the driver's side a hundred yards or so farther down the highway. They were falling all over each other in the cruising lane trying to hitchhike themselves out of the situation. The car finally came to a dead rest against the guardrail.

As fate would have it, a police car stopped to pick those guys up and the three went on down the road. With hearts still pounding we decided to sit down and collect ourselves. Shamefully we had known they were drunk before getting in the car and we swore to never make that mistake again, that we'd never, ever get into a car with drunks. We agreed to be more careful about who we rode with.

In a short amount of time we worked up the nerve to start thumbing another ride and thought to open the hood of the wreck, to make it look like our car had broken down. We figured we'd make the best of it, like seeing the silver lining in a black cloud. Just minutes later someone stopped to give us a lift.

Perhaps a ride or two later we found ourselves once again in the middle of heaven on earth. Having passed Butte and the Anaconda mine to the north, we were surrounded by a dreamy landscape. The light was perfect with long, beaming shadows across the evening cumulus sky, a big sky. In the distant west was a mountain range unlike any we had ever seen before cast beneath a Prussian-blue storm and a peeking, streaking sunset. The sun gleamed against the brilliant spring grasses and gently rolling hills surrounding us for many miles in all directions. As far as we could see, we were alone, just we two. Our world was suddenly way different than Centre County or even Delran, New Jersey, where I had spent the greatest part of my childhood. Delran was minutes north of Camden, which was an industrial wasteland. Yes, we stood in heaven on earth.

Even the traffic had become scarce, maybe a car every five minutes or so. No one seemed interested in us and we weren't anxious to leave. We gave up on hitchhiking at least for the moment having patience on our side.

"We'll use discretion from now on," I thought as I started to draw the scene with pencil and pad. You see, having no other skills to market, I was set to become a famous artist, one whose works would eventually be on display in the greatest galleries on earth, certainly in my postmortem. There was one mountain, maybe even *the* mountain we were looking for, the one that we'd set out to find.

The quest for the mountain in my mind had begun six years earlier and though she had never seen it, Libby was fully committed to finding it as well. It gave our journey more reason than just honeymooning. We had a sense of purpose and drive, though we lacked any real direction.

Libby was playing her flute. Her cowgirl hat was missing, probably still in the back seat of the wreck on the divide. She stopped playing to ask me something. "Do you think that's the one?" referring to the mountain centered in my drawing. "Is that the one you saw in the library?"

"I'm not sure," I said. "It could be, but I'm not really sure."

A car was slowing in our direction and I could hear the tires roll onto the gravel berm though we had not hitched anyone to our aid. I looked up to see flashing red and blue lights. It was a cop, a state bull. *Oh boy!*

The officer got out in his spit-polished uniform. I was so impressed with his professionalism. I wanted to be him. I recalled being taught to always address the police with respect as he asked to see our driver's licenses or any other identification. "Yes, sir, officer," I replied. I had mine in my wallet and Libby was sifting through her pack to find hers.

"What are you two doing out here all by yourselves?" he asked.

"Officer, we're hitchhiking to Oregon," I replied. I knew he wouldn't buy some lengthy explanation about a mountain quest.

"We've been having a lot of problems around here lately. You guys haven't been causing any trouble, have you?" he asked.

Libby walked up to him and threw her head back in pride unveiling her face. She handed him her papers. "Here's my license and our marriage license too. We're on our honeymoon. Our wedding was on June third. Look at the date, you'll see," she said with a confident smile. She put it to him almost like she was expecting some type of "congratulations." I felt a little more comfortable that our chances of going to jail were somewhat lessened.

"Well, you kids set down and I'll run these through," he said as he returned to his patrol car. Minutes later he came back with our documents in hand as our story had checked out, just as Libby had said. We weren't a threat to anybody.

"You kids be careful now," he said as he got back in his cruiser and rolled westbound.

The trooper hadn't cleared our sight when we heard the low rumble of a white Dodge Tradesman van rolling in the eastbound lanes. As it passed by, I saw the driver looking our way. He slowed the van, drove left across the grass median in a U-turn then pulled right up to us.

I had never seen a car drive across the grass median strip before and though it was certainly illegal, it made us both chuckle a bit. We hadn't moved an inch from our footsteps with the trooper. *We'll be discreet, no more drunks. We're going to be more judgmental about things from now on.*

The van came to a full stop right in front of us, partially on the highway and partly on the gravel. I opened the door to find a respectable, sober guy perhaps eight or nine years our senior, maybe twenty-eight years old. He looked kind of like a mix between Mick Jagger and David Soul, the blonde cop from one of those Clint Eastwood cop movies. His face was clean-shaven, his hair, so typical of 1970's length, was recently barbered and he wore mirrored sunglasses.

Sure, I thought. *This looks like a fine, respectable person who is willing to give us a lift.*

"You guys want a ride?" he asked.

"Sure," I said. "Thanks for stopping."

I slid open the side cargo door and threw our packs into the van. Libby hopped on top of the packs and I loaded into the passenger bucket seat. No sooner did we start rolling out when the driver said, "Are you guys okay? I saw that cop was checking you guys out and I got worried. I thought I'd better double back and see if you guys needed some help."

"What, you passed us?" I asked, a little confused.

"Yeah, I thought I'd better, thought you were in trouble and might need some help."

We never really understood what he meant by all that until the following day. He introduced himself as "Mack James;" the name, the person we would never forget. Small talk with new people always started out a little awkward and so we just blew his remarks off as some strange caring. Anyway, we were going somewhere again and began to talk at length about many things, our travels, possible destinations, our wedding, honeymoon, and the like. We told Mack about the wreck on the divide and how we were still a bit freaked out by it all, but had settled down considerably. We thanked him for stopping to give us a ride.

The sun had set and looking back on another hard day's work, we'd started out at the KOA campground just outside of the reservation at the Little Bighorn; it had been a long day.

Mack then offered us a lengthy ride by saying, "Why don't we get some grub, have a few beers, and roll out the bags on the side of the road? If you want, you can ride with me tomorrow, north up to Libby," referring to a small mountain town in northwestern Montana.

Mack looked like a comfortable guy with whom we could both relate. Besides, Libby was Libby's name and again it seemed right, destined. We agreed to his plan and found a roadside bar to shoot some pool over beers. Bored with it all we rolled down the road a ways and set our bags out under that big, starry Montana night sky.

Staring straight up to the heavens I sat and wondered what would become of us. We really didn't know where we were going, but we were clear on where we'd come from. I recalled all of our friends at the bluegrass wedding, all huddled amidst those great trees in the front yard of our family farm in Centre County. We had moved to the farm when I was thirteen to give my dad a chance at peace and serenity after his many painful years in the V.A. hospital in Lyons, New Jersey.

We got married in a light rain, in the sight of God, beneath the great oak trees of that old farm. Actually there weren't that many people at our wedding, but there were new and old friends alike. Our new friends were folks we met while working the graveyard shift in an assembly line factory. Libby and I were the newcomers on the job. We made, tested, and packed electronic capacitors, which we all thought were actually weapons parts destined for the more troubled corners of the earth. We used to pack them in vacuum-formed, clear plastic trays that had army men, tanks, and exploding bombs as the background print. Each tray looked like some kind of bizarre kid's game. We made tens of thousands of them.

For Roberta, our wedding was certainly her year's highlight. She ran the corona machine, staring untiringly at the glare of a strange green oscilloscope to discard faulty capacitors, night after night, year after year. Roberta was well into her seventies, skinny as a rail with gaunt cheeks and pale, white skin that rarely ever saw the light of day. We often thought that the fine pink dust billowing from the electrostatic coating room next to her workstation would eventually kill her from lung cancer. That was if her chain smoking didn't take her sooner. But like all others at our wedding, she found herself wrapped in the warmth and love of friends and family. I suppose my sibling's and neighbor's bluegrass band and a dram of Jack Daniels helped warm her as well. The band started playing at two that afternoon and reluctantly stopped sometime well after midnight.

I pondered on while staring into those endless Montana stars. *Where and when will this journey end?* I heard in my mind's ear the jolly roar and laughter of my lifelong friend, Gene Rudzinski. Gene was a mountain of a man, bigger than life itself. He was somewhere between being a great, big uncle and a best friend in my life. We used to hunt deer and small game together. I think my mom had him tag with me because I started sporting at fourteen and spent a lot of time in the woods alone. I think she was worried about my need for supervision in the field, especially on season opening days.

The memory of Gene's words and great voice was so comforting. The evening of our wedding I asked Gene for some heartfelt advice. We were all pretty lit by then and the band was playing "Fox On The Run." With a sigh and a befuddled look, I asked him, "So what do I do now? Your best advice, big guy."

Gene asked if I had any money. I told him that we had saved a thousand dollars working at the factory. He said to take off, to travel, and not to worry. He said to forget about everything for as long as we could, to travel as far as we could go and think about only one thing, to love each other and to forget about everything else. I asked him what to do when we ran out of money. He said to forget about that entirely and to just love each other and don't worry about anything at all. He said that in time, all those things would become clear, but for at least six months we weren't to think or worry about anything at all. He said that we'd never get another chance, for the rest of our lives to live so freely.

"Once you settle down, that's it," he said. "You're in for the long, hard grind from then on."

I knew deep down in my heart that he was right as he always spoke with absolute and jovial Polish certainty.

Libby was already out like a light. She always slept well. I lay down on my back and pulled the sleeping bag up to my neck. I knew that we were honest and trustworthy people, but except for our love of each other and the clothes on our backs, we had no real identity. It was 1978 and most of the hippies were well on their way to selling out. Disco had finally dethroned The Beatles on the charts and we were neither beatniks nor Bee Gees fans. We were both twenty years old though Libby was three months older than I.

The truth is that we were homeless but we never felt so because we always had our two-man tent. We could pop it up in the dark of night beside the road almost anywhere, any time, and by dangling that crucifix necklace from the top of the tent, it was a home, fit for a king and queen. But on that night we didn't need our tent and the crucifix stayed around my neck. The days were long, sometimes fearful, but always exciting and in my heart I knew that Gene was right. There was nothing to fear because our hearts were good and we had faith that our chosen path was right. I fell asleep that night knowing that we were good people.

The heat of the western morning sun was abrupt and we rustled up our bags to get a hot cup of coffee. Within minutes we were again rolling north in Mack's Tradesman. We drove through increasingly remote wilderness on a road that cut through massive stands of spectacular fir trees. We hadn't ever seen timber before and were awestruck.

Mack said, "Wait till we get up by Libby and Troy. They get even bigger up there."

We jumped right into the morning's small talk. Mack was a little hard to read because of his shades. He wouldn't look at us when he talked and never called us by name. Our topics were common, though, and our talk was comfortable. We started sharing experiences and talked of wildlife, of deer, elk, and bear. We knew nothing about western big game and were captivated by Mack's stories. Mack and I were hunters. Libby was a wanna be and you could see her eagerness to know more as we spoke. Then our conversation turned to guns.

"Do you like guns?" Mack asked.

"Sure," I said.

"Check this out," he said as he reached behind his seat and handed me a briefcase. His eyes were fixed on the road ahead through his mirrored shades. To my surprise, I opened the case to find a Thompson Contender complete with scope. It was fully disassembled in the gun case and had two short barrels, one for a large-caliber pistol and the other for a center fire rifle cartridge. I was amazed.

"Do you mind if I have a closer look at this?" I asked.

"Go right ahead. Put it together," he said.

I had only seen those pistols in hunting magazines and catalogs. I had always wanted one but never really figured I'd ever touch one let alone assemble one. My dreams were coming true, kind of like what Gene said. I assembled the short rifle barrel on the pistol.

I felt great, like I was in control of the world. I pointed the Contender out the window and at approaching objects down the road. I marveled at its craftsmanship and respected that it was surely a very lethal sidearm. I broke it down and carefully placed it back in its case. I was gloating over it and thanked Mack for having shared it with us. I closed up the gun case and handed it back to Mack who tucked it safely behind his bucket seat.

With his left hand on the steering wheel while driving on down the road, Mack said in a calm voice, "You like that one? How 'bout this one?" In slow motion Mack reached for something near his left hip. All sounds went mute. In one long, sweeping move, Mack drew a large-bore revolver from a holster, swung it across himself, extended his arm, and pointed it directly at my face. His head swung in perfect synchrony with the arc of the moving revolver. He abandoned all attention to the road and for the first time looked directly at me down the snout of his piece.

In seconds that lasted a lifetime, I sat motionless, frozen, unable to even breathe and my heart may have skipped a beat. The instant that Mack's attention returned to the road, something foreign took me over. It could well have been that my guardian angel jumped right into my skin and took over because I had a surge of courage I'd never felt before. My left hand swept up to meet his and as I leaned forward in my seat, I palmed the revolver and instinctively twisted it toward his thumb.

I'd learned at a young age about the thumb's weak grip from my karate instructor, Kenny Taylor. He used to show us all how to break a stranger's grip by twisting your fist toward their thumb. I used to show off the move to all my friends at school. It worked every time and it worked on Mack. I had completely forgotten that Kenny Taylor also told us never to challenge someone holding you at gunpoint, but knives he considered to be fair game. Needless to say, Kenny Taylor was one bad dude, a great friend, and one heck of a mentor of the martial arts.

In an instant, the revolver was mine. I had palmed the cylinder with my index finger firmly behind the hammer and my thumb under the trigger guard. I held it flat in front of me with both hands open-palmed like I was reading the Good Book. *What do I do now?* I continued to react without decision and stayed very calm. With the butt of the piece in my left hand and the barrel pointed at my opened window I picked up where I had just left off with the Thompson Contender. I resumed admiring the new piece in my hand. It was indeed beautiful, a Colt .45 with a gorgeous, perfectly crafted abalone handle. I rolled it around slowly to find that it was fully loaded, all six chambers.

Looking at Mack, who was again attentive to driving, I carefully pointed its muzzle at targets down the road and out the window. As I chose new targets, I'd briefly glance over at Mack. He was without expression and wouldn't look at me. He knew the power was mine and though I felt that power, I was still petrified inside. I could not let him see my fear and soon paid him no attention at all. Having that revolver in my hand made it easier to mask my fear. My brain went gray and having to act without thinking, I rolled the piece around and casually handed it back to Mack grip first.

Mack's blank face showed a hint of a smile. He reholstered the pistol at his hip then said, "I can trust you."

Libby was absolutely cool and together. She was sitting on the packs between us and to the rear a bit when all that came down. Mack placed both his hands on the steering wheel and she leaned forward to hear him better as he'd begun to speak in a different tone. We both listened very carefully over the rumble of the van's engine as Mack made us a proposition.

"I'm going to rob a grocery store up in Libby tonight. If you guys want, you can make enough money tonight to travel for years. All you have to do is drive away when I come out." He went on to tell us of his profession, the jobs he had done, the process of robbery, and nefarious situations he had gotten into and out of. He made it clear that he wouldn't hesitate to shoot his way out of trouble if and when the need arose. Apparently, he had some sort of network that kept him steadily employed and we had no doubt in our minds that he was very serious about his work, that he was very serious about the night ahead, and that we needed to take him very seriously.

I wanted to die right then and there.

He said, "I bought a totaled CJ5 in a junkyard just for the title. A couple weeks later I went to a car dealer and picked out a brand new one just like it. I even found one the exact same color yellow. I asked the dealer if I could take it for a test drive. The guy threw me the keys and I took off with the Jeep and never went back. The cool thing is the title of the junker matches the description of the one I stole except for the VIN number. Cops never check those at a routine stop. It's already up in Libby parked in front of the store. "

We both knew that this was no time to be speechless and that we had to appear to be comfortable with the situation, but inside, my stomach was wrenching. I so wanted to talk alone with Libby and she stayed as cool as a cucumber. I could hear my mother's voice saying something cautious in my head. *What about the new in-laws? What would "mom" and "dad" think? Everything's gone very wrong. It's not supposed to be like this. We're on our honeymoon, damn it.* We shot west thinking things were still like Bonanza. You know, horses, cowboys, and Indians. *And guns. Sure.* That pulled me back into the reality of the moment.

"So how far is it to Libby?" I asked.

"It's just up the road, maybe ten minutes," he replied.

I wanted out of that van and out of the situation at once. Mack never asked us if we wanted to do the job, he just laid out all the details. I felt a little comfortable that we weren't forced to a point of decision while still in his van. We remained calm and all conversation dropped off, and as we neared town, Mack put on a stone cold face.

We pulled into Libby, which was of course a quiet, warm little town, big enough for a bus stop but not much else. We made a couple of right-hand turns and slowly drove by the grocery store. Mack pointed out the yellow CJ5 right where he said it would be. Ironically, we passed right by the jailhouse too. *Where is that state trooper when you need him?*

About that time Mack asked, "You guys wanna go for a cup of coffee?"

"Yeah, let's do that," I replied, being careful not to show my elation at the thought of being in the presence of others.

We doubled back to a little cafe that we'd passed when first entering town. Mack rolled the van to a stop and asked us to lock all the doors. Casually, I hopped out and immediately slid the cargo door open to get my hands on Libby. I could see in her eyes the very same fear and emotions. We were surely soul mates. Mack lagged behind a bit as he put on a fake but very convincing wig, then pulled down a brim hat.

The three of us walked into the cafe and took a booth on the south wall. It looked like a typical Saturday morning at the smoky western small-town cafe with maybe a dozen people about including the waitress and cook. We drank coffee and Mack ate a full breakfast. The mere thought of food made me nauseous and just having a waitress frequent our table was a relief. We drank coffee like sons of bitches. We would have sat there and drank coffee for weeks if it meant that we wouldn't have to get back in Mack's van.

He finished his meal and said, "Well, why don't we get out of here? I gotta use the bathroom. I'll just be a minute." We offered to pay for his meal as a genuine offer of appreciation for having given us a lengthy ride, but he just shrugged his shoulders as he left for the bathroom. We paid the bill then scampered outside at a quick pace. You can imagine the frantic dialogue that passed in the minute or so that we had to ourselves. That was our first chance to talk in confidence since the previous evening's roadside police check.

Libby asked, "What are we going to do, John?" All semblance of calm was gone from her face. Her beautiful eyes were wide with fear.

I was equally afraid, but seized the moment. "We're not going to get back into that van, under no circumstances. Do you hear me? You understand?"

She nodded her head committing fully to my direction with the situation, giving me strength. "What do we do then?" she asked.

"When he comes out, we'll wait for him to unlock the side door. I'll grab our packs," I explained.

"What then?" she asked.

Mack came out the cafe door and was approaching the van. I lowered my voice. "I don't know, just remain calm. We'll figure it out. Do not run and do not get back into the van, no matter what. We're safe right here, right now. He won't pull anything with people around," I said.

I knew that getting our gear on our backs was crucial, not that we had much. Our gear was all of two packs, a couple of bags, a tent, a canteen, a change of clothes, two flutes, a camera, some trinkets, ID, about nine hundred dollars in cash, and Granny's afghan. The canteen, tent, and one bag were wedding gifts. The packs were heavy and we were in great shape from lugging them around. But without those things, we were screwed. It was our property.

Mack walked toward the van with his hands in his pockets. He had a slow, steady gait and a bit of a shrugged posture. We were anxious to hear his door unlock. He then pulled himself into the driver's seat and in a stretch reached over to unlock the passenger door, then the cargo door behind. I opened the cargo door, pulled out our only belongings, then promptly slammed it shut.

I heard Mack mumble something inside the van as he looked at us. Our intentions were known; the play had been called and the ball had been hiked. There was no going back and we would have to be unwavering, so we were. Mack walked around the front of the van to talk it over. I started to pull on my pack and Libby did the same.

"What are you doin'? What's goin' on?" he asked

"Nothin' Mack. We're just gonna head on down the road," I replied.

"What are you talking about?" he asked.

"No big deal. We're just gonna move on with our honeymoon," I said with confidence and as a matter of fact.

"Just get in the van," he said. "Don't worry, everything is all right. There isn't going to be any trouble tonight at all. I promise," he reassured.

"Mack, listen. We're on our honeymoon. We saw some big trees coming into town that we want to go check out. It's really no big deal," I restated.

The words and courage of my big friend Gene came to mind and stiffened my posture. *"Just take off for six months and don't worry about money or anything."* I could see Mack was concerned about our decision. I read in him that we were suddenly a problem for his evening's plans. Not only had he divulged his intentions but he had also revealed other incriminating details from previous robberies. He even had disclosed a number of jobs that were set for the coming weeks and months. To Mack these were "jobs" and this was indeed his "work."

"Just get in the van, everything is going to be fine. Trust me," again he said.

I cinched down the belt strap of my pack and tightened up both shoulder harnesses. Libby and I were in sync and Mack could see that we were determined. We were strong from carrying the extra weight of those packs. It was almost like we were suiting up for work, like soldiers setting to the field. With our packs on tight, we were complete, ready for anything.

"Where are you gonna go?" he asked. I sensed that he was concerned that we might go right to the police.

Libby said, "We don't care what you do with your life. But we're on our honeymoon and we're not ready for anything like this."

"Look, Mack, your business is *your* business," I said. "We don't have any interest in all that. Don't worry. We're not gonna go to the cops. We're just gonna head on down the road and continue on with our honeymoon. That's it." My tone was friendly, compassionate, but not convincing and he saw that we were certain to leave.

He then offered to help us out, but with Mack it seemed would always come some sort of proposition. "Well, if that's what you want to do, why don't you let me take you up to this beautiful campground I know? It's way up in the mountains. It's really a beautiful place. There's nobody there. You'll love it," he said. "Just get back in the van. I'll take you up there," he insisted.

I shook my head and without turning I started to back away from him. I raised my hand, showing him my palm, and thanked him for the ride. We both wished him well. Mack just stood there and said nothing as we turned and walked out of town.

Within minutes we were alone, surrounded in timber and walking back down the deserted two lane that we'd ridden into town. There was no traffic at all. We walked about a half mile talking back and forth the whole way and were really glad to be rid of Mack. We felt like we were in the clear, our pace was quick, and our hearts were light. At first, we thought the faster and farther we walked the more distant was our brush with Mack.

But as I was walking in the lead, I stopped momentarily to weigh our situation when something unnerving suddenly dawned on me. We were a long way from being out of the woods so to speak and no matter how far or how fast we walked, we were not escaping the situation. The slightly uphill road back into town was a long arcing curve to the right. I turned and told Libby, "You know, there is nothing to stop that guy from driving out here and blowing us both away right on the side of the road."

At that very instant, we heard approaching the signature low rumble of Mack's van. Libby looked over her shoulder, back toward town and where the road disappeared into the trees we saw Mack's white Tradesman van appear roaring our way. We had no time to talk or plan. He came to an abrupt stop right before us with the van only partially pulled off the road. We were absolutely petrified and couldn't have run even if we wanted to as it all happened so fast. My stomach was gone entirely.

As Mack walked around the front of the van, I saw the fingers of both his hands were tucked into his pockets, not his thumbs. I also noticed that his shirt was no longer tucked in as it was at the cafe just minutes before. *For sure that Colt .45 is under his shirt, tucked into his pants.* He was a little hunched over and walked toward me with that steady, slow step. I knew that if he even so much as moved his right hand toward his belt buckle I would take him down. I would have to.

As he got near I stepped in front of Libby closing the distance between Mack and me a few more inches. The hair on the back of my neck was stiff, my eyes were fixed on him, and I was never, ever more ready for anything in my life. My whole body was coiled hard, like a predator ready to pounce. I knew no matter what, Libby would be able to get away. I would deny him, at all cost.

Mack said, "I've been thinking about that job tonight. I'm not going to do this one."

"Hmm. Why not?" I asked, not caring whatsoever his reasons.

"Well, it just doesn't look right to me. It doesn't feel right either," he said. "I think I'll just go up to Sand Point and visit my grandpa."

"I didn't know that you had a grandpa around here," I said.

It seemed like a change of subject was a welcomed relief. I didn't want to know any more about his evening's plans and while Mack went on a bit about his grandpa, we never heard a single word that he'd said. He broke his words with another request.

"Why don't you guys just get in the van and let me take you up to that campground? It's a beautiful place way back in the mountains," he offered throwing his head back and to the right. By his gesture I could tell that the campground was in the opposite direction than we were walking. "You'll never see another soul up there," he said.

"Thanks but no thanks, Mack. There's a lot of country we saw this morning that we want to take another look at. We'll be heading down the road that way," I said as I tipped my head southeast.

"Fair enough," Mack said, shaking his head slightly. He then shrugged his shoulders walking back around the front of the van, hopped in, wheeled the rig around, and rumbled back toward town. All things considered, I thought he took rejection pretty well.

Just as quickly as he had appeared, Mack was gone, but we still knew that we weren't safe on that road. We thought of just running straight uphill into the forest but decided that we needed to immediately be near more people. We turned around and started walking right back toward the safety of town. Our walk turned into an all-out run with me in the lead. We stopped to catch our breath just before reaching the cafe. We hunched over ourselves panting hard with hands on our knees and though neither of us was laughing we weren't without words between breaths.

Libby said, "My God, John." She took a long, deep breath between phrases. "Did you feel your knees knocking back there? Mine are still knocking. Are yours? Are your knees knocking too?" she asked with an astonished look.

I knew exactly what she was talking about and nodded my head up and down in full acknowledgment. It was like one of those old Krazy Kat or Bugs Bunny cartoons. You know, when your knees shake uncontrollably out of fear. Neither of us had ever experienced it before. We thought it was some imaginary depiction of fear until that very morning on the side of the road with Mack. Lucky for us that we were wearing full pants instead of shorts or Mack would have seen us trembling in our tracks. As our breathing slowed so did our knee knocking and soon we gathered ourselves together and walked as we talked through an alternative plan to get out of town.

We thought about going back into the cafe, but decided to look for a bus depot instead. Riding a bus would get us out of town and off the road for a stretch. We found a Greyhound station immediately across the street from the jailhouse we'd passed earlier that morning scoping out the "job." The station was a dank, worn, and dark office. We walked into the station and inquired about the very next bus out of town and not caring where it was headed, we couldn't have boarded soon enough. The clerk told us that the bus was scheduled to arrive shortly before noon but sometimes it ran a little late. He said that we could buy tickets to just about anywhere and so we had to settle on a destination.

We bought two, one-way tickets to Pendleton, Oregon. Why Pendleton? It was cheap and it was far, no other reason. Waiting for the bus, we took a couple of seats and held each other loosely. Noon was a couple hours out and it could well have been a century. The morning's events, the caffeine, and the paranoia were overwhelming.

The bus arrived slightly late, as expected. We threw our packs into the luggage compartment and found the very last seat in the rear of the bus. It was one seat wider than all the other seats on the bus, kind of like a mini sofa. We rode from town to town not knowing where we were headed and all we knew was that we'd have to get off the bus at Pendleton, wherever that was, somewhere in Oregon. We crossed the Washington state line with a sigh of relief and with every new town and every mile, we felt more relieved that Mack was farther behind us.

We talked long about the day and about Mack and started to lighten up. At least Mack was not on that bus. Despite the day, we were both so glad to be gone from the east, gone from Bucknell. Yeah, we met at Bucknell University. It was a beautiful campus. I was a sophomore and Libby was a junior. We talked long about our college experience on the bus. We figured that Bucknell was where folks went to become well spoken, but we never really understood just exactly what the heck that actually meant. Most of the time we couldn't figure out just exactly what our professors were talking about. Unfortunately, we couldn't read fast enough to keep up with everybody else. I fell behind and started partying way too much.

Libby never messed with drugs or alcohol. For her school was an atrocity for different reasons. She felt unhappy from the time her parents sent her to boarding school when she was fifteen. She had been molested twice as a child, once by a stranger and once by one of her professors at boarding school. "Molested," might be a little soft. From her account, the professor attempted to rape her. When Libby told me, I was shocked and it was no wonder why she had such disdain for education. I knew why she was so shy and cold to me at first. She wouldn't even kiss me under that big, full, Halloween moon the night we met on campus. I so wanted to make up for all the shortcomings that had been dealt her way. We struggled so with college life and successfully transferred to the old school of hard knocks instead. And meeting Mack was one of those hard lessons. We realized from the back seat of that Greyhound bus that it was far easier to get into trouble than it was to get out of it. We learned that we could get into deep trouble without even trying if we weren't careful, but the day was slowly improving, all things considered.

We started to think things through, over and over again while rumbling around on that Greyhound. We were mutually impressed with our ability to stay calm back in Montana. Libby was always naturally calm. She had learned from experience at a young age that remaining calm was the best way to deal with child molesters. For me it was also learned behavior. As my mind drifted back in time, I remembered how my mom dealt so cooly with a deranged mental patient from Dood's hospital.

Oh yeah, Dood was my dad. He was a paranoid schizophrenic patient in a V.A. hospital for many, many years. Long before he became "Dood," my dad graduated from the Naval Academy at Annapolis. Lieutenant Commander Robert John Riger became an officer in the United States Navy and was well on his way to a remarkable career. Well, while flying copilot at critical altitude, he suffered a permanently debilitating anoxic event that destroyed a portion of his brain. He was never the same after that and a decade of hospitalization had taken its toll on him. His fingers and mustache were stained brown from the nicotine and caffeine he chose as part of his self-medication. He preferred Kool filter kings, one after the other, all day long, every day. My sister had coined his nickname in the fifth grade when she made him an ashtray with the name "Dood" written in rolled clay on the bottom. None of us knew how she ever came up with his name, but it stuck for the rest of his life.

For Dood, the smoke went well with sweet, iced coffee. That was his nutrient staple. The nicotine and caffeine were in addition to an ever-changing cocktail of prescribed, hard tranquilizers to help make his voices go away. All told, his life was rotting away as fast as his teeth were and we all knew it. For many years we visited him at the hospital monthly on weekends. Sometimes he was on furlough from the hospital. Other times he'd escape to come home for a few hours. Once he arrived, my mom, my little brother, and I would have to immediately make the three-hour trip to take him back to the hospital. Dood was truly a wonderful and loving man despite that he thought he was a spy for the pope and heard voices instructing him to kill my sister.

Well, one summer night, one of his friends from the hospital decided to pay us a visit. We heard the front door of our house open while my mother and my other four siblings were seated at the dining table in the kitchen of our home in Jersey.

My mom said, "Did you guys hear the front door open?" I think we all did, but none of us wanted to believe so. About that time, a man, a stranger, with dark hair and wild, crazy eyes, walked right into our kitchen and started in on my mom in a threatening voice. My older brother Charlie was coming into manhood and stood up to the intruder. The guy reached across the kitchen table and grabbed brother Charlie by the collar with one hand and raised his other huge right hand.

"These hands are registered with the FBI, boy. I could kill you with one clean swipe," the stranger said aloud.

My sister and I started to cry when my mom in her calm, loving voice stepped in. "Oh, now that's okay, you guys. There won't be any need for that. Hey, why don't you kids walk on up to the pool? I'll stay here and have a talk with Daddy's friend," she said.

None of us wanted to leave her there, but we knew we had to do as she asked. We had an unspoken understanding to *always* do just exactly as she asked. It was kind of like a code for us and we'd been through it before with Dood a time or two.

We ran up to the pool at Riverdel and got the pool manager to call the cops who escorted the intruding mental patient from our home. My mom seized control of the situation by nature of her ability to stay calm. Had we not stayed calm that morning with Mack the day's outcome could well have been different.

Time and again we came to the same conclusion that Mack wanted us back in that van for one and only one reason. Though he said that he'd changed his mind about robbing the store Mack had to certainly be unsure of our intentions. He had to wonder if we would go to the police and tip them off. Mack couldn't afford that chance. I was thinking that we had been very lucky to get away scot-free when a new swell of fear surged in me.

Could Mack have learned that we'd left town on a bus? There'd be no other likely explanation for our disappearing from such a small town so quickly. Surely, he would inquire at the bus station about his camping friends who left without his saying, "goodbye." He'd learn that we were bound for Pendleton.

The fear was so strong that we knew we couldn't ride the bus to Pendleton. Mack would likely be there when we got off. Perhaps it wouldn't be Mack at all. He could just phone one of his associates to do his dirty work for him, with us never knowing the difference or even seeing it coming the next time. We had to err on the side of caution. We thought of getting off the bus in Spokane but feared that he or another hit man may be following the bus to take us out at the first opportunity. Surely his patience was wearing thin trying to follow us or run us down. We agreed to get off the bus before reaching Pendleton.

The bus stopped in a small jerk-water town in western Oregon called Spangle. We chose Spangle because we could see that there was no one trailing behind the bus. We pulled our packs out of the luggage compartment and slipped right into the closest open establishment, which happened to be a bar. It was late Saturday afternoon and the bar was slow with business. It had that dusky smell of dirt, smoke, and old, rotten beer. We found a booth in a far corner of the bar and ordered a couple beers. Happy hour brought more folks to the bar and before long there was a small-town Saturday night party in full swing.

We partied well into the night with dozens of folks. The atmosphere was loud, warm, and very friendly. We were pretty used to drinking and rarely ever drank excessively because our road budget didn't really allow it. By later that night, we had made friends with a number of folks who were buying us beers just to hear our road stories. Still disturbed by it all, we hadn't spoken to anyone about Mack.

Suddenly, the front door of the bar flew open and the place fell silent. Two "customers" entered and walked over to the bar. They were both wearing fully   rubberized Halloween masks that covered their heads and hands. Looking hideous, like a pair of old, decrepit cadavers or something, they walked slowly and steadily with a slightly hunched over posture. As they crossed the room, they were peering about in all directions, almost like they were trying to find someone. They peered at each and everyone in the bar, one by one; their faces were fully hidden except their eerie eyes peeking through the small holes in their masks.

You could have heard a pin drop because everyone was taken aback by their ghostly presence. They approached the bar, stopped, looked around, walked from table to table, then left the bar without having said anything to anyone, ordering a drink or exposing their identities.

We started to freak out! We were sure that it was either Mack or a pair of his accomplices. A couple that we had befriended immediately picked up on our fear and we unloaded a summary of the day's events to our new friends. We briefly told them about Mack.

They were thoroughly convinced of our predicament and shared our fear. The husband said, "Hey, we gotta get you guys out of here. Right now."

We were already headed for the door, shouldered our packs, and headed out to the street. Our new friends followed us out of the bar and as we walked down the street further into town we continued to describe the whole of the day's events. The husband, whose name I can't recall, and his wife, Pam, suggested that we head over to their house to be on the safe side.

I stopped in my tracks and looked the husband squarely in the eye. I assured him that we would be forever grateful and no bother at all if he could provide us sanctuary for a few hours. They were both glad to help and the fear dissipated in minutes. They were shocked and scared for us and by the time we'd reached their home they'd offered us safe haven through Sunday. The husband said that his brother was headed for the coast on Sunday afternoon and that we could catch a ride with him. Mack would soon be forgotten once we were safe and in the clear on the coast.

We were so appreciative of their offer. It was a great change of luck for us. We walked a few blocks under streetlights in the dark of night to their home. They were a genuinely thoughtful couple in their mid-forties. When we arrived at their home they made us comfortable, giving us clean towels and showing us where we could sleep. They opened right up to us and offered us everything from food and drink to a hot shower. We preferred to roll out our bags on the carpeted floor rather than further impose on them. Libby showered before going to bed that night.

I got up early the next morning to clean up. While showering I finally discovered the source of what had become an annoying, persistent itch in my groin and leg for days. I was covered with ticks. I had picked them up that one late night west of Fargo when we had hopped out of a semi and crawled off through the brush to camp. I knew that I had a few ticks, but in the shower I could see they were fully engorged with blood and that many had already embedded their heads beneath my skin. In fact they were already dead. I pulled them off and cleaned out the sores as best I could. I asked Libby if she'd found any on her but she hadn't. They must have been all through the clothes in my pack and I didn't know it.

We had learned that Pam and her husband were avid bridge players and since we both grew up in bridge-playing families, we spent the greatest portion of that day playing cards while doing our laundry. Pam told us that her brother and his wife were also sharp bridge players and encouraged us to play a rubber or two with them.

By Sunday noon we were ready to move on but sad to leave our new friends who could well have saved both our lives. We were forever indebted to those folks and while waiting for their relatives to arrive Pam's husband, worried about us, offered some words of advice. He tossed me a heavy metal bearing. It was the shape of a small barrel, kind of like a whisky keg that was only about an inch and a half long and about an inch wide. It fit perfectly in my clenched fist. He told me to always keep it in my pocket and said it might come in handy if we ever found the need to punch our way out of a situation.

"Hey, it's better than nothing," he said. The bearing was heavy and clumsy in my pocket, but I knew he was right. I agreed to his advice and thanked him. If nothing else, it was a great souvenir reminder of those two.

The brother and his wife arrived after lunch. We said our farewells, hopped in the brother's car, and the four of us traveled down the Columbia River toward the coast. The Columbia is an immense river. I recall endless fields of irrigation, orchards, power plants, and breathtaking landscapes. They were a genuinely friendly couple that was well aware of our situation and we got along as well with them as we did Pam and her husband. Her name was Marilyn and his name was Randall, Randall and Marilyn Vaughn. They were from McMinnville, Oregon, about an hour from the coast.

Randall was sympathetic to our situation because he'd ridden into McMinnville on the rails just after the Depression. He started life anew there and had become the mayor of their town. They were happy to help us out, to hear our stories, and play a lot of bridge once we got to McMinnville.

Along the way, our new guardians asked us if we wanted to check out a waterfall on the way, a feature of the Cascade Mountains. Time was again on our side. We had nowhere to go and no time to be there. We were free and willing to see and do whatever. They pulled their car into a large, curved parking lot. There were lots of people with cameras walking about. Strikingly distinct were the lush, forested woods and the soothing sound of falling water originating unseen from several hundred yards behind a wooded knoll.

It was a special place for sure. It was a peaceful place. It felt like a place of love and inspiration. We followed Randall and Marilyn to a bridge that perfectly framed one of the most beautiful sights we'd ever see. Libby and I stood there speechless, arm in arm, in full embrace as we stood before a great cascade fall at least five hundred feet high, perhaps even taller. We already knew this place well. We stood before what we had seen in a huge poster within reach of Libby's bed at Bucknell. Though she had no other pictures in her room, a poster of this very fall was on her dorm room wall at Carey House, the international dormitory. We used to stare at it and wish that we could be in that ever-so-inviting picture; we always wanted to jump right into that poster. She would often touch the cascade and gently run her fingers over the trees on the paper. The fall was not identified in the poster but as we stood there in tears Marilyn told us the name of the fall, "Multnomah." The name was so fitting though we never found out what it meant.

The world stopped. The only hint of time was the powerful sound of the water plunging into a pool beneath the great fall. We held hands at arms length on the arched bridge and in a moment that could have lasted an eternity, I was fixed on Libby. Her profile was tall and proud. Her brunette hair was cut in a long, gypsy shag and flowed freely from the misty, plunge-pool breeze just a hundred feet to fore. She was an incredibly strong and courageous woman. Her features were purely Celtic, perhaps Welsh. She was a lass for sure and I was awestricken by her beauty.

I thought back to college and all that we had overcome. I recalled those nights when we walked the railroad tracks under the grey of an eastern fall night and how we stared into each other's eyes under moonlight. In the light of day Libby's eyes were unlike all others. The outer rim of her iris was green and changed to blue then brown then black at the pupil. In fact, her eyes had all the colors of all the eyes I had ever seen. The strength in her chin and nose complemented her high, rosy cheeks. Her skin was as soft as silk and fair like the wool of a newborn lamb. She was wearing her green turtleneck, army sweater, and khaki pants. Her clothes were freshly laundered at Pam's.

It's amazing what a little soap and water will do to renew the spirit, I thought. *Beneath her clothes, my God, she's a masterpiece.* Libby was a work of voluptuous perfection. She had all the right curves that extended from the various dimples where her muscles met. I never understood what a foot fetish was until I met her. Not that I had a craving for women's feet, it's just that Libby's feet were so unlike all others. Her Vasque Whitney boots only hid her adorable toes, as we'd go about the day. *Libby is the complete woman.* Quite bluntly, she was very well built. She had become quite strong from walking great distances and carrying her hefty pack, bringing out her very best.

Frank Frazetta's women have absolutely nothing on her, I thought. She had a distinct sweetness about her taste and smell that hinted of something distantly familiar to my memory. She was a living, breathing pheromone in the flesh, a sensual attractant, like the rarest of fine saffron. Her smell was almost like that of an infant but it was hers and hers alone.

I am immersed in this woman and can't get enough of her. She is mine, and mine alone, my woman, my betrothed, my wife. For heaven's sake this will certainly become a problem from time to time living this way. But I do have that great barrel bearing in my pocket ready for any and all would be wrong doers, God forbid that I should ever have to use it. I know what it means to be in love at first sight. I can only imagine what lies before us in this walk through life, but right now the world is still.

I knew that Mack was well in the past and we would never see him again. Though our troubles were few, you could probably have bowled over us with a steamroller and that would have been infinitely better than being trapped by circumstances back east. We were so damn glad to be gone from the east and all our failed challenges back home, let alone to be at Multnomah. *What must lie ahead?*

We walked around the plunge pool to the west side and viewed the cavity behind the falls. We were getting soaked and perhaps the chill brought us back to our senses a little. We thought it best to run down Marilyn and Randall who had encouraged us to explore a while. We found them at the car, anxious to get on the road again. They had stopped at the falls many times before and could not have known how special the moment was for us.

We got in their car and told them about our revelations at the falls. It was getting late in the afternoon and they encouraged us to spend the night at their home and play some cards. We accepted and thanked them for their offer assuring them that we would set out on our own again first thing in the morning.

We continued on down river and arrived in McMinnville later that evening. As we pulled into their driveway we noticed that they had carved out a pretty descent life for themselves. Randall broke out his special homemade beet wine for the occasion; its sweetness we'd never forget. They had a small barbecue for us and we all enjoyed a night of wine, supper, and cards. We played bridge well into the night as Randall and Marilyn taught us a unique convention for bidding aces and kings in one bid. Through all of our future years playing bridge, on occasion even with world dignitaries, we would meet no others who knew their convention. We called it the "Vaughn Convention."

Marilyn asked us about our families and it became clear that she was worried about us so we took a break from the bridge table to talk of heart. She convinced Libby to call her mother, to spare her any worry, and though Libby was reluctant, she agreed. That was the first night Libby had spoken with her mother since our wedding. I could tell that Libby was down after her conversation with her mother.

I took her aside and asked, "How did it go?"

"Oh, okay, I suppose," Libby replied.

"Did you tell her we're in Oregon?" I asked.

"She doesn't seem worried where we are or how we got here. She did say 'hello,' though," Libby chuckled.

Libby didn't want Marilyn to know that her conversation didn't go so well and because Marilyn felt good that Libby had called home, that was good enough for us. We finished the rubber of bridge and then turned into our bags on their floor for the night.

The next morning, Marilyn and Randall were worried. It was raining and they feared that hitchhiking would put us back into harms way. They knew all about our brush with Mack. Randall said, "You just can't go out there an' start walkin' and hitchhikin'." He wanted something more, something specific, and something known, like where we were going and how we'd get there. He even offered some employment prospects, but none sounded good enough to defeat Gene's plan. Where we were going and what we were doing was still a mystery to us and we liked it that way. Our immediate goal was the coast, to maybe even try to start a new life, but that was a fleeting idea at the moment.

Randall asked if we had any money and I told him that we had a grubstake saved up. He said, "You can't go on hitchhikin'. You must go buy a car, or something. You'll be a lot safer if you travel by car. I'll take you to a car dealer and maybe you could get a used car."

We could see that his concern was taking him over and we agreed to at least check it out, more just to lay in a plan that would lead us away and put us back on the road of discovery. It had stopped raining when Randall pulled into the car dealership and bid us a sad farewell though he was relieved to drop us off there instead of roadside. It became increasingly apparent that a lot of folks we met were reluctant to see us go on our own again, even Mack. I suppose they each had their own reasons but there was an attachment that was sometimes tough to break.

We weren't accustomed to folks wanting us to become part
of their lives. It seemed like Libby's folks were delighted to
see us go on our own. Her father was a decorated veteran
from World War II who had fought in the Battle of the Bulge
against the Germans and knew well that strength of character
came from establishing one's own independence. Libby had
acquired her father's courage and I not only admired her but
admired her father as well. I so wanted to be like them both.
My first meeting with her dad was to explain that we'd be
dropping out of school together and to ask for his daughter's
hand in marriage. As you can well imagine, I was pretty much
a worthless case and I knew that ever gaining his favor would
take some doing, if it were at all possible.

Neither of us had ever bought a car before, let alone from
a car dealer. At that, we weren't really sure we wanted a car.
We scanned the lot and realized that price would well limit our
selection. We looked over the used car section and started to
get excited about rolling down the open road in our brand
new jalopy.

*Funny how style can suddenly take you for a ride when in the last
two weeks it meant nothing at all. Should we settle in on the Civic?
The better mileage makes sense. We can easily fit our packs in, but
what about that Oldsmobile, that Delta Eighty-Eight, a true classic?* It
was a '66 or '68, a real chunk of Detroit steel, white with lots of
chrome and a great interior, all in all in great shape, like 80,000
miles. I found myself peering down its lines appreciating the
times of her assembly. I could almost hear Diana Ross and The
Supremes in the back of my mind. *This could be our car, an act to
mark a positive change in our life, one that will bring us great fortune
and a new future of limitless opportunity and excitement.*

We walked into the dealer's office and set our backpacks
on the floor against the wall just inside his door. We found a
well-dressed gentleman behind a desk who gave us a look of
weighing curiosity. We explained that we were passing through
town and had decided to buy a car to finish our honeymoon
and were really interested in the asking price of the used cars.
His curiosity turned into general disinterest and while looking

at us both he tilted his head back and called out loud for a different salesman to cut our deal.

A much younger, well-dressed man perhaps in his thirties greeted us with a smile and a handshake. He led us out of his boss's office to sit down at his much smaller desk in the open floor of the showroom. Libby and I were both relieved to learn that the Civic was actually two hundred dollars more than the classic.

We had no idea that haggling was expected when buying from a car dealer, especially used cars, and we were a little reluctant to make the purchase at all. He wanted $600 for the Oldsmobile and we had little more than that left to our name. Doubt started to creep into the dream of being car owners so we told him that we wanted to go back out and look the lot over one more time.

I sat down on the curb. Overlooking the used cars, I started to think back to our wedding day, cruising around in my old '54 Chevy my grandma Mary had passed down to me. We were riding in the back seat while Mark and Kathy escorted us down Tadpole Road. They were the only friends from Bucknell who came to our wedding; we hadn't invited anyone. How they learned of our day was a mystery but we were glad to see them both. We were all glad for the day of celebration. They'd given us a great wedding gift of a pair of knit baby booties. In one of the booties was a big, fat bone, which we passed around as Mark chauffeured us in the back seat. He was asking a lot of questions about just what we were going to do and Kathy was completely turned around in the front seat as we careened down that old country road.

"Well," I said. "I think tomorrow we're gonna head west."

When they learned that we were prepared to head out by foot and thumb they both tried to convince us to take the Chevy. We were almost set in our decision, though, as the car would eat up all our money in no time. We could go farther and travel so much longer without the car, or any other liabilities for that matter.

"What will you do with the car?" Mark asked as he drove.

I told them that my little brother just started driving and could use the car more than us.

But then again, what about Mack? Lord knows we don't want to run into his type ever again. And Randall and Marilyn? We don't want those guys to worry either. What about all the travel that may lie ahead without wheels under us? Our vulnerability? What I'd give for my old Chevy right now.

The fear overcame me, but Libby wasn't fully convinced that buying a car was such a good idea. Nonetheless, we agreed to buy the Eighty-Eight.

We went back inside and shook hands with the car dealer, "$600 it is," I said with a lukewarm grin. We went back outside to load our packs in the cruiser while the dealer drafted the sale. Signing the paperwork with hesitation, the reality didn't set in until we shucked out $600 in cash into the hands of the dealer. He left the room with our money. The cash that we had left, all that we had in our possession, was suddenly pretty meager. It wasn't the amount of cash, it was the amount of time; our freedom horizon was shortened by two-thirds with one swipe of a pen and a fist grab of our dough.

The dealer came back to the desk and we reviewed various documents. He then gave us the keys and wished us luck on our adventures. We left feeling as though our travels were of no interest to anyone there and as we walked out of the dealership we knew that we'd given in to both those guys who were on some kind of city trip. There was no attachment or human connection with either of them. It was business. I felt almost filthy, used in a sense. Something wasn't quite right because new car owners were supposed to be really happy. We disguised our frustration under frostbitten pumpkin smiles then jumped into the rig to roll off for parts unknown, without a direction or plan.

We didn't go one half mile when I glanced down at the gas gauge which was only a hair above "E," and filling the tank ate another chunk out of my wallet. While pulling out of the gas station we passed by some hitchhikers. We wanted to stop and pick them up, but strangely we were afraid of them and in less than a mile our fear turned into envy. We knew nothing about the place through which we were driving. While hitchhiking we had become very trusting of others, people would tell us about jobs, history, landmarks, natural features, and such. Our trust didn't need to be earned and we benefited from being so blatantly open. But suddenly we knew nothing and we had no means of learning about the area.

Do we really want to live here? Who knows? The car changed all that.

We talked openly about our purchase as we headed toward the coast, which was about an hour west. Then we started talking about auto insurance in as much as we were driving illegally without it. Within miles, maybe thirty minutes after the sale, we were both convinced that the car had to go. *Maybe we could sell it to somebody for a profit when we get to the beach.* We didn't really want to stop traveling. I remembered Gene and how we were supposed to go for six months without worry of money or anything and the car had definitely compromised that plan in one ill-thought moment. We had abandoned our heart's desire and gave into fear instead. We yearned to reinstate our lost sense of totally irresponsible freedom.

THE COAST

The rain returned as a soft, persistent drizzle and by the time we got to the coast it turned into a drenching fog. The car was an anchor, dragging behind, dragging us down, and slowing our progress to nowhere to become nobodies. The coastal inland was a real let down too with lots of towns just like New Jersey.

Do we really want to settle here? This is just like where we came from.

The West Coast was very different, though. There was a lone, small bar and restaurant that abutted the beach at the ocean's shore. It looked pretty dead but it was Monday evening. I guess we were hoping to see a boardwalk with lots of people in swimsuits and suntans all wanting to buy our car, you know, like at Wildwood or Atlantic City. But there was no one, no salt water taffy, no amusement rides, no hustling or bustling anywhere, no such luck, not even any Beach Boys playing in the background.

We walked into the bar and found one grumpy old guy. He may have been just a bartender, but he could have been the owner. I think he was grumpy because business might have always been slow. We weren't hungry and bought nothing. It was obvious that we'd have no luck of turning a profit on our car there.

Well, what the heck, we're here. Let's go and check out the ocean. It was the first time either of us had ever seen the Pacific Ocean so we took our boots off to walk in the sand down to the water. We could hear the ocean better than we could see it through the mist; the clouds were low and the wet sand was cold on our bare feet. We stepped ankle deep into the decaying rush of waves that had traveled a lot farther than we had, from somewhere way beyond the water's foggy horizon. *The earth is a big place.*

The water was ice cold. We were all in the moment, our feet, the water, and the cold. There's something about the ocean that makes you feel real small and in the moment we realized that making it to the coast was not to be the end of our journey. It was to be just the first leg of one much longer.

We were determined to get our money back for the Eighty-Eight. *Tomorrow it will happen. Then we'll set out for the next leg of our honeymoon.*

We were relieved by our shared self-confidence and pulled back to the sand to sit on a driftwood log. Our thoughts perhaps would have been different if the sun was shining over a setting sea or the water had been warmer, but it was not to be.

I scrounged some more deadwood for a fire as night closed in on us and our beach. There was no one else about, it was too late and we were too tired to go in search of a meal. We had some dried meat in our packs and a couple cans of beans and vegetables that cooked damn well over the campfire. We opened the lid of a can about three-quarters of the way around; that way we could use the lid as a handle. We ate right out of the can with a camp fork and, with a little water from the canteen supper was served.

We ate as we talked through the day's events and shared our fork back and forth for a bite of grub. The day was turning to night and it had been a long, strange day in a strangely new place. New faces and new places had become the norm for us. *What would tomorrow be like?* We committed to converting the defeat and exhaustion of the day into success the next day. Sitting right there on that stump we rationalized that we had made it. We were at the West Coast of the United States of America in Oregon! We made it. Somewhere in our minds two weeks earlier that goal was nothing more than an idea at best. At least we'd gotten that far and so we celebrated with laughter still unknowing who and what would come our way the following day.

The day ended on that up note. We had issues to deal with but we decided they could all wait until the morning. Then we suddenly realized that the car would give us immediate shelter in case it started to rain again. We didn't set up the tent but rolled out our bags by the campfire. No need for a tent, not that night.

We had become quite used to sleeping right on the ground. I went to sleep that night thinking how important those bags had become for our survival. Without them survival would've been a lot more difficult. How lucky, I thought, that we had the warmth of down. We were lucky, so lucky. I doubt Libby's mom would've ever thought that her sleeping bag would someday become her shelter and warmth. What tremendous foresight she must have had. We went to sleep without worry or cause.

The next morning we woke at the dawn of day. It was a clearing fog and the sun shone through to promise drier weather. We had slept well and were fresh when we piled into the cruiser and headed right straight back to the car dealer in McMinnville. We wanted to be at the door when they opened. *Maybe they'll have coffee and donuts for their customers.*

We arrived early and waited. Planning to request a refund because we just simply did not want the car, we decided that if they wouldn't agree that we would have to play hardball. We devised a plan B just in case. Soon the younger salesman arrived and while unlocking the side door we approached him. He met us with a smile of familiarity. We were kind of getting used to seeing people two days in a row now. It started with Mack in Montana, then it was Pam and her husband in Spangle, and then Randall and Marilyn. And suddenly it was the car dealer guy. He was less familiar to us and we kind of liked it that way. We had a growing need to be alone, just we two. We didn't want anybody else to have an "in" to our world. That was part of the reason we set out anew in the first place.

As we entered the dealership we started making our case, which turned into a polite plea. The dealer explained that he'd have to discuss it with his boss, the other guy from yesterday. He said that the boss wasn't at work yet but should arrive shortly. He offered us a cup of coffee as we waited. *Free coffee, what a concept, you bet.* As I mixed in three tabs of sugar and dry, nondairy creamer into my cup I recalled the very first fruit I ever picked off a tree.

I told Libby about my friend of youth, Sammy Mullin, who told me about a tree with pears on it. He said that I could pick and eat as many as I wished, for free. In disbelief we rode our bikes to the end of Whittaker Street in Riverside, New Jersey, to find just as he'd said, a tree fully laden with ripe fruit. I'll never forget the happiness and fulfilling grace of that moment. I bit into that soft, warm pear to savor its unmistakable sweetness. I ate pears with Sammy, my best friend, until I could burst. Then I put extras in each pocket of my jacket. Sammy already had his fill earlier that day and wasn't so greedily-hoarding. I remember being most impressed that the pears were free, that we didn't have to purchase them with money at the store. But on that day it was a free cup of coffee. I was equally grateful of the moment, the coffee, and the memory.

We sat for almost an hour before our dealer explained to us that they'd buy our car back for two hundred dollars. We were appalled and asked to speak with the big guy. Within a few minutes the big guy came to us with our dealer. The big guy explained the simple matter of facts of doing business in the sale and resale of automobiles. "We buy cars for so much money. Then we sell them for so much more. That's how we make a living," he explained. There was no tone of compassion in his voice despite our case. We wanted to rescind our sale of less than twenty-four hours but he said that they'd be more than glad to purchase our car for two hundred bucks and that was that. "Take it or leave it."

Libby stiffened in impatience with the dealers who both seemed amused, almost delighted, at our predicament. She stood up and pulled out all the stops. She also pulled out a signed affidavit confirming the functionality of the odometer and the recorded mileage at the date and time of our sale. When she claimed that the odometer had not moved one tenth of a mile since our purchase yesterday, the big guy's mouth opened the size of an ostrich egg. She then stood up and announced to us all that if they didn't refund our money in full, that she was going to march right on down the street and report to both the state police and the local newspaper that the dealer had fraudulently turned back the odometer of our car to improve its value.

Furthermore, she said, "How do you think it will look coming out in the newspapers that you also took advantage of an out of town couple on their honeymoon? Mayor Randall Vaughn is a great friend of ours and he will certainly take a direct interest in this case."

Both dealers said nothing, looked at each other, then left the room. Within a minute or so, the younger dealer returned alone. In a meager voice he said, "My boss has agreed to give you five hundred dollars for your car. The difference of $100 is my commission for the sale. He doesn't want to pay that out of his pocket." He started to plea with us. "You know, I don't make much money here. Mostly I get to handle the used cars. My boss almost always handles the new car sales. I could really use that commission."

A car is never an investment; you always lose. On some cars you just lose more than others. This was yet another lesson in the school of hard knocks; we had just completed our first detailed lesson in haggling. We agreed to the dealer's terms. We figured, *so we lost a hundred bucks. Hey, easy come easy go! At least we're getting rid of that damn car.* We settled up accounts, pulled our packs out of the car, and hiked right on out of town. We were again free, back to Gene's plan, no more deals, no worries, and no fears.

The very first thing we did was load up on dried meat and canned goods. We always had some grub in our packs thereafter. That really gave us freedom and range. We decided to head back to the coast for another look because time was once again on our side. There seemed to be more of our kind on the coast, hitchhikers that is. Most seemed to be West Coast locals instead of transcontinentals and we were different than most in many ways. Most of our conversations with other hitchhikers were very brief and everybody else seemed to be heading somewhere on a timeframe. There was a lot of talk going around of The

Dead in Eugene and some kind of gathering, but we gave it all little attention.

We arrived at the coast late that afternoon and decided to find a restaurant for supper. We found a great place just a few miles from where we'd spent the previous night. We had a nice sit-down seaside dinner on the twenty bucks Uncle Howie spotted us at our wedding for just such an occasion. With an ocean view table we ordered white wine and a full plate of Dungeness crab in celebration of our renewed free-spiritedness.

It was evening when we came out of the restaurant. We chose to find new country to the north and traveled right along the coast. Soon night settled in so we found a knoll of large pines near the shore to spend the night.

We woke the next morning to a light and lifting fog. Our bags were soaking wet from the condensation of dew in the morning air. Libby awoke with an intense allergic bout and had slept poorly all night from pollen, most likely from the pines. I had heard her sniffling and sneezing most of the night; her eyes were puffy and she was still tired. We thought to walk across a meadow to the seashore a mile or so to the west, but found the wet, tall grass was just a bit soaking for our leg gear. We were already pretty wet just from the ambient moisture in the air. The grass was full of huge banana slugs, which were just a little creepy and somewhat intimidating too. Neither of us had ever seen slugs so big, and the tall, wet grass was loaded with them. They were harmless for sure but they still freaked us out with their slow, huge, creamy-banana yellowness.

We chose instead to walk further north on the coastal road, eventually coming to a nifty old house on the east side of the road. There were cats and dogs, chickens, and loads of plants, trees, and floppy old sheds and shacks about.

What the heck? Let's go check this out, we thought. There was a guy coming toward us in a car on the driveway. He stopped to greet us and we presented ourselves as passing through. He said his name was "Freedom" and he politely invited us to the solstice party that evening. That was our clue as to the date of the day. He said to go up to the house and meet the others.

The closer we got to the old house the more weathered it appeared. We heard some folks talking inside and it sounded like many different voices taking turns speaking. We knocked on the screen door and a hippie gal came to the door with a toddler in her arms. We told her we were invited to the solstice party, so she let us in. We left our packs outside the door and found a number of folks sitting in the living room in a circle talking about the day's duties. We had obviously walked right into the morning meeting of a commune. We took seats on the floor in the background of the largest room in the house.

There was some lengthy and calmly debated discussion about whose turn it was to clean the cat box, do the dishes, etc. We could see they were big-time issues, that somebody was pretty chapped about getting stuck with more than their share, and that obviously no one person was in charge. We silently observed for about an hour and quietly slipped out the same door we'd come in. We were convinced that the cat box discussion would surely take the rest of the day perhaps with no resolve.

So much for commune life, we figured. It certainly was not for us. It all seemed maybe a little too slow and boring. We scrapped the hippie commune solstice party idea because we thought it could've probably gotten pretty weird. Besides, we had no patience to wait around all day. We figured that if we stuck around much longer, we'd have probably gotten stuck with cleaning out the cat box.

We walked back to the road and heading south got a great ride from a guy in a new Volvo with a sunroof. That was our first sunroof. I never saw one before and it was quite a step up from convertibles. He was a businessman and had little to share other than a long, comfortable ride down the coast.

By that afternoon, we found ourselves in somewhat new terrain. It was more mountainous and woodsy. A salt-and-pepper bearded guy in a beat-up pickup gave us a ride. He looked a little grubby, kind of like a woodsman and said he was making a whole lot of money as a lumberjack. We talked some and he asked if we were interested in making some money too.

Wow, a job prospect, I thought. He said there was good money in cedar shakes. I didn't really understand what he was talking about but it involved swinging an axe and my beard was already well underway. *Sure, I could become a lumberjack. This might work, good hard work. In no time at all I'd rival Paul Bunyan in logging skills. This might be a job worth writing home about. "John Riger has become an Oregon lumberjack" is what they'll be saying.*

The more our new friend talked, the better it sounded. He said to start he'd have me "set chokers," whatever that meant. He said that Libby could work at the camp doing laundry, cooking, etc. It was too good to be true. We agreed to give it a try.

He pulled off the paved road onto a climbing dirt road and as we drove further into the mountains, perhaps a good ten miles, the forest just got enormous. I noticed that we passed a government forest boundary sign and a warning that lumbering was strictly prohibited beyond that point. Several miles later we were surrounded on all sides by absolutely massive trees. He parked the truck and we started bush whacking through a thicket to the other side of a timbered mountain.

We fought through thorny briars on a trek off trail until we came to a freshly-cut stump of a tree. The stump was as big around as our kitchen back in Pennsylvania. We climbed up on the stump and were speechless with amazement. I really wanted to see the chainsaw that was used to fell such an enormous tree. The tree was gone but you could easily see where it had fallen.

We started asking lots of questions and our would-be boss was smiling.

"What are chokers?" I asked.

He told us a helicopter would fly in to hook them up. He said it wasn't too dangerous as long as you were a pretty fast worker. "Make sure you don't get your hand hung up in the cable or you might lose it," he warned.

"I saw a sign back there that prohibited logging in this area," I mentioned.

He said that we'd be just barely inside that boundary by a quarter mile or so. "Don't worry," he said. "Nobody'll know 'bout us till long after we're outta here."

He wasn't very reassuring. I told him that I couldn't afford any trouble with the law and inquired to know more about all that money that could be made chopping shakes.

"Let's head down to camp an' I'll show you," he said.

I guess we both had visions of a lumber camp with lumberjacks and horses and a cookhouse with a saloon and lumberjack games going on about. As we turned into a dead end dirt road, we found an old yellow, school bus amidst a couple of rusty junk cars. A rough looking woman and several children poured out to meet Dad and there was smoke billowing out of the stack halfway down the bus. The windows were just plain old glass bus windows. It was obvious that the bus was not drivable; it was missing the rear axle. They were a family and they lived there.

He never really introduced us and went right over to a cedar stump and started to chop off thin sections that instantly became roofing shingles, "shake shingles," he called them. We soon realized there wasn't any money to be made and our trust in him died on the spot. Looking at each other we knew this was another failed attempt at opportunity and for several hours that afternoon we had again abandoned Gene's plan. No harm though, as it was just a strange acquaintance and we got the chance to stand atop a mighty stump truly unlike any we'd ever seen before. It was worth it.

The woodsman drove us back down to the paved road. When we unloaded and grabbed our packs he walked around the cab and asked if we had any spare change or a couple of bucks we could loan him. He was broke so we shelled out five bucks for gas. He sped off into the woods in his old, rickety truck.

There was very little traffic and so we talked and laughed as we waited for another ride south on the coastal road. We had actually spent the better portion of the day with the logger and we learned quite a bit about the area. Had we been stuck with the car we dumped that morning, we'd have missed all the day's events. We knew that we'd better start sizing people up a little more discriminately. Looking back, he didn't really strike either of us as a wealthy, timbering entrepreneur though he presented himself as such.

Our first impressions seemed to be pretty darn accurate but we ignored them. *Perhaps we should just trust our first impressions, go on instinct. Sure why not?*

Later that evening, we found a coastal bar with a local guitar band so we had a few drinks and talked with a few folks. It was great to meet locals and learn the details of our immediate vicinity. Some talked about politics or religion and we found that most had a casual openness about them. Not too long after dark we left the bar and walked a few miles north. We rolled out our bags on a small roadside hilltop in a grove of large coastal pine trees.

We woke that morning again soaked in our sleeping gear. We'd had good weather all night but the morning dew had dampened all but our spirits. A sunny morning on the rise was certain to dry us out in no time so we rolled up and headed out shortly after sun up. We stumbled through tall grass and over rocks a hundred yards or so to the road and headed south. We passed through a number of small towns, hitching rides one after another, and most folks that obliged were friendly locals. We were very much in the mainstream of coastal life. Logging was locally strong in a few places but growing environmental concerns had much of the economy on the ropes in most others. Everybody assumed that we were headed for Eugene for the concert the following day. The Dead were going to be in town with Santana, The Outlaws, and Eddie Money. *When in Oregon...*so we set our day's efforts for Eugene.

We arrived in Eugene in the early afternoon. It was a great little city resembling a college town though we had no knowledge of such. The concert wasn't until the following day,

Saturday, and we needed to get our tickets, find the stadium, and locate a place to spend the night. Somehow, we ended up in a residential part of town and were trekking to a ticket window a mile or so east. As we walked, we noticed a fellow coming our way on the same sidewalk. He was dressed all in white, in a long, immaculate white robe. I'd never seen someone dressed like that before except in Ben Hur. He had shoulder length brown hair and a short beard and mustache. He wasn't well groomed and hadn't shaved in a month or so. He was Hawaiian complected with real white teeth and he walked right up to us with friendly body language.

As he approached we could hear that he was talking. At first we thought he might be talking to us because his voice was clearly audible, but the closer we got it sounded as though he was talking to someone else. He closed within a car length when all our eyes met. By then we could tell that he was talking very much to himself. He reminded us of a guru with a big smile and it put us both at ease. He was cool. He was gone.

We shook hands and were able to connect with some friendly small talk. We asked if he was going to the concert the following day and, though we never really got a clear answer, we could see that he was alert, coherent, friendly, very interested in us, and still definitely in another space. We told him that we were on our honeymoon, just passing through, but were seeking a ticket booth for the following day's events. He reached into a small, leather satchel that hung over his shoulder on a long strap and handed us two small, white pieces of paper. Each was about one quarter of an inch square. There was nothing on the paper, just two tiny, little squares of white paper.

He said, "Take this tomorrow at the show. It is very, very clean." We thanked him for his giving then shook his gentle hand as he walked on past and resumed talking out loud to himself.

We finally found the ticket window at a local record store. We asked the saleswoman for directions to the stadium and a nearby campground. She directed us further east. She said a few miles past the stadium was a fish hatchery with a campground. *Perfect,* we thought and headed out of town that afternoon on a road that took us right past the stadium. Soon the two-lane road began winding about as it paralleled the meandering of a sizable river. Within minutes we saw the fish hatchery and hopped out of the car.

The hatchery was unlike anything else we'd ever seen and we felt that there was something very unique about it. We sensed it was a very special place; that something very positive was working there. It was the feeling that surrounds you with good comfort. The grounds were impeccable. The trees were grand. By the layout of the buildings and concrete work, we could tell that some serious forethought had gone into the development and construction of the hatchery.

This must be a very important place, I thought. Even though it was a fish hatchery, there weren't any fish in any of the runs. Our curiosity was strong and so we made sort of a self-guided walk-through tour. As we walked around we hoped to find someone who could tell us more about the hatchery, but there was no one.

The road to the campground doubled back downstream of the river adjacent to the hatchery grounds so we walked a stretch and found a place to camp. The river was a big river; the water was crystal clear and huge boulders lined its banks. We dropped our packs at the campsite and anxiously climbed atop a huge boulder for a better look at the river. As we sat there, every now and again we could see some huge, silvery flashes on the river's bottom. Instinctively we knew they were fish of some sort. Many were at least two feet in length. There were lots of them and the more we watched the more intrigued we became. Some were flashing close to shore in gravelly backwater eddies. I thought for sure I could catch one with a spear.

Spear, heck, I thought. "They're close enough to catch by hand," I said to Libby. I must have laid belly down on one of the boulders until my fingers went numb from the cold water. While rethinking the spear method, Libby gave up watching and went to our campsite.

I looked up to see a fisherman downstream about a hundred yards or so. *Little chance I'll bet of hooking one of those,* I thought. I was a little defensive about someone approaching "my" fishing hole. Believe you me, all my primal instincts vanished when I watched that guy set the hook on one. I had never seen a pole bend like that before. He played that fish like he'd done it a hundred times before, jumping from rock to rock, upriver, then down, and then back up again. I found myself hoping that he would land that fish. I wanted to see that fish and I wanted to know every single detail about that fisherman. *What type of tackle is he using, what pound test line, where's he from, is the fishing always this good?* I wanted to know all about him right down to what type of car he drove and what side of the bed he slept on. You see, fishermen and hunters tend to be really superstitious. What works for one should almost always work for another and I would've traded him places for the moment.

With absolute expertise he worked the fish to the calm of a backwater pool. With one long, scooping motion he lifted the fish from the water with the largest dip net I had ever seen. The fish wiggled futilely in the bottom of the huge net. As the fishermen laid down his rod I started toward him; I had to see that fish. I got to him just in time to see him slip the fish with a two-handed release back to the river. I caught a fleeting glance of the exhausted fish as it went straight for deep water and disappeared.

I asked him what kind of fish it was. "Steelhead," was all he said. I asked him what he caught it on. His reply was short and nothing that I recognized. My first impression was that he was really not interested in getting to know me. This guy wanted to fish and rightfully so. My higher education of steelhead fishing would have to come another day.

I doubled back to find Libby sitting on her pack resting. I told her about the fisherman and the steelhead. We talked about fishing when we were younger. We liked to share our stories of such things and as she was telling me about trips to Canada, big, old bass and snapping turtles, I drifted back in my mind again to Bucknell.

I recalled being seated with my student advisor in one of the classrooms. He asked me what my declared major would be and I told him that I wanted to be a biologist. A lot of my classmates were doing fruit fly genetics experiments. I told him that I wanted to try that. He asked if I wanted to become a doctor. I replied that I didn't ever see myself as a doctor. He explained that the fruit fly studies were reserved only for those in the pre-med program and that there wasn't really a school for biology. He then asked what else I was interested in. Behind him was a seven-foot grand piano used for teaching music. I told him that I really enjoyed the piano. I told him that almost every night I could be found playing one of the several grand pianos in the carpeted rehearsal rooms on the ground floor of the same building, the music building. As I pointed over his shoulder at the piano and told him that I would like to study piano, he shook his head.

"We don't really have a school of music here," he said.

Hmmm... Strike two. I paused, took a long breath and exhaled aloud. "You know this is not going very well for me. Why don't you tell me what I *can* do and I'll figure it out from there?" I asked.

"How about Spanish?" he asked. "You're really doing well in Spanish. Why not declare that as your major?"

I told him that I loved Spanish. "But I've studied Spanish for eight years already. If I really want to study Spanish, I'd have to live in a Spanish speaking country," I added.

"What about economics?" he asked. "You're doing well in economics. Why not declare that as your major?" I had flash visions of being stuck in traffic at five o'clock on the sure kill expressway in Philadelphia trying to get home from some stock market, life insurance, desk job deal. *No way,* I thought.

I left his office knowing that I'd have to choose the untraveled fork in the road. School was not working out and I knew that I would have to leave. There was no other way. As I looked west across the campus there was a spectacular view of the western sky and the very distant Blue Ridge Mountains. I knew that out there somewhere was a place for me. I prayed to God for strength because I knew my parents would be so disappointed. In that very moment I decided to quit school, to "drop out" as it was called. I really did enjoy just working for a living; making money to get by was okay with me. A feeling of closure and comfort came over me.

I returned to my room at Carey House and described to my roommate, Taylor, my meeting and discussion with my student advisor. Taylor could see and feel my confidence, but he knew that my meeting was a flop. As usual, our discussion led to women. We were both frustrated with women. I told Taylor that I didn't care if I ever dated another woman in my life. The women of Bucknell weren't my type. Sure, I had girlfriends and dated a lot, but none seemed to have the values I shared.

"Just what're you looking for in a woman?" Taylor asked.

"I'm not real sure, but I just want a woman that likes to fish," I replied.

"Likes to fish?" he chuckled. "Well, good luck finding that here."

"Yeah, I know. But I want a chick who isn't afraid to put a worm on a hook," I added. "I figure that if she'll hook up a worm, hey, we're good to go."

Though Taylor laughed, he knew that I was right and he knew exactly what I was saying. We always had a kindred understanding of each other.

Minutes later we decided to head over to the cafeteria for supper. Walking down the hall at Carey House, we caught the smell of home-baked bread. As we passed the small kitchen we found Libby making bread. She wasn't on the meal plan and had chosen to cook for herself. We'd seen her off and on and she had a precious shyness about her that made her, oh, so attractive. *Not likely that she would go for likes of either of us*, I thought. Taylor asked about her bread and she offered us each a piece with melted butter. It was delicious and we savored in its every delight.

Libby said to Taylor, "Hey, you're wearing a fisherman's bracelet."

My eyes jolted and my jaw dropped. *Maybe an opportunity, no?* Taylor had a bracelet of fishing swivels on his wrist that he always wore. I didn't even know that's what it was called. I just noticed that it was a fun piece of jewelry that generally spoke well for Taylor. But I was fixed on Libby and immediately interrupted their conversation.

"How do you know those are for fishing?" I asked.

"Those are fishing swivels. I used them all the time when I was a kid. We used to go fishing for pike and largemouth in Canada every summer," she replied quite matter-of-factly with her head high and chin strong.

On the bank of an Oregon river east of Eugene, I heard her stories once more and relished in them, in her, and in our union. Surely, we agreed that fishing would be an important part of our future. It would have to be.

Who knows, maybe Eugene, but the West is big. And what about Alaska? We'd had a great day and fishing drew our personal compass to a new and distant direction with intent. We would follow that thought, but The Dead and Santana were playing the next day and so fishing had to be postponed. Town was easy, just a few minutes away and we thought it might be more fun kicking around with others converging on the stadium so we hitched back into town for the night.

It was dusk when we got back to town and a fun ruckus was on around the stadium. Cars, pickups, vans, buses, and Dead Heads had assembled a makeshift camp in a field across the road from the stadium's gate. We joined the crowd, which was a collage of countless small parties. People were clustered about and music was playing from all directions on various car stereos. There was a lot of laughter in the air. Some groups were just talking while others were in full meditation. All in all it was a very unique collection of all types of people. We bounced around all night long from group to group talking, singing, running, laughing, and sharing. It was a great place and our choice to come back into town was right.

Things started to mellow in the wee hours as many had folded up for the night, but we stayed right with it enjoying a night like none other. At one point there was only one car stereo still playing and the music was so awesome that we walked closer to get a better listen. A guy I figured to be the owner of a decent pickup was reclined on the hood with his back to the windshield. Both doors of the cab were wide open and I was amazed at the music pouring out.

I asked Libby if she knew who was playing.

"Yes," she said.

A pause in her reply prompted me to ask again, "Who is this?"

She again said, "'Yes', this is 'Yes.' 'Yes' is the name of the group."

My light switch immediately went on. Though I had never heard them before, the signature of their sound was ever after unmistakable.

By dawn we were among the few lively souls still stirring but a little weary from the night's excitement and unrest. Daylight brought a lot of folks back to life and by midmorning the place was again a buzz of activity with legions of newcomers arriving for the day. The cops showed up at nine o'clock and they made everyone clear the asphalt area leading to the ramp and the gate. Their crowd control measure was to force everyone, every single one, back to the parking field where we had all spent the night partying and though the gates were not scheduled to open until noon, they strictly enforced keeping us all on one side of the road. As more and more concertgoers arrived it turned into a huge mass of people on the one side of a four-lane highway. There was a lot of traffic. Across the highway were acres of vacant pavement leading up to the entrance gate. Whenever someone tried to cross over, the cops would stop them short and make them fold back into the mass assemblage of people.

We definitely were not the type of people that liked to follow the masses. We had to be different from the rest and we couldn't take it any longer. We were shoulder to shoulder and came up with a plan. Libby and I talked about it and decided that no matter what, we had to break free from the crowd and get over on the other side.

A guy standing next to us had a Frisbee and I asked if we could borrow it for a few minutes; he gladly obliged not knowing our intentions. I hurled the Frisbee across the highway far into the vacant lot on the other side of the highway. Just as we had planned, Libby, without her pack and in all her cuteness, started to run across the highway. An officer yelled at her to stop, which she did, but she turned to him with Bambi eyes and then pointed at her Frisbee. The officer gave her a nod of approval to go get her Frisbee. She ran out into the huge, vacant lot then picked up the Frisbee and started waving it back and forth while dancing and jumping up and down. The crowd starting cheering at her defiance or so as most had perceived her act. She took the Frisbee and hurled it to no one in the direction of the gate. That's all it took! One, then two, then three started across the highway to play Frisbee with Libby. Within seconds the entire mass of bodies surged in unison across the highway, stopping all traffic to rush the gate.

I suppose it was true that we were beginning to better understand people in general, their motivations and fears, there likes and dislikes. Though different than most, we shared many of the same motivations and fears, otherwise our honeymoon might have gone on forever. But on that day, one week after our brush with Mack, we were among a vast host of friends, none of whom we'd ever known before. We thought there was a good chance of running into old friends from back east at a large Dead concert and for the rest of that day we caught ourselves scanning the crowd for familiar faces, any familiar face. And in all those tens of thousands, we knew no one.

"Hey is that so and so?" we would ask each other. Our hopes repeatedly faded, time after time.

As the mass of Dead Heads packed into the stadium, we continued to play Frisbee instead. *Why rush the day. Time is on our side.* Within an hour the gates had opened and the crowd had filled the stadium. As the crowd thinned on our playground we could throw the Frisbee farther and farther and soon there were but few of us still outside the stadium. We could hear the muffle of speakers from the beginning of the day's first act.

We bid thanks and farewell to the Frisbee's rightful owner then finally headed for the gates as well. We were different than the others, or so we thought, and being either first or last was our goal. We didn't want to be part of a multitude. If all were headed in one direction, we always had to be the first to turn about, to go against the grain. It had to be because, well... it was right.

We were surprised that they let us in with our full pack gear. We pleaded a good case in that our home was on our backs. They briefly checked everyone's belongings for alcohol as they were trying to keep the crowd from becoming unruly. Security had lapsed; we were among the very last to enter the stadium and they didn't even search our gear. I was worried that they might find our small bottle of tequila, which we had carried for weeks and never touched. We weren't big drinkers. The days were always moving, very physical indeed, and there really wasn't time to drink. We would more often offer a quick snort of hooch to an acquaintance as a sharing, giving gesture.

Selecting the right seat at the concert was vital and the only place for us was stage front. Being last in the crowd we thought making it to the stage would be virtually impossible. After all, wasn't that the reason that all others were in such a rush to be the first in line? Slowly and politely we stepped over seated fans toward the stage. "Excuse me," was all we could say, over and over as we made our way forward. In no time at all, we were up front. We never really made it to the security line but were within fifteen tightly packed, body widths from the stage. At stage front at a Dead concert, you didn't sit down; you danced throughout. Sometimes it wasn't really dancing, but more like an undulating mass with those around you. The first act for the day, Eddie Money, was well into his set.

The Outlaws played second and during the break between bands we got acquainted with those around us. We met the guy on our right who seemed like a nice enough fellow and broke fairly interesting small talk. There was a long break after The Outlaws to set the stage for Santana.

The stadium erupted when Santana took the stage. In total fascination we watched arm in arm. The last musician to take the stage was the drummer. Not a note had been struck. He looked to be in his mid-twenties. *Of course,* we thought, *he was only sixteen when he played at Woodstock.* We could see that he was seasoned. *What an honor to be witness to this event,* we thought. With our mouths wide open we watched as a stagehand opened a blue velvet-lined drumstick case that had only two, polished silver sticks inside. The drummer gracefully rolled each stick about like batons, raised them over his head and opened the set with a drum solo. Percussion joined him, then bass, and finally Carlos entered the mix with the signature sound of his guitar. With the band in full gear I turned to Libby and with each of us smiling, I gazed deeply into her kaleidoscope eyes.

There was a big, heavy, bearded fellow clear up front who passed around a plastic baggie during the stage break between Santana and The Dead. We didn't really know what was in it, but by the time it got to the guy on our right we could see that it was a light, greenish powder of some sort. The guy on our right didn't know what it was either but he ate the bag's entire contents.

When word got back to the heavy, bearded guy up front he said out loud, "Good luck, pal. You just did, like, a hundred hits."

The Dead were masters at feeling the crowd and selecting a set of appropriate songs. Everyone was calling out their favorites but Garcia, Weir, and Lesh stayed true to a selection that best fit an overcast, near summer solstice mid-afternoon. They kept it pretty mellow and never really stepped it up to a rock concert. After all, Santana had already done that up tough; they kicked total butt. We really weren't familiar with many of the songs chosen but they all had that Dead improvisation feel for which they'd become famous.

Meanwhile, the guy on our right wasn't doing so great. He sat down amidst all others still standing and wiggling about to the music. His head drooped as he stared at his feet. I kept checking him to make sure he was okay and though each time he would acknowledge, we could tell he was very far away.

The Dead finished with one encore. The excitement of the day's events began to unravel and in no time at all there were just a few of us remaining on the stadium floor. We were, again, in no hurry to leave and stood watching with amazement as the stage crews wrapped cables and started boxing up equipment. We could see they had a full shift of work ahead of them so we just sat on our packs watching while we talked. We talked a lot and for the first time we found new emotions in each other.

On our way down, Libby got worried. For the first time, I heard a true sense of hopelessness in her voice. She told me that she didn't think that we'd ever make it. "Making it" was still an unknown to us both. We didn't really know what making it meant.

Libby said, "John. Do you really think there's a chance that we'll make it? There are so many people, all seeking the same thing. Do you really think we can make it? It seems so impossible." There was a serious tone of resignation in her voice. For the first time, I could tell that strength was needed and it had to come from deep within me.

I told her, "Honey, I don't know. But we're gonna give it one hell of a try. We're gonna have to get right back out there and keep lookin' for that mountain. I know I'll recognize it as soon as I see it. It's out there, somewhere."

Part of her despair was from fatigue. The other part was from the disappointment of not seeing a single, familiar face in such an immense crowd. Funny though, we decided that we shared a basic human need for some sense of familiarity. All day long we could have sworn that we saw dozens of people we already knew but at each closer look we realized that our minds were playing tricks on us. We noticed the same thing occasionally on the road when a car would drive by amongst so many others and we'd almost swear that we saw a relative or close friend from back home at the wheel or as a passenger. We were convinced our minds were reaching for something that wasn't there, to fill a void. We were definitely alone and a long way from home, with no means of heart of returning and had deprived ourselves of any single repetitive event, be it a place or face. Neither of us had ever gone more than just a few days without a trace of familiarity before and though we both felt a sense of liberation, it came with a heightened feeling of loneliness. But Gene's plan was reassuring.

"Remember, Gene said 'Don't worry about anything, money, work, nothing. Just travel as long as you can'," I reminded her. "Remember he said that we'd never, ever get another chance to do this once we settle down." Gene's words were so right on. He might just as well have been speaking right through me. Gene feared nothing and the thought of his huge, jelly bowl laughter gathered us up. I helped her strap down her pack, and then threw mine on. We headed out of the deserted stadium for parts unknown. It would soon be night and we had to get out of town and find some rest.

We got a ride in the bed of an older pickup truck with half a dozen other concert fans. The overcast sky had thickened and had begun to drizzle as night was settling in. We had learned in rainy Wisconsin that we could stay a little drier in the back of a moving truck than standing on the side of the road thumbing for a ride. We all huddled close to the cab as we went down the road. We had absolutely no idea where we were headed and a light, misty rain came and went as we traveled. At dark the rain stopped so I asked the driver to let us out. We hurriedly jumped out, grabbed our packs, and crossed the highway fence to find a place to pitch our tent. In less than five minutes we were reclined safely inside; moments later we were asleep.

We woke to a clear day and having had a full night sleep we rolled up and headed out anew. We grabbed a couple of eggs and a cup of coffee at the nearest roadside cafe which cost all in all about six bucks. Breakfast was easily the cheapest served meal so we tried to take advantage of it whenever we could.

Libby sadly realized at the cafe that in the previous night's shuffle she had left her jean jacket in the back of the pickup. My grandma Mary's wedding band, given to Libby by my mother the night of our wedding, was still in the pocket, gone forever. When road traveling an insulated jean jacket is priceless for warmth and durability. To lose the ring and the jacket at the same time was disheartening for us both. I tried to reassure her about the loss but I could see she was pretty down in the dumps about it all.

The landscape of our surroundings wasn't too impressive so we set our day's goal for distance. We never carried any road maps because the local maps would only last us a day or two and the full-blown atlas was just too big to afford in our backpacks. By noon we found ourselves traveling an incredibly winding road through some spectacular mountains and impressively timbered woods south of Medford.

This must be Northern California, we thought. We passed through a little town called Happy Camp as our driver relayed a familiar theme throughout the great Northwest. Lumbering was declining because of environmental concerns and the prospect of finding gainful employment was doubtful. We were both feeling a little grubby from road wear and neither of us had bathed since Randall and Marilyn's so we asked the driver if he'd let us out at the next creek's crossing. He stopped at a tall, spanning bridge over aptly named "Clear Creek" which was a tributary of a much larger river it joined just below the bridge. We found our way down through the rocks and brush to a small cobble beach at the creek. It was perfect. The highway was far overhead and no one could really see us so we dropped our packs and our britches right there, creek side. There was a sunny plunge pool under the bridge deep enough to dive into. We waded thigh deep into the crystal clear, ice-cold water. I plunged head first into the water. The rush of the cold was more than refreshing and I surfaced immediately as the shock of the cold completely took my breath away.

"How is it?" Libby asked.

"It's great," I replied.

"Is it cold?"

"At first, but you get used to it," I said, still struggling to fully inhale.

She dove in after me and surfaced with a laughing shriek that echoed throughout our private, wooded canyon. A few minutes later the cold became tolerable and then comfortable. Libby had joined my full embrace. We felt the warmth of our bodies fighting back the cold making us hold each other even closer to share our warmth, flesh to flesh. We hugged and kissed and by her rosy cheek-to-cheek smile, I could see that her troubled worries were gone for the moment.

As cold water always does, a fresh comfort soon turned into a bone chill and Libby was first to exit the creek to sunbathe on the rocky bank. As she sought a place to lie down I couldn't help but admire her full nakedness. I hadn't seen her naked since Bismark, North Dakota, some weeks back and though she'd retreated from the cold water at Beaver Island, on that day in northern California there she stood, dripping wet from head to toe. Her body was perfect in every way, the only perfect thing I had ever seen. Her well-defined muscles from the back of her neck and shoulders poured down her loins and joined two distinctly pronounced dimples just above her flawless rump. Her hips, thighs, and calves were perfectly fit and formed. Sporting a forty-pound pack over hill and dale had transformed her into a masterpiece. As she lay naked in the warmth of the noonday sun her misted breasts stood firm. Her erect and engorged nipples slowly released tension, as did the goose bumps on the skin of her firm and beautifully robust breasts. I was the envy of Eros.

I dove down once more and shook the water from my hair and beard as I surfaced. When my eyes cleared, to my amazement floating down stream a foot or so in front of me was one of the largest insects I had ever seen. Perhaps three inches long, not including its antennae, it was slender and brown with long legs sprawled out on the surface of the water to keep it afloat. *What a great bait*, I thought. Surely it wouldn't drift too far downstream before one of those great steelhead in the larger river just below the bridge would chomp him down. I told Libby, who shared my fascination. We talked again about fish and fishing as we dressed.

There was scant traffic outside of Happy Camp and once again our impatience overcame us. We chose to hitchhike in both directions to take the first willing ride and ended up hitchhiking right back through Happy Camp. We gave up early that afternoon to set a full camp and enjoy the wild surroundings. We found a flat spot on a blind curve amidst coarse, small trees just off a windy country road. The camp was above a steep embankment that led down to a dry gulch. We relaxed and talked all evening and built a small fire to cook a can of creamed corn and a can of beans. As usual, we ate right out of the cans. That always made for an easy after supper cleanup, just the spoon we shared.

The following morning was sunny and clear and promised to be a gorgeous Northern California day so we rolled up camp and headed for the road. A used flatbed with stake sides rolled past us on a blind curve, and then screeched to a stop to pick us up. It was full of others like us with packs, sleeping bags, etc. All were headed to a "gathering" it was called, the rainbow family gathering. We had heard a lot of talk about it in recent days, but weren't really interested in the gathering as much as the ride. They were all headed for the mountains around a place called "Roseburg."

Libby struck up a busy conversation with an older, bearded fellow as we bounced on down the road. I couldn't quite pick up on their conversation so I tuned out to take in the passing trees overhead while reclining on my pack. I felt comfortable and relaxed. I remembered how comfortable and relaxed I used to feel while lying down in the back seat of our station wagon when I was a kid. I remembered how the vibration and turning of the car used to roll me to sleep just like the rocking of a baby in a cradle. From the back of the old flatbed, I watched as the power lines started to hump and bump by, peak to valley in their passing, sagging droop. I recalled watching the same drooping power lines whiz by when I was a kid, how they used to oscillate, peak to peak on each passing power pole. I could sometimes tell just exactly where we were on our route to and from Dood's hospital just by the familiarity of those power lines. *Some things are the same now as they were then,* I thought.

The old truck pulled into a grocery store parking lot where everybody bailed out to load up on grub donations for the gathering. All the food was donated in-group then shared in common. It all sounded a bit too weird for us so we hopped off the flatbed and separated from the group. Libby wanted to dispose of our charred cans from the previous night's supper so we headed for the nearest trashcan. She grabbed my arm and I could see that she wanted to tell me something in private. The older, bearded fellow had given her a small crystal ball and told her that he was one hundred seventy-five years old.

We opted to head south and got a ride through Crescent City, a coastal town, giving us some natural bearing as to our whereabouts. It wasn't much of a town really. Not a bad town for sure but it just seemed kind of worn in a sense. It seemed like it had seen both better and worse times. It was full of good folks with lots going for them, but there was just nothing really distinctive about it otherwise.

A ride took us the whole way through Crescent City where we saw a sign for a town called "Eureka" and decided to head that way further south. After all, "Eureka" was the name of a female raccoon I had raised from a bottle-fed cub back at the farm in Centre County. A car killed her mother, and our neighbors thought I'd make a good surrogate. Eureka was absolutely adorable for about two whole days. Her meanest of wild instincts surfaced and prevailed from then after. She was often unpredictably and furiously uncontrollable if things didn't go her way.

Though the pace of traffic was faster out of Crescent City, the hitchhiking slowed way down. Through most of the northern tier and the Northwest we could easily make several hundred miles a day. That afternoon we noticed that it took a long time to find fewer people willing to take us just a few miles at a time. There were no long ride prospects at all.

Well into the afternoon we were held up on a fairly busy interstate on ramp with lots of cars but no takers. Finally, an old army jeep pulled up and stopped dead, right in the middle of the on ramp. The driver made no effort to pull off the road as was typical. The jeep had no top on it and was just like the one Radar used to run around in on "MASH." The driver wore a grimy baseball cap and overall, he looked a little scruffy, but he seemed friendly so we threw our gear in and headed down the road south for Eureka.

The driver lit a joint and passed it to me. I took a hit and passed it back to Libby. It tasted strong and sweet, unlike pot we'd ever tasted. We got real high, real fast. The driver called it "sin semilla" which I knew translated in Spanish to "without seed." He told us it was homegrown from all female plants, which were denied the pollination of male plants. He said that if you didn't remove and kill every male plant, one would fertilize all the female plants. Much of their potency would be compromised to afford the production of seed. We'd never heard of any such thing and were absolutely fascinated and completely stoned. His explanation detailed a lot of science but fell well short of the killer buzz we were all feeling.

As we drove down the road, the fields gave way to forest. The further we drove into the forest, the sparser and larger the trees became. Within minutes we were driving through woods unlike any we had ever seen before. The forest consisted of tree trunks, massive tree trunks that reached to a distant canopy. Libby and I were speechless in awe. I stood up completely in the front seat holding the windshield and Libby was up on her knees in the back seat. The driver looked at me with a great grin. For the second day in a row we'd had our breath taken away. I sat down and put my palms to each side of my forehead in complete and total wonder.

The first words I could find were, "Are these the redwoods?" The driver gave me a nod. "My God, what the earliest Spanish explorers must have thought when they discovered these trees," I said aloud.

The driver glanced to me as he drove and said, "Probly wasn't any differn't than what you're feelin' right now. Did you guys have any idea that the redwoods was on your route?"

He was so right. We both knew that the redwood forest was somewhere in the West, but we never gave it a remote thought as a honeymoon destination. It just never crossed our minds. Most travel to the redwoods by intention, as a vacation or holiday getaway. We stumbled into the redwoods purely by accident. Or was it? Their magnificence and grandeur was indescribable, especially in a top-down jeep, unexpectedly and delightfully stoned. In that moment we felt once again that our travels had become a journey guided by a much greater Hand, the Hand of creation and power who had planted the original seed of such awe-inspiring trees. All fear and frustration was gone. We couldn't have imagined discovering the redwoods under any other circumstances.

We stopped along the way to feel the forest. The driver took us on a back road, which led to a sharp rock escarpment that faced a wide, flat pool and bank of another grand river. He said it was a great steelhead fishing hole.

Imagine that, I thought. The air was completely still so Libby took her flute out into the woods and played an enchanting, soothing melody. Her song gently echoed throughout the forest's great and distant tree trunks. The driver and I stayed near the jeep. Libby removed from her pocket the crystal ball that the ancient one had given her earlier in the day. She said a prayer to be forgiven for having lost Grandma Mary's ring and promised herself to never again idolize material things. She then smashed the crystal ball down onto a huge boulder at the foot of a great tree. She walked away in total absolution and returned to us at the jeep.

We rode with the jeep driver out of the redwoods to just short of Eureka where at dusk a newer four-door sedan picked us up. We had to ride in the back seat because the driver had already picked up another female hitchhiker who was riding shotgun in the front passenger seat. We sat with our packs on our laps so it was hard to get comfortable. The driver was clean cut, wore a business suit, glasses, and was all jacked up about working for Revlon. He gave us a quick ride across Eureka and it was nightfall by the time we reached the south end of town where the pace of traffic was much faster and frantic. We could only imagine intensifying traffic further south on our course so we decided to hole up for the night under a tree just off the interstate. The traffic and noise never really subsided all night long and it never got dark because mercury streetlights put a yellow-orange glow over everything, including us. We hadn't really camped in a setting as urban since leaving Pennsylvania and decided that in the morning we'd take an opposite course. We both slept very light.

We woke to frantic, fast-paced traffic so we joined the rush hour early and headed right back north, back through Crescent City. On our way up Grants Pass, which we'd missed on our first southern trek through Oregon, a busload of hippies stopped to pick us up. As we ran up to load we noticed a hand-painted sign on the back that said, "Don't laugh, your daughter may be inside".

The bus was headed to Roseburg and as fate of the great Hand would have it, we boarded the hand-painted-with-flowers bus loaded full of rainbow gatherers. There was a lot of talk of beautiful, high mountain meadows, waterfalls, love, and peace. The more we talked with others the more the gathering sounded, well...maybe okay. It sparked our reserved curiosity. *When in Rome*, we figured. *Fine*, we thought and headed to the gathering with so many others like us.

The bus pulled into a grocery store parking lot just as had our bus ride the day before. It struck us both as being a somewhat structured stop for people so carefree and spontaneous. We were also told that donating food and money was important to make the gathering work. We were told repeatedly that if you couldn't assist with either of those basics that you probably shouldn't participate. We were okay with donating food so we bought a sack of potatoes for thirty-five cents. The money part was a whole separate issue though. The thought of being taken twice in one week (once by a used car dealer) was certainly out of the question. We were told that eventually we'd have to take a mandatory shuttle that'd cost ten bucks each.

As we introduced ourselves as "Libby and John," it clued them in that we were a little out of step with most everyone else. Almost all others headed for the gathering had names like "White Sky" or "Running Tree" or "Star Flower." After a while we found shared delight in relaying back to each other the strangest names of our new acquaintances. We thought about coming up with earth names of our own but gave up on it as we'd already begun to introduce ourselves by our birth names anyway. Few would admit to any other common or birth names, as did we. With our sack of raw spuds we climbed back aboard the funny old bus with the rest and headed for the gathering.

The bus came to a stop some ten miles up a seriously remote forest road. We all got out there and the bus headed back down the road having left us amongst a crowd of perhaps a hundred others. We were staged there to wait for the fee shuttle that would take us to the trailhead. The staging area had a refugee feel to it. All of our food, fees, and any other donations were collected. As we waited, we talked with others to learn more about what we'd just gotten ourselves into. We were not surprised to learn that we had little in common with others. *What the heck, we're here. Let's make the most of it. And so far it's only cost us twenty dollars and a sack of russets, right?* There was no real schedule for the next shuttle to take us closer to the gathering and that seemed AOK with all.

Libby broke out her flute to pass the time. A grungy little toddler, covered with dirt and dripping snot all over her mouth and chin, walked up to Libby and held out her hand. Libby maternally asked the little gal if she would like to play the flute. As soon as she handed over her flute to the toddler Libby knew that she'd made a big mistake. She put the end of the flute into her snotty, dirty, little mouth and started to slobber all over it. When Libby asked for it back the little girl turned away with possessiveness.

The little girl's mother came over and dissuaded Libby from trying to get her flute back. "In time," her mother said, "she'll get bored with it and just put it down."

In the dirt, I thought.

Our frustration got worse from a guy sitting on a stump just to our right. He looked pretty rough, like in his mid-forties. Most of those years it appeared he may have spent wandering through the woods with a dirty, snotty flute of his own stuck in his mouth. His hair and beard were long, unkept, and hideously dirty. In fact he had sticks and dead grass in his hair. His clothes and skin were soiled. His mind was in trouble too.

He kept saying the same phrase over and over again in a fairly loud, clear, laughing voice. "Everybody's somewhere," he would burst out. "Everybody's somewhere," again and again and again while staring into blank space. He decided it was his turn to slobber all over Libby's flute and grabbed it from the toddler who immediately began to cry. Holding the flute backwards, he started blowing air, and Lord only knows what else, into the flute's aperture. He failed to produce a single tone.

Libby had had enough. She walked over to him and grabbed her flute out of his hand in mid "melody." She marched back to me with her head high and her chin firm and upright. She sat down on a dead tree, cleaned the flute, put it back in its case, and then put the case back into her pack.

A group of shuttle vehicles consisting of another bus and two large flatbed trucks arrived to finally take us all to the trailhead. There wasn't enough room to load everybody at the staging area but there was enough room for everyone who wanted to go. Some had to stay behind for reasons unknown but didn't seem to mind. The shuttle took us a couple of miles farther up the mountain where we unloaded at the trailhead. The trail to the gathering was a gentle, three-mile hike downhill that came out at a Cascade Mountain meadow valley. Were it not for so many people, it would have been an absolutely magnificent place, but such an intense human presence was taking a temporary toll on the otherwise pristine surroundings.

As we walked down the trail, we'd stop and talk a bit with folks who were ascending the trail out. It gave us a chance to catch our breath. We met a guy named "Moon Bear" who seemed to be fairly with it. We asked him a lot of questions. Moon Bear told us that no drugs or alcohol were permitted at the gathering. No one was to eat meat or adorn any leather garments. There were other rules too, like don't bathe in the creeks or streams, use only the latrines, and stuff like that. After all, there were thousands of gatherers. It was kind of like a mini, West Coast Woodstock without the music or the drugs. It was a new mass gathering of casualties from the anti-war movement born from the ashes of an emerging American counterculture.

Moon Bear told us that we should only eat the food that would be provided and that we should forfeit all of our consumables. The gathering was intended to be a spiritual and body cleansing of sorts. He said that he thought its organizers were based out of Hawaii. Moon Bear honestly tried to fill in all the gaps and our growing reservations. He said to definitely check out "Kid City," as he called it. It was a day care center set up to attend the needs of small children. He also relayed word that a woman had been seriously injured, perhaps killed, earlier that day. She apparently had fallen from a cliff or cascade. He asked us to be very careful as we checked things out.

It was dusk when we arrived at the gathering. The huge mountain meadow was filled with tipis or "lodges" as they called them. Perhaps thirty tipis formed the circumference of the meadow. The smell of wood smoke almost masked the smell of a trampled meadow that was well on its way to becoming a mud bog in many places. We saw no tents among the lodges. All the tents were tucked up on the hillsides in the timber. We had learned along our road of travels that a flat spot made all the difference in sleeping well in a tent. Even the slightest slope would have us both climbing out of the tent's lowest corner all night. We decided to pitch up between two lodges on the flat of the meadow.

We stood outside our tent just kind of taking in the entire scene. There were people everywhere, and like the Dead concert in Eugene, we knew no one. There was no music, no laughter, no crying, and no activity of focus. Neither of us had ever seen anything like it. We always figured that folks retreated to the mountains to get away from other people, to commune with nature. It was so unusual, almost like everybody was on some kind of city trip, but in the mountains.

We both wanted to check out one of the tipis because we had never really seen one and shared a passion for Native American culture. We asked a guy coming out of one if we could go inside to check it out. "Sure thing," he said and gave us the go ahead. We found a group of perhaps ten adults and two small children seated in a circle around a small fire. We soon felt out of place and no one offered us the smoke of their peace pipe. We stayed only minutes, just long enough to appreciate how much work it must have been to get all the poles and canvas to such a remote location. Apparently some had been camped there all month and planned to stay all summer. We exited the lodge feeling fortunate that we didn't have to live like that despite it being a shared dream of ours at one time.

For lack of anything else to do, we stood outside our tent talking. We wanted to build a small campfire of our own but the woods had already been picked over. We couldn't find one burnable stick of wood within a reasonable search from our tent and gave up on the idea.

Out of nowhere a guy walked up to us and said, "You can't camp here." We were both taken aback by his remark.

"Why not?" I asked.

"The meadow is for lodges only. Tents have to move back into the woods," he said in an enforcing tone of voice. I explained that it was too dark to even walk through the woods let alone find a campsite. I went on that we came to the gathering to escape the rules of civilization. I explained that had we known that zoning laws were in place we'd have probably foregone the entire thing. He backed down and agreed to let us spend one night among the lodges but that we'd have to move our tent first thing in the morning. We'd only been there a few minutes and had already worn out our welcome. He tried to make us feel privileged, almost like being allowed to live amongst the upper class, just that once. We crawled into our tent and broke out some beef jerky and our Tequila bottle, took a few snorts, and crashed out. It had been another day.

We rose at first light the next morning being reminded by somebody outside our tent that we had to move. As we rolled up our bags and tent others were looking on with blank stares of apathy. It was time to leg motor out of there and we knew it would consume most of the day. We each adorned our leather belts as an outward statement of disrespect and blasphemy. After all it was a little hard to swallow being the only two people in history to ever get kicked out of a rainbow family gathering, or so it seemed. We walked with a steady, sure-footed step toward the trail out.

We were hungry and breakfast, we were told, would be served at sunrise in the great meadow. *Damn right,* I thought. *I want to get something for that sack of spuds and the twenty bucks we anted up yesterday.* I told Libby, "Maybe they'll have some pancakes with real butter and maple syrup. Or maybe they'll serve some scrambled eggs and bacon or sausage, yeah, with hash browns from the spuds we brought." We headed for the meadow where most had already gathered. There really wasn't anyone in charge and as the sun came upon the meadow, everybody held hands in a huge circle and chanted.

"Ohhhmmmmm…ohhhmmmmm…ohhhmmmmm…" echoed across the valley as everyone chanted aloud in long and continuous unison for several minutes. We both thought that was pretty cool. *Now, what about those hot cakes?* A small group of four men were approaching us as they worked their way around serving the great circle of people. As they waited on those before us, I stood in Pavlovian anticipation for those scrambled eggs and ham that were surely coming our way. As they got closer I could see the first guy was handing out bowls. He handed us each a bowl of our own. The next two guys were carrying a huge, aluminum kettle. The fourth guy was working between them and, in assembly line fashion, scooped out a cup of oatmeal gruel. They were good at it and worked well as a team, almost with assembly line synchrony.

When they got to us they plopped a cup of porridge into our certainly filthy bowls. I looked into the kettle and thought I saw raisins in there, but a closer look proved that they were only ash and burnt chips of wood. They no more than served us when Libby said, "Don't look now, but I think we just made one of those CARE commercials." You know, like one of those old ones where they're feeding the starving masses in Biafra, or something. We noticed that our breakfast had a peculiar after smell.

My hunger overcame me and I took a healthy bite up tough using my fingers as a spoon, as was customary. *Yep, oatmeal,* and bad oatmeal at that, no honey, no raisins, just burnt, ashy oatmeal with something else unusual in it. I tried to take another bite, but Libby would not touch hers. We agreed that pancakes, eggs, and juice would not likely follow. We offered ours to others who looked hungry and set out again for the trail up and out.

A short walk took us right past "Kid City" where there was even a rustic sign for such. It was fantastic. It was kind of like a corral made of dead tree branches to confine little kids. We didn't see anyone supervising except for one younger male teen and a couple of pre-teens all looking like they desperately needed a cigarette. There were several dozen kids inside. Some were crying hard, like the kids I remembered that couldn't really hack the first day of kindergarten. Others were playing with sticks and stuff and each and every one of them was covered with dirt from head to toe. The day care was an organized effort to look after children while their mommies and daddies communed.

As we were leaving Kid City we ran into a familiar face. *What a treat, someone we know!* Moon Bear was headed back to the

great meadow gathering for morning leftovers. His was one of
the few faces we'd seen twice since leaving back home almost
a month earlier. I could see he had curious interest in the
beef jerky dangling from the corner of Libby's smile. While
gnawing, she politely explained that we were on our way out;
that we didn't really fit in but that it had been an interesting
foray.

Moon Bear said, "You *must* go check out the detox station
before you leave. If you didn't like this, you'll definitely dig the
detox station. I just came from there. It's awesome."

Fair enough, I thought. But we were a little confused about
his prior recommendation to check out Kid City and were still
determined to leave. We shook hands with Moon Bear and
headed on up the trail.

I was so set to get out of there that I failed to notice the
delousing station. Libby later told me naked adults were
checking each other's privates for parasites. Apparently I had
walked right past it and never saw it. I wasn't sorry I missed it.
Maybe for them it was all just good, clean fun.

Perhaps one half mile upstream of the gathering, on our
way out, we saw a hand-painted sign that we'd missed the day
before on the way down to the meadow. Just as Moon Bear said,
we found the "Detox Station." We looked maybe a hundred
yards across a meadow to see a small tent. I looked at Libby
and she looked at me. We figured, *Hey we've come this far and
Moon Bear seemed like a pretty good dude. Sure, let's give it a go.*
We traipsed across what was once a marshy meadow that had
turned into a soupy slog from foot traffic.

We approached the tent to see a woman dressed in a
robe and headband seated lotus before a small fire talking
with a patient. We quietly sat behind the gentleman. She was
asking him a lot of questions. I paid little attention to their
conversation to try to respect their privacy, but couldn't help
but overhear some of their conversation. I was more interested
in the fire and the small metal saucepan that was beginning to
boil water. There were little white things in the water but for
the boiling I couldn't see them clearly.

Eggs! I thought. *She probably starts the cleansing with hard-boiled eggs. Count me in.*

She asked us if we'd come for detoxification to which I eagerly nodded. She said that she'd be with us shortly and asked the guy before us to go inside her tent and drop his drawers. When she removed the saucepan from the fire, I could see that the little white things were not hard-boiled eggs at all. They were three little, white plastic rectal probes that apparently she had been reusing to deliver enemas to any and all willing partakers. Any notion of their use on me was well outside the range of my personal, moral flexibility and as she closed the flap to her tent, we high stepped across the slog and scurried up the trail. We could contain neither our disbelief nor our laughter.

We found our way back to the trail leading out, and near the rim of the valley the trail began to switch back to gain in sharp elevation. On one switchback we encountered two men both of whom traded off eager, full hugs with Libby.

"Welcome home, sister," they each said as they hugged her back and forth between them. Their welcoming was a customary greeting at the gathering, but their embrace was a tad more elaborate and hands on than normal. We took a break from the climb to catch our breath and to get to know them better. There was something about them that was different from the rest. They suspicioned the same of us. They saw our leather belts and asked us if we were rainbow family.

"No," Libby replied with a chuckle.

"Neither are we," they somewhat embarrassingly admitted.

"What are you doing here?" I asked.

"We work for the United States Forest Service," the smaller man replied. "We're supposed to keep an eye on things up here," he went on. "You know a woman died up here a few days ago. We're supposed to just make sure nothing gets out of control."

I wasn't sure just exactly what all that meant but Libby did. "So you guys are like stool pigeons?" she asked with a chuckle.

We were fascinated with their job descriptions. *What an ideal job, to hang out on a mountain trail and keep an eye on things, for money,* we thought. It all sounded pretty good to us. That we all felt outside the rainbow family membership gave us a commonness to share, talk, and laugh about.

The taller guy asked if we had any hooch.

"Sure thing," I said. We set our packs down and I broke out the tequila. The sight of the small bottle put a smile on both of their faces. They started passing it back and forth just as they had been hugging Libby only minutes before. As the bottle came to me I tilted my head back and pretended to take a pull but just let the tequila touch my lips instead. The sharing felt good.

We wanted to know more about their jobs. While asking lots of questions, our conversations were frequently interrupted by trail walkers mostly descending into the valley of the gathering. As people approached, the two would cease their talking or change the subject altogether so as not to blow their cover. They really weren't dressed like rainbow people either, jeans with flannel shirts, leather boots, and belts. They looked more like lumberjacks than hippies.

We asked them forest management questions too, to share in their expertise. In mid-sentence the tall, dark fellow grabbed his coworker's arm to interrupt him. The taller fellow had seen a group of fresh young women approaching us as they descended from above. In the lead was a young, buxom woman. It was as though they scented estrus. The little guy handed me back the empty bottle of tequila while looking up trail with his nose into the wind. They abandoned us entirely and ran uphill to meet the clan of young women.

"Welcome home, sister," they each said as they went back and forth hugging and groping the various girls. They did not share their greeting with all, just the cutest of those en route to or from the gathering. The older, less attractive women were lucky to get a head nod at best.

We pulled our packs and walked past them as they continued greeting other ladies on the trail. We bid them farewell with smiles. Theirs were certainly the best job of any we had known so far. *Perhaps even Mack would have turned straight given an employment opportunity like that,* we thought.

We decided not to wait for the shuttle ride back to the highway, choosing to walk instead and soon caught a ride anyway as most downhill traffic was without passengers. In no time at all we were back on the comfort of hard pavement and chose to continue north since abandoning a southerly route the day before.

The sky was graying and a chill had set in. We caught a ride in an old white beater van. We piled in to find three other hitchhikers and a driver. The van had sort of a crashing bed built into it. There was one strange character reclined in the rear of the van on the bed. Two small, square van windows lit behind him on either side. He was opening, folding, and wielding a large knife. He didn't really bother me much but Libby said that he was mumbling some strange things.

I asked the driver if he knew him but the driver said that he'd picked him up a ways back. I found the heavy steel roller bearing that was given me. It had been a cumbersome object bouncing around in my khaki pants pocket for weeks. It seated perfectly in the palm of my right fist and though I was ready for trouble, there would be none.

We got out of the van in a small, convenient town just off the interstate north. It was soon evening and we ducked into a homey restaurant to eat supper. We were both hungry and as we were setting our packs in the corner of the greeting room the hostess approached and said in a very matter of fact tone, "I'm sorry but I can't serve you."

My first impression was dead wrong because I thought there was a problem, like they were out of food, or the kitchen was broken, or some other problem. She repeated herself, "No, I'm sorry. I just can't serve you."

We realized that what she really meant to say was more like, "Look, you dirty, filthy, road trash, hippie bum wannabes, get your tick-infested bodies out of my restaurant."

Our light switches went on as we gathered up our packs and left, embarrassed. Apparently we looked much the worse for the wear. She'd probably had enough of rainbow family types that had virtually taken over her town by the thousands.

As we walked toward the interstate we passed a fast-food burger house. Neither of us really liked fast food so we opted to move on to another, more welcoming town. By the time we got to the on ramp it was dark and drizzling light and steady. We had no luck getting rides though the traffic was ample and the interstate was loud and fast. We sat on our packs beneath the streetlight of the northbound on ramp.

Out of nowhere a small, thin gentlemen appeared and walked toward us. At a short distance in the dark he appeared neat, in a suit and carrying a small suitcase. As he neared our eyes met with friendly curiosity. We could see that his suit was actually tattered and torn from wear and that his face was unshaven for several days. His hair was ruffled but somewhat barbered and he tried to keep it combed. When we shook hands I could see his were dirty, as were mine.

He shared with us his most unusual story. Apparently, he was from Louisiana though his speech was without accent, slang or dialect. He spoke with educated clarity. He told us that his wife of thirty-five years had passed away six months earlier. He was traveling admittedly with little, if any, reason. He didn't seem at all distraught. To the contrary, he was the friendliest road traveler we had met. He told us that he missed his beloved wife dearly and we both felt the love that he lost with his wife's passing. His kindness we'd forever remember. He asked us if we needed some money and his question was extraordinary to us.

I told him, "No, we're okay on money, thanks."

I thought a moment about Gene's plan, not to worry about money. No one had ever openly asked about our finances before and neither of us felt at all threatened by his inquiry.

He pulled out his wallet and opened it before us. His wallet was as worn as his clothes. He had only two dollars in his wallet, which he removed.

He said, "These are my last two dollars. I want you to have them."

We struggled to believe what he was saying. I told him thanks but no thanks. I really didn't want his money; I didn't want to be indebted to him or anyone else. For the first time in my life, these values emerged and I declared them. They were strong feelings. They were very strong feelings. He went on and insisted as he placed his last two dollars into the palm of my hand at my side.

How strange, I thought, we both thought. Every time I tried to politely deny his offering he'd as kindly explain his case. His offer turned into a gentle plea and we could see in his weary eyes that within him was a desperate need to be so giving of his very last money. He was convincing as well as reassuring that the acceptance of his generosity would be a righteous thing for us all.

A swell of guilt rose in me that a refusal of his offer would be insulting. Reluctantly we thankfully agreed to accept the gracious offer of his last two dollars. That brought an immediate, huge smile to his face and so to ours. We thanked him over and over as I stared at the money in my hand. We could see the reward for him as he was helping us on our way. He then walked on passed us with his small suitcase up the on ramp to the busy highway and disappeared into the dark, rainy night. I couldn't help but think how my instincts and actions were so opposed from a short meeting with a strange, loving, little fellow. Our total encounter was less than five minutes. His name neither of us ever got.

The burger stand had closed for the evening and with its lights out where we sat got even darker. The streetlight directly overhead illuminated only us in the steady drizzle of rain. We sat on our packs pondering our last acquaintance. There seemed to be a spiritual component to his persona. We felt so grateful for our shared love and commitment and the thought of him made our tears well. The thought of losing either one of us after thirty-five years was unthinkable. We started to get

wet and the drizzle made us pensive, dampening our spirits to
talk much.

The drizzle soon turned into a light and steady rain so we
tried to seek shelter. An overpass by its design provided relief
from rain. There was often a small, flat concrete slab at the top
of the notch of the embankment just feet beneath the highway's
overpass. I'd often thought it to be a great place to seek shelter
on a rainy night, but we'd never needed to before.

As we approached the overpass, the police had pulled up
to the same area under the highway with their lights flashing.
Apparently, they knew the same as we did. A paddy wagon
pulled up behind them with lights ablaze as well. Two officers
went up the embankment and arrested a number of homeless
people. They'd already found shelter there and were being
hauled off to jail for the night. Neither of us was willing to go
to jail, not for one single night, not for one single minute. We
summarized that the presence of tens of thousands of rainbow
family people may have put that little town over the top and
a zero tolerance policy was likely in place. The thought of
Libby's parents getting a phone call from the Roseburg police
was absolutely out of the question. We opted instead to stand
roadside of the on ramp thumbing for a hopeful ride, which
was a completely legal activity. It was raining. It was raining
hard.

By midnight it was doubtful that anyone would stop to pick
us up and as the saying goes, it was a night neither fit for man
nor beast. But there we were, in the steady downpour of a
Northwest summer rain. The numbers of cars taking the on
ramp had slowed considerably to perhaps one every twenty
minutes or so. The chill of night started to creep in as our
rain gear began to fail. All we really had for wet weather was a
poncho and a jacket.

Libby's poncho was the kind you throw over your head. It
covered her shoulders pretty well but not her legs or her feet.
Libby's was made of waterproof plastic and mine was a navy
surplus duck cloth that soaked clear through once it got wet.
I put my Chevrolet baseball cap on Libby's head to warm her

some. The cold, steady rain was beating us and beating us bad. We'd not prepared for a night like that and we had no place to go.

In desperation we sought a flat spot in the dark to maybe pitch our tent. We walked up to the interstate to see cars careening north and south on four lanes, but the splash and low visibility made the notion of hitchhiking anywhere but at the on ramp just downright unsafe. No one would stop in that rain even if they could see us in the black of night. We could tell by the steep drop off of the highway's embankment that the highway was built by huge earth moving equipment appreciably by design to allow for drainage so apparent on that night. We literally couldn't find a flat spot to set the tent and time was running out on us.

We opted to run across both lanes and the median to hopefully find a place for the tent on the other side of the interstate. *If we can just get that tent up maybe our bags will be dry enough in their wrap to provide some warmth.* The steep embankment of the southbound lanes offered a few trees but no flat spot. We ducked down into the trees, but there was nowhere to go.

The cold of the night overcame us so we huddled together, arm in arm, on the embankment in a crouched position until our legs became numb. We pulled out the tent and just draped it over us hoping that any of its non-existent water repellent properties would work. We pulled our sleeping bags out and covered ourselves in a mat of soaked holofil and collapsed down. The tent and slicker we draped over them. Our bodies lay right on the soaked ground. We were wet and cold from our heads to our toenails. The rain caused sheer and utter misery once we'd had enough of it and there was a sense of unrelenting power in its demand for our full attention and submission. But no matter what we could not make it stop.

"Surely that's how they used it in the old Chinese water torture. Drop, drop, drop on the forehead," Libby said. The constant sound of its pounding and the way it seeped down our necks, backs, crotches, and ankles. Neither of us knew how they used water as a torture but it must have been similar to that night. We'd had enough but there was no stopping the rain.

Sleep was out of the question and from the fatigue of the day and the cold of night, I begged for morning's light that was hours away. *Surely this weather will break with the warmth of the rising sun.* I started thinking back on the day. *I was wrong to take that lonely fellow's last two dollars. I should've just thanked him but walked away.* I thought of the lady hostess at the restaurant. *She was well in her right not to serve us and it wasn't right of me to be offended. All those lodges that I ridiculed last night, what I'd give to be warm and dry in one of those right now. What about all of those rainbow family folks? What a fool I am to think that I'm any better than the least of them. Yes, I am judgmental and I am wrong. I'm tired. I'm afraid. I'm angry, hateful, jealous, envious, prejudiced, lustful, selfish, greedy, and proud. Here I sit in the rain in complete, stupid, humble, humility. This is certainly destitution. They all warned me of this and I wouldn't listen. What I'd give to be sound asleep in that Delta Eighty-Eight. The lumberjack and his family, they're all snug in their old school bus. Even Mack offered me something other than this chosen misery. Libby's folks were right. We should've stayed in school. Yet, I drug her clear out here to share in my meaningless self-pity. My life is a grand delusion. I'm a stupid jerk living a loser's life. I'm a completely worthless waste of space.*

As I lay sopping wet and sleepless I realized that they were all right and I was wrong, all along. I had let my ego and my stupidity put us both in a hopeless predicament. *Libby's fears after the Dead concert,* everybody was right except me. I was wrong. It was wrong and every single choice I'd made over my whole life that led up to that night was wrong. I resigned to the night and its hell and prayed that tomorrow, which had already become today, would be better. Never again would I take the simplest things for granted, a roof over my head, my health, and a hot meal.

At very first light we tied down our gear and headed for the northbound on ramp. We were completely wet, soaked to the skin. The rain hadn't let up one bit and the sky promised that we'd be denied the sun. The burger stand was still closed so we stood proud with our thumbs extended hoping to catch a ride with a commuter. We'd have gone anywhere just to get into a dry, heated car, but, as fate would have it a flatbed pickup truck pulled up and offered us a ride in the back.

As we rolled north in a downpour huddled up to the cab my hope faded to anguish. Not only was I cold, wet, and tired, but I was sick as well. My stomach started to twist and turn with pain. I fought back the nausea in denial that something, that anything else, could be wrong. I felt the sensation of a cold sweat, though I was already cold and sopping wet from the miserable night in the rain. Apparently I had picked up some kind of bug and it was beginning to demoralize me.

We pulled off at an exit without utilities; there wasn't even a gas station. In the unrelenting rain, I found the occasion right then and there to vomit in the weeds as the driver pulled away. Libby held my forehead as I released. There is always relief after throwing up, that passing that takes the weariness away so that you can sleep and sleep well for a while.

No such luck today. We got right back to roadside and hitched for a ride. Relief came in the way of a guy in a pickup truck and the instant we threw our packs into the bed and hopped in the cab, we felt the warmth of his truck's heater. He was headed for Portland and gave us a long, great ride. Libby tried to make small talk but as the windows steamed up we both fell asleep.

By the time we got to Portland it was midday and still raining. The driver exited the interstate eastbound. The first motel we passed, I asked him to stop and thanked him for his kindness. My stomach was still wrenching and I needed to vomit again. I found some bushes as Libby went inside the office to check us in. It wasn't much of a motel but on that day it could just as well have been a five-star resort. There is much to be said for a roof over your head and a dry, warm bed in foul weather and rough times. I was worried they might turn us away like they did at the restaurant the previous evening, but Libby came out of the office with a key. We walked to our room, opened the door, dropped everything, stripped ourselves of clothes and piled shivering into soft, dry sheets.

I awoke that evening to the sound of television and the smell of warm food. The sound of the TV was comforting, but the mere thought of food made me sick. Our bags were strewn about the room drying as Libby, the angel that she was, had just cleaned them at a nearby laundromat. By midnight the nausea had stopped but sparing of detail, diarrhea had set in at the other end. My body was purging.

The next morning it was raining still so we rented our room for one more day. I remember little except that I rested and ate lightly that evening. Libby had gotten some soup for me and though it tasted so good, her loving-kindness and caring I remember most. We talked about the coming day, what we'd do. Feeling a bit better and dry and warm, we could deal with tomorrow then, we figured. *Sufficient for today are its own troubles, which are fairly few.* We both got another full night's sleep.

We slept in a bit the next morning giving the weather a chance to break inasmuch as check out was at eleven o'clock. We rolled up all our gear and went for coffee and a cinnamon roll and were back on the road by midmorning. Feeling renewed with fresh clothes, clean bedding, clean bodies, renewed health and spirits, we kept heading east to avoid Portland. The weather was clearing and sunny.

A long, shiny blue Cadillac Fleetwood convertible with the top up pulled alongside to give us a ride. Libby got in the back with our packs and I rode shotgun. Our driver's name was C.J. McMurphy. Small talk about our honeymoon, the gathering, Mack, and me getting sick led us to a conversation about employment.

"All you're going to find out here is picking apricots in Yakima," he said. "Not really a lifelong career but it might give you some bearing," he added.

The thought was actually okay with us. Mundane, repetitive work might be spiritually therapeutic, we agreed, and picking ripe fruit from a tree was always a pleasure. We wanted to pick Washington apples but it was too early in the season.

Apricots will have to do, we thought. Anyway, we thought it might look impressive on a resume someday. C.J. let us out headed for a new experience with a destination after about a half hour ride.

The road to Yakima was a four lane the whole way and the traffic was sparse. We expected the hustle and bustle of a lot of migrant workers but there was absolutely no one there. Apparently the picking of apricots was either finished or it hadn't yet begun, but there was no one tending the orchards. We walked right into the first orchard we came to and there was plenty of ripe and green fruit on the trees, but by late afternoon we could see that employment prospects were slim. We did pick apricots though, maybe a half-dozen. We ate them all; they were as sweet as honey. We took no more than just a few and ate them right then and there. We doubted that an orchard grower would be very understanding of others raiding his crop, as well he shouldn't. Besides, a pack full of ripe apricots wouldn't fair so well, all things considered.

By evening the weather in Yakima was overcast but not threatening, and a high, rumpled blanket of clouds suggested a nearby ocean's origin. We slept in the open just off the interstate on ramp that night.

The next morning was a clear blue day. For the second day in a row there was very little traffic in and around Yakima. There was so little traffic that we figured something must have been wrong. It was not Sunday, it was Tuesday, but there was absolutely no mid-week traffic. Mid-week traffic was usually busy with folks going to and fro, but not so on that day. That's when we figured out that it was actually the Fourth of July. That explained a lot. The day being a holiday might present a very unusual ride.

Maybe we'll be lucky and catch a ride with others headed to a boat party at the lake? But most folks were already where they wanted to be for the fourth and that, we figured, was the reason for so little interstate travel. Anyone traveling out in the middle of nowhere, like we were, on the Fourth of July might need to be a little more careful, we agreed. We were also at a bit of a crossroads. Traveling east meant Mack, south was been there done that to nowhere, and the odds of traveling north were very slim because there was no one traveling that way. We decided to head for Seattle via Portland for an evening of fireworks. We walked down the on ramp so that the few passing cars already eastbound could see us and stop if so inclined.

A dilapidated green Datsun B210 rolled to a stop without passing us. That usually meant it would be an honest ride. We had learned that cars that passed us before braking might be more troublesome. Even worse were those that doubled back, like Mack, who could be outright threatening. Anyone willing to change the course of their travel definitely had questionable intentions. Somehow we managed to stuff all our gear and ourselves into the cramped little car. And just as we had suspected, our driver was recently released just days prior from the Arizona State Penitentiary. He was trying his first chance at freedom after five years of imprisonment. I found the roller bearing in my pocket and rolled it about, though as it would turn out, there was no need.

He was a smaller, thin, average-looking blonde man of about thirty years. Aside from his stubble beard he didn't look at all like an ex-convict. He was on his way back to his hometown of Portland. How he got his car and how he ended up in Arizona we never understood but all of his stories were captivating. He had a long history of drug abuse and associated crime. He told us that his very first day in the Arizona pen, when he went to stand in the chow line for lunch, just two positions ahead of him an enormous black man grabbed an inmate from behind and cut his throat from ear to ear with some type of blade. The poor fellow died choking in a pool of his own blood on the prison floor. He said it made him lose his appetite; he couldn't eat for days.

He went on to explain how he'd gotten busted by robbing pills from a pharmacy. As it turned out there was one pill in the batch that was a sort of beeper radio tracking pill that could be traced anywhere the pills went. He said that by noon the following day, the cops had him in handcuffs. He told us that they were using the very same technology, micro transmitters, with money robbed from banks. His knowledge of crime and crime-related subjects was scary, but fascinating. Most interesting was his openness and trust with two passing strangers. Likewise, we shared with him our brush with Mack and he assured us that not getting back into his van most likely saved our lives. Admittedly, his stories had a scared straight affect on us. We asked if he was going to resume a life of crime since he was finally out. He said that under no circumstances was he going back to prison. He said that he was going straight from then on.

He then asked, "Hey, you guys wanna smoke some pot?"

I looked to Libby in the back seat in a little disbelief. We each had smiles and snickers so we laughingly agreed.

"Sure, why not?" I replied.

He reached under his seat and pulled out a small baggie, handed it to me and asked me to roll one. I could see that the pot had like oak twigs and scrubby, leafy crap in it. It was hardly a clean bag of pot. I smelled it and indeed there was some marijuana mixed in with who knows what else.

"Where did you get this stuff?" I asked.

"It's homegrown," he replied. "We had a small patch of it growing right on the prison grounds in Arizona," he went on. "It's not great, but hey, it's something, it's got a real mild buzz."

It tasted really bad and all it gave me was a nagging headache.

Arriving back in Portland late that afternoon, we worked our way into downtown Vancouver, a smaller city in Washington just north of Portland and across the state line on the Colombia River. Vancouver was a full-blown city of its own complete with all the bells and whistles. It was Tuesday night, the Fourth of July, and our first Fourth of July together. We decided to make it a memorable one and celebrate so we found a cozy little

Chinese restaurant that was barely within walking distance of a cluster of major interstate thoroughfares. The hostess was nicely dressed and greeted us with a smile. We felt welcome. The lighting was romantic and there was oriental music playing in the background. It was such a relief to just sit down for supper in a relaxed atmosphere. We ate to our fill of great food and spirits.

After supper we headed back toward the river where the fireworks could be seen later that evening, but perhaps a half-mile on our way, Libby realized that I'd left my jean jacket back at the restaurant. We were limited to how much gear we could carry and my insulated jean jacket was invaluable. I had to get that jacket back and would have gone great lengths to do so.

We were walking near a small, open space park beneath a labyrinth of concrete skyways and overpasses. I told her that I had to go back to get my jacket and that she should just wait in the park for me. Walking in the reverse direction to get the jacket, I didn't go one full block when our separation over came me. I looked back to see her puppy dog eyes when we both realized that we'd not been apart for many months, perhaps since February. I ran back to her with hugs and kisses then told her again, that she must *stay* at the park under a specified tree waiting for my return. We'd both flunked obedience school and I feared that should we lose each other by accident, we might likely never see each other, ever again. We agreed to the plan.

I ran back to the restaurant and went inside to retrieve my jacket, which the hostess gladly handed to me with a smile. I walked outside and turned south to meet up with Libby back at the open space park. There was a bar on the very same block next to the Chinese restaurant and as I walked passed, I noticed a group of four cops who were frisking a guy they had spread-eagled up against the brick wall outside the bar. I did a double take at the suspect as did he me. It was C.J. McMurphy!

Seeing a familiar face unexpectedly in an unfamiliar place gave me an immediate connection, a sense of kinship, if you will, and though C.J. wasn't "family" at all, in that moment, he might as well have been my uncle. Except for seeing Moon Bear twice in two days at the gathering, C.J.'s was the first familiar face I'd unexpectedly run into since leaving Pennsylvania. It was kind of what we'd hoped would happen at the Dead concert.

C.J.'s eyes opened wide and his mouth dropped as he recognized me. Ignoring the cops completely, he took two full strides to give me a bear hug. He was obviously sauced. Apparently he'd gotten an early start on celebrating the fourth and frantically asked if I would drive him across the state line.

"Sure," I said not knowing any of the specifics of his plea but feeling somewhat still indebted from his generous ride the day before. While pointing his index finger right at one of them, C.J. told the cops that they couldn't hold him because I was willing to drive him back across the state line to Oregon. He was clearly not welcome by authorities in the State of Washington, but spoke to the cops almost as if he knew the law inside and out.

The cops checked out my ID, which they found to be free and clear, and agreed to let him go. C.J. practically thumbed his nose at them laughing as we strolled away arm in arm.

As we walked he started pouring out his gratitude and went on and on about how I had just saved his hide. He never really disclosed any particulars as to why they had him up against the wall in the first place so I didn't ask. I guess by then I didn't really want to know anyway. I was more anxious to get back with Libby who by then had to surely be wondering what was taking me so long.

Around the corner angle parked to the curb was C.J.'s midnight blue Fleetwood convertible that had the top down. I had told C.J. all about my jean jacket and that Libby was waiting for me at the open space park. Excited to see Libby again too, he threw me the keys then hopped in the passenger seat while I fired up the Cadillac. He wasn't real sure how to get to the park for one-way streets and the left turn only traffic design and somehow got us onto a monster of a freeway maze. As we were jammin' down the super slab the sun got in my eyes so

C.J. lent me his sunglasses. The whole setting was fast and fun perhaps amplified by his outrageous and drunken elation.

We rounded a great skyway overpass and I could see Libby far below patiently waiting beneath the tree. I blared the horn and yelled over to her.

"HEY LIB! YO LIB!"

I could see her mouth open wide in unbelieving recognition as I wolf whistled a loud, high-pitched shrill and waved my left arm extended with an outstretched hand.

We pulled up to the park where she jumped into the back seat. We had a hilariously joyful reunion. C.J.'s reputation with the Vancouver police was rich and as we drove him back to Portland, across the river and back to Oregon, his gratitude intensified. He explained to Libby that the cops at the bar had ordered him to leave the state immediately. C.J. knew that the instant he got behind the wheel the cops would have cause to arrest him for drunk driving.

He had us pull into a Holiday Inn where he bought us a room for the night and in his drunkenness offered to give us anything and everything we'd ever wanted. He even bragged about being a millionaire and promised that if we called him in the morning, he'd make good on his offer. We could see that he was anxious to get on his way, to resume his evening's celebration and so we too were looking forward to getting to the fireworks display as evening was setting on. We all hugged, high-fived and bid farewells waving as C.J. McMurphy drove off west into an urban Portland sunset.

We checked into our room, dropped our bags there then headed right back out to the frontage road to thumb a ride to the fireworks display. The show was a good five miles deeper into the city and we were getting impatient because no one was interested in giving us a lift despite the fact that there was a lot of traffic.

At dusk a long, faded, late-model station wagon braked to stop well past us. We ran up to the car to catch a quick ride to the fireworks display that was surely to begin at any moment. As we approached the car I had an instinctive feeling overcome me; it was unlike anything I had ever felt before. The driver was a black man. I saw another roll over the front seat to join yet another already in the long seat behind.

I looked through the open passenger side window to the driver who ordered me to, "Get in," as he bluntly put it. The two in the back seat who had their eyes fixed on Libby said nothing. My prejudice welled up and out of me as I took Libby by the arm and backed away from the cruiser.

I waved them on and said out loud, "No thanks. You guys go on ahead."

The driver again in a direct voice said, "Just get in the damn car."

I said nothing as I turned away and started to walk up traffic. I could tell he was disgusted with me as he sped off. Libby was curious about my decision; that was the first time we'd ever thumbed a ride to turn it down. I felt awkward about it as well and couldn't really explain my actions except to say that I was afraid and that it didn't feel, well...right. I couldn't recall ever acting out of prejudice before in my life, but I chose to on that night and I didn't really have an excusable reason. I had no reason whatsoever to be untrusting of them but I certainly was and there was no way in hell that I was going to get us into that car. In all probability they were just three guys on their way to see the fireworks too and stopped simply to help us get there on time.

We talked long about it roadside while watching the fireworks over the river miles off in the western night sky. Trust, and the nature of trust, started to roll around in our minds and off our lips. It was definitely the theme of our day starting with the former inmate from Arizona. We agreed that trust was at the core of our journey. After all, there we were, day after day with thumbs out roadside soliciting for assistance in the way of a ride. We might as well have held up a flashing neon sign that read, "Please stop and help us. We are two homeless and worthless people without direction, cause or self-esteem. We trust that you'll share with us something rewarding about yourself, if nothing other than a short ride."

Our shared experiences were forever changing us in profound ways. Suddenly we were aware of our vulnerability and no longer felt naive. My act of prejudice somehow made me feel competent, tempered in a sense. We agreed that we greatly benefited from being so trusting of others and however difficult were our circumstances on occasion, our open trustingness of others had really made for a memorable and fulfilling stream of human experiences. We agreed that it was indeed a misfortune to not trust others and we felt pity for those who insisted that their trust must be earned.

We thought of all the fascinating things we would have missed out on if we walked through life with our "shields up," so to speak. Those openly pronounced to not trust others were themselves untrustworthy, were usually selfish, were sometimes just outright snobbish, and probably struggled with emotions like unconditional love, compassion and forgiveness. We were better off to avoid them, but they weren't likely to pick us up anyway. We understood how people could lose their trustingness of others and perhaps in our case all it would take was one bummer encounter with a person we really trusted. But so far we had fared pretty well. *What is life without risk?* We accepted the risk of getting burnt once in a while and figured that perhaps two rides in fifty were rides that we could have foregone, our rides with Mack and the drunks. Those odds were improved by trusting each other, our first impressions and our openness were being well-rewarded by the majority of those lending us their hands.

That all spoke well for human behavior, we thought. We talked long about the parallels between trust and love. *I suppose you can't expect to be trusted, no matter how trustworthy you are, if you yourself are not trusting. Maybe the same can be said for love,* I thought.

And as ironically, that revelation about trust had come out of an act of unprecedented, willing prejudice on my part. We knew that it was born of instinctive fear, of judgment, but not hate. We agreed that fear and hate were two distinctly different feelings that didn't share the same space of mind. We knew that fear was largely a natural response, but that hate was a chosen ugliness. We agreed that no matter what, if either of us felt uncomfortable about a car, a driver, an encounter, a situation or any experience before us, that the act of waving it off and walking away without reasonable cause was warranted and unquestionably justified. We agreed to trust that spark of wild instinct embedded perhaps in the ancestry of our genes, to help us correctly judge and weigh each and every new situation ahead of us. We shook on it and agreed to pay close attention to our first impressions.

We would never be the same again from that moment on. In time we would be very hard to fool and we knew it. We found ourselves looking forward to new encounters with the challenge of understanding the core motivation of others in a very compressed time frame and amid new and ever-changing circumstances. We knew that along our way we could expect encounters with those wanting to exploit, take advantage of or just outright prey on our vulnerability. Our senses were tuned and we needed to be alert at all times.

The value of our first impressions was undeniable. Not only would our first impressions of others be irrevocably fixed, so would the first impressions we put forth to others be so subconsciously irretrievable in their mind's judgment. A lot of folks along the way told us that they never picked up hitchhikers but had stopped to pick us up for some unknown reason. Maybe it was because somehow we gave them a good first impression.

We walked back to the Holiday Inn on the Fourth of July, compliments of our new friend C.J. McMurphy. We were fulfilled with the rewards of our courage that had trickled in from all the day's affairs. *What will tomorrow bring?* We went to sleep that night happy and excited for the coming day because with our new perspective we were ready for anything.

We woke the next morning renewed from a night of hot showers and clean sheets. It was foggy and by mid-morning the weather clogged in on our way north for Seattle. The interstate was busy and we had luck thumbing a ride before the rain set in.

We got to try out our newfound skills on a heavyset fellow in a small sedan. He wore a suit and was headed north on a business trip of sorts. He was a friendly and jovial fellow who laughed a lot. What we were most impressed with was that he knew everything. It seemed that no matter the subject, he knew something over the top about it. He talked of everything from thermodynamics to precious metals and he earned our full attention through his being so thoroughly convincing. His glasses were very thick and coupled with his weight, character, and IQ he was quite unique. He knew a lot of scams too and laughed as he relayed them, one by one.

Somehow I felt that was how he made a living. Had we anything of value we thought he could surely find one way or another to turn it for a profit. A con if you will but a friendly one at that who would gladly take your money with a smile on his face. Never no mind to us, though, as we rolled up the interstate warm and dry in what had become a steady, hard rain.

Somehow we got on the subject of diamonds, perhaps from his learning about our honeymoon. We had no rings to exchange at our wedding ceremony and he prowled through to learn that Libby had lost my grandmother's wedding band along the way. He played our shared guilt and played it well.

"As an investment," he said, "there is none better than diamonds." He quoted us figures that somehow exacted the value of cash we were carrying. "Had you purchased diamonds two months ago you could have doubled your money by now." I was almost taken in by the thought; doubling our money for nothing, now that is an investment. He appeared to have no stake in his pursuit, or so it seemed.

The weather had opened up and while rolling to a stop to let us out, he suggested that we have lunch at a nearby restaurant that served good, cheap food. He said that he could contact his diamond broker if we wanted to talk further about making an investment.

"Sure, why not?" I replied.

He said his broker could meet us at the restaurant. He dropped us off curbside right in front of the restaurant in Tacoma. Not really giving it much further thought, we thanked him for the ride and he rolled on.

The restaurant was clean and we were their only patrons for lunch. It seemed that different parts of the country were renowned for certain local, savory dishes. Neither of us had ever heard of Crab Louie Salad before and lucky for us, that was our lunch order for the day. We feasted on bread and a bowl piled high with fresh vegetables and crab.

As we waited for the check, a tall businessman in a plaid leisure suit came in the restaurant looking about. His white shoes were clean and unscuffed. His one eye fixed on me as he walked our way, but the closer he got we could see that his other eye wandered out and away to nowhere. It was really hard to connect to him because his eyes were so weird, but we tried. He was in his late fifties, wore thick, black-rimmed glasses and was as friendly as they get. He introduced himself and sat beside our table then explained that his colleague had just called him. It was his understanding that we might be interested in investing in the "diamond market" as he put it.

I bobbed my head up and down and side to side so as not to show any convinced commitment. He started in on a spiel that sounded almost too good to be true. He explained that in as little as a few weeks we could double our money or even better by making an investment within the diamond market. Libby asked him how a typical transaction was made.

"Do you sell stocks in diamonds?" she asked.

"No. It's a whole lot simpler than that. Here let me show you," he said with a grin. He reached into his suit pocket and pulled out a small, neatly folded piece of light blue paper. As he unfolded its creases, his tone took on a surreal, almost fairy tale quality about it. Finally, and in slow, rehearsed motion he revealed its priceless content, one single diamond. It was beautiful and large, perhaps just smaller than a pea. It rolled around freely on its blue paper mat and caught the sun from every direction. We "wooowed" and "ahhhed" simultaneously as an almost sarcastic audience.

"How much is that diamond?" I asked.

"Four hundred dollars," he said. "But the market is rising with no end in sight and it could well be worth six hundred by the end of the week," he added.

We were absolutely amazed at what had come of our day. We thanked him for coming and told him that we needed his card because we were definitely going to be in touch very soon. We told him that it indeed looked like an excellent and rare opportunity for us and that we would be closing a transaction with him later that same day.

He gave us his card but we both saw disappointment in his face as we did not let him get to the, "You have to buy this diamond right here and now with cash or the whole deal is off," part. We escorted him from the restaurant reassuring that he would be hearing from our investment broker within the hour. We paid the lunch bill, gathered up our gear and headed out for the second half of our day.

THE PENINSULA

It was a good time to change direction. The thought of a night in Seattle was grim so we headed for the Olympic Peninsula instead. Libby had a cousin who lived near the coast so we thought it might be kind of fun to try to look her up. Life slowed considerably once we crossed the sound so we stopped to buy some dried, smoked salmon, some canned vegetables, and a couple of ice cream cones. We talked long about the day's characters, how we were on guard, and laughed at the day although our caution was certainly warranted.

Hitchhiking also slowed on the peninsula with short rides to nowhere really, but the scenery was building and spectacular. Early in the evening a gold station wagon pulled over well past us to a stop on an uphill, rounding curve. We both walked up to the passenger side door a little bit cautious. I opened the door and never really acknowledged the driver's face because all I could see was a pair of handcuffs tucked into the seat cushion, a length of rope wrapped up with a slip knot at the end and a pair of black leather gloves on the front seat.

The driver asked in a very friendly tone, "Need a ride?"

"No thanks," I said.

I closed the door with a firm slam and motioned for him to move on as we both backed away from the car to the berm of the road. We looked at each other with astonishment as he slowly drove off. We were a little freaked out by it all and gave up early on any further travel for the day. Several hundred yards into a beautiful, evergreen wood we threw out our bags for a long night's rest beneath moonlight and pine.

The next morning we again woke to fog. Our bags were soaked with condensation so we slept until the sun was bright and warm to dry things out a little bit. We eventually rolled up and started trekking. We had to get to a phone to contact Libby's cousin and gave up on any thought of covering huge miles on the peninsula; it was almost as if we had flipped a switch and turned the traffic off. There was no traffic noise either, which was a welcomed change. Everything else was slower too. Speed limits were lower and no one was really traveling long distances nor on schedule or deadline. There was very little employment and many folks were retired.

We finally got to a phone booth and sure enough Libby found her cousin's listing. She called and got general directions to her town so we headed that way though it took us almost the entire day to travel less than a hundred miles. Across the northern tier we could easily cover four or five hundred miles a day with a few adventures thrown in to boot. Our progress was slow, but the landscapes were so beautiful that the change of pace and scenery was welcome.

Late that afternoon on the north side of the peninsula we found ourselves in her cousin's town that actually more resembled a hamlet with little or no municipality. We found another phone booth at the ferry dock but had no luck at all reaching her cousin. There was no answer. We were disappointed so we decided to hold out until she got home. We tried calling about every hour until dark set in, but still no luck so we spent the night right there in a cluster of mixed trees about two hundred yards from the ferry's loading ramp. The ferry dock was well lit throughout the night so we slept lightly.

The next morning was overcast and we decided to try Libby's cousin one last time before hopping the ferry. I could hear Libby holding conversation on the phone as I ate a couple of pecan pie snacks at a small mom and pop convenience store. She hung up the phone and relayed that her cousin was home, but had voiced some reluctance in having us visit. Libby said she'd explained that if it were too inconvenient we surely understood and would just move on. Apparently her cousin gave in and extended a lukewarm invitation to stop by.

Surprisingly, as it turned out, their home was within walking distance of the convenience store.

We approached their home with an open curiosity. Their house was a small cabin that set back in the woods just off the road. Moss and climbing vines were claiming the shady sides of the house. It had small windows and looked quite peaceful. We knocked on the door, as there was no doorbell. The door opened to reveal a beautiful and smiling, familiar face. Lisa met us on the threshold with hugs. We offered to set our packs down outside so as not to intrude. Lisa and Libby were very much alike except that Lisa was perhaps fifteen years her senior. The love and affection of family took them over in a grand reunion. It had been many, many years since they'd seen each other.

Lisa introduced us to her husband, Gary, who was shorter but equally as warm and as friendly a fellow. They took us into their living room where we all sat and visited over hot tea. We explained ourselves as best we could. We talked about our days at Bucknell, our work in the factory, our wedding, and some of our experiences on the road. They listened in captive fascination about Beaver Island in Lake Michigan, our escape from Mack, and the gathering. We all laughed to exhaustion.

It had been a long time since they had seen any family. Their life on the peninsula was slow and peaceful, but at times had become downright sedentary. Though they were guarded at first, our presence had provided them with a much-needed breath of fresh air. Within an hour their apprehensions vanished and they asked us to stay a day or two. We gladly agreed and planned for a short, two-day reunion. They made us feel very comfortable and we thoroughly enjoyed our break from the unknown.

We headed for a place called Hurricane Ridge where Gary, who was very knowledgeable about wildlife and such, suggested an afternoon outing. Though the weather offered little visibility, the ride to and from gave us all an opportunity to recount days of old and new. We stopped at a grocery store on the way back and put together a supper that we shared that evening. As we lay down to sleep on our bags on the floor of their home that night, a comfort that all was well fell over us.

The next day we sat about and talked inasmuch as the rain had stalled any outdoor activity. Rain played a huge role in the laid-back lifestyle of the peninsula because there was so much of it. By noon we could tell they were becoming a little envious of the excitement of our travels. They had become fairly recluse people and had few dealings with their neighbors. Somehow they managed to survive without regular, steady employment. Lisa was an artist, living a moderate artist's life, and Gary was able to do just about anything for several months at a time, but regular, gainful employment was hard to find on the peninsula. We could tell that for them, life's complacency had become boring at times.

That evening we drove to bathe in some natural hot springs. We parked the car at a small, unmarked lot and took a short hike to the springs. They were beautiful springs, surrounded on all sides by great stands of Northwest timber. Libby and I chose the first bath while Gary and Lisa went on further, disappearing into the woods. While stripping down I could not help but notice once again Libby's transformation into womanhood. She could remove her pants without unbuttoning them from weight loss. I noticed that she'd been walking about every day with one hand clenching her khaki pants at all times to hold them up. Every ounce of fat had been replaced with muscle in her shoulders, neck, back, torso, legs, and keister. Right down to those toes, she was so beautifully proportioned in every respect.

I slipped into the hot spring. The water was hot. It was very hot. I could only submerge for a second or so before being overcome by the heat. Libby, in her naturally cold-blooded state, could immerse in the hot spring indefinitely. After only a few minutes I sat poolside on a rock to cool down. But my energy had drained completely and I got very light-headed; the whole world went white on me. I got dizzy and actually lay down because I almost fainted from the out of body feeling

taking me. I told Libby that I wasn't feeling quite right but
spared alarming her. My temperature recovered a bit and as
I dressed I could tell that something within me was not right
still.

We met back at the car and decided to go for supper at a
crab house on the waterfront. All were eagerly hungry and
refreshed, but I had a strangeness about my body that was not
subsiding. I kept my discomfort to myself so as not to spoil
what was otherwise a great day. We pulled up to the fresh
seafood restaurant on the coast and when I stood up from the
back seat of their car I immediately got faint and broke into a
cold sweat.

We were seated inside and we all ordered Dungeness crab,
fresh from the ocean but to me it did not matter. My anxiety
was intensifying and about two bites into my meal I had to leave
the table to vomit in the men's room. I barely made it. *This,*
I thought, *is a repeat performance of the bug I picked up a few days
ago. It sure feels the same.* I cleaned up a bit and returned to the
table as white as a ghost. They all cut their meal short and we
headed back to Lisa and Gary's nest. I went to sleep as they
stayed awake talking.

We decided to move on the next morning though I was
still weak but no longer nauseous. Gary directed us to some
particularly beautiful country. Lisa bid us farewell at their
house and Gary drove us to a trailhead that started deep in a
heavily wooded rain forest. It was raining lightly when we got
there but we opted to start a lengthy hike despite a reluctance
to exert myself. We hugged Gary goodbye and headed off into
the wilderness.

The rain forest was indeed a unique place. There were
mosses and ferns and things growing on other mosses and ferns
and things that were growing on other things that grew off of
other things that all grew on trees. The forest floor was a diverse
carpet of flora, thick and lush with countless green species.
The trail that Gary had suggested was arduous and climbed
about ten miles in length to an uncertain destination.

We started in at a comfortable pace with Libby in the lead and immediately, as mountain trails do, we started to switchback to gain elevation. My fatigue was suppressed by the sheer beauty and serenity of such massive wood. Looking out from a switch point we noticed that the rain forest had changed into tree trunks, just massive, Pacific cedar tree trunks, dispersed and without branches. They were huge, standing tall and straight and reached to the sky. They were separated only by the void of moist, wet air.

We paused many times along our way to catch our breath and take in a short view. The moisture was thick, more than one hundred percent humidity for sure and our visibility was limited by an ever-thickening fog. The higher we climbed the denser the fog such that you could actually see each and every individual drop of water in the mist. It might as well have been raining and we got thoroughly wet. We had gained several thousand feet in elevation and covered perhaps three or four miles before the fog set in so thick that our visibility was reduced to only a few feet. Libby was in great condition, and as she trotted on I struggled to keep pace but focused on her pack and feared losing sight of her. The trail changed from dirt to solid rock then back to dirt again, time and again. We walked for miles not acknowledging any of our surroundings just staying focused on the trail at our feet and moving up and ahead. We had hoped that the fog would lift with elevation, but it only thickened so we stayed right on the trail because leaving it would certainly disorient us in no time. My mind overrode my body's need to rest as I was still sick and Libby was a strong source of renewable endurance for me.

By mid-afternoon we figured that we had to be in the vicinity of our ten-mile destination. We had risen above the trees and though our visibility was zero, we could tell that the terrain had leveled off. There were small, dense patches of snow here and there so we decided to unfold our gear and camp up on a small flat spot, at least until the fog broke. We tented up and rolled out our semi-dry bags. I fell into the tent and collapsed from total and complete exhaustion.

I was awakened by Libby several hours later who, while standing outside the tent, said in an almost frantic voice, "Oh my God! John, come see this."

I thought something was very wrong by the tone of her voice. I opened my eyes to see an artificial, brilliant orange flood light had illuminated the tent and all things in it. I sprang out of the flap door of the tent to see what was wrong. I thought I was dying because the setting was so unreal. The fog had lifted and we were camped on a pinnacle that reached far and away in all directions. Vast timbered valleys reached perhaps thirty miles or further to the Pacific Ocean's horizon and the brilliance of a yawning, setting sun. The entire sky was ablaze with a full palette of every color. The distant valleys were cloaked in soft, settled clouds so wispy that they seemingly could have been blown away with a light hush of one's breath while vast stands of timber seemed to clutch them still for their moisture. The clouds eventually broke in elevation to the climbing reaches and glaciers of Mount Olympus far and across a great and tremendous span of crystal clear space.

As it turned out, we had found the only flat spot large enough to pitch our tent in all visible directions for many, many miles. My sickness gave full submission to the beauty of our world as we hugged in speechless awe sharing our love for each other. The sun soon set and as we drew back into our tent with night closing in, we fell asleep thankful and overwhelmed by the likes of a Greatness unlike any we had ever known before.

The next morning we woke to a crystal clear day, ate some dried, smoked salmon and wandered from our tent. We could see that any extended trek from camp would lead us far down in elevation so we opted to sit and explore the beauty of our immediate location instead. We were surrounded by spectacular mountains though none of them was the mountain we had sought. Unfortunately, a national park is for visitors only so we'd have to look elsewhere for the mountain of our journey.

Surely, we thought, *mountains like these will have to be a fixed part of our future and the immediate journey ahead of us.*

We walked to the head of a nearby glacier where we met a park ranger. We talked some and he taught us how to descend a glacier using an ice axe in a maneuver called a "glissade." It was kind of like skiing in your hiking boots while using the ice axe as a rudder. If your feet got away from you and you started to slide down uncontrollably, he taught us to roll over and spike the ice axe right into the glacier to stop. We had no ice axes but he let us use his. He then taught us how to do the same with a walking stick as glacier travel requires one or the other we learned. He continued on down the trail and we headed back for camp. We sat and talked as we watched a red tail hawk soar effortlessly over the valley and before the sparkling white mountains in the distance. On the same lift of air we whiffed the smell of a herd of Roosevelt elk rising to our senses from the green valley far below.

Libby said, "I was worried about you last night. I thought you might need to be airlifted out. You were so pale. Are you feeling better today?"

I let her know that I did feel better, somewhat transformed by the spectacular scenery the likes of which I could never have imagined. I reassured her that I was AOK. The trek back to civilization was long, but literally all downhill so we decided to break camp and head out for new parts.

Perhaps two miles back-tracking we could better appreciate some of the pure danger of which we had been unaware on the previous day's ascent. The solid rock trail was actually a fracture in a great slab of rock that made up the face of the mountain we had climbed. The face was very steep, without a single feature to break one's fall. Had either of us stumbled yesterday and fallen a foot off trail there was no way to stop your free fall. Had we seen that feature of the trail we might have refrained from any further ascent. But the fog was so thick yesterday that we trudged on without fear or worry of a threat unknown to us.

At the base of the mountain Libby wanted to try taking a shortcut and we ended up regrettably walking thigh deep through a rain forest bog. When we emerged at the trailhead we were covered in huge, black leeches from the waist down, which was a little disappointing after such a great overnight camp. Not only were we soaking wet but also we had to strip down to our toes to get them off of us and out of our clothes. Libby was a little freaked out and frustrated by it all.

"I can't believe this. It was such a great day, right up until now," she said as we stood about half-naked wringing out our clothes.

I looked over to her with a grin and said, "Hey, what's so bad about a few leeches?" That made her chuckle and put a smile back on her face, but I wasn't kidding. Before long our clothes dried out enough to don and we headed out on a damp, two-mile trek on asphalt to the nearest highway.

CANADA, EH?

We got a quick ride to Port Angeles and hopped the ferry into Canada arriving in Victoria, British Columbia, around six o'clock. We stood on the red brick sidewalks noting the wonderful layout and design of the city's harbor and gardens when I realized something. "This is the city Dood used to tell me about when I was a kid," I said aloud to Libby. "Yeah, of course, Victoria!"

Dood had told me on several occasions as a kid that Victoria was a beautiful city that I should someday see. He told me about cobblestone roads, the red brick walkways, and flowerpots hanging from every lamppost. And just like that, there we stood on the lovely streets of Victoria. I never knew before exactly where Victoria was on earth, let alone British Columbia. I thought of Dood and how proud he might be of us finding our way there by accident.

While walking about we encountered another backpacker who suggested that we stay the night at the youth hostel. He said that it was very clean and affordable. We had never heard of one before and, for us, there really was no other alternative. We arrived at the hostel at dusk. It was cheap, only costing two bucks each for the night; another dollar and a half bought you a hot shower. Our married status made no difference so we had to sleep in separate dormitories for men and women. We each claimed a bed, took a shower, and agreed to meet up in the television room.

I got to the television room before Libby and sat on a picnic bench next to a woman who was well into her seventies. I thought it strange that a woman of her age was hanging out at a youth hostel as it was. I looked at her with a smile and said, "Hello."

Apparently I said something very wrong. She turned her head slowly toward me. Her eyes opened wildly as she stared right straight through me. She snapped back in a very commanding voice. "Don't you say 'Hello' to me. You have absolutely no right to talk to me like that and I'll have none of it!" She turned away in disgust and lit a cigarette. I noticed that her head was partially wrapped in a black turban of sorts. There were others in the room and she bolted out in bitterness at every single remark anyone made about anything. She was obviously disturbed and I felt for her. She was the most irritable, sarcastic, and mean-spirited person I think I had ever met in my life. My first impression was that she was irrational and could potentially be dangerous.

Libby arrived and we left the hostel for a short walk around to see and feel the city of Victoria before turning into our dormitories. As we walked I told Libby about the disturbed lady at the hostel and to be very careful about saying anything that would upset her because everything to her was upsetting. It made me think about my roller bearing. It was gone! Thinking back I figured that I must have lost it the night we spent at the ferry dock waiting to connect with Lisa and Gary. I didn't recall it bumbling around in my pants pocket all the way up or down the mountain in the national park. At first, I was a little saddened that it was gone, that I had lost it. It was more of a souvenir than a weapon of mass destruction. In another instant, I was glad to be rid of it. It was always heavy, clumsy, and bothersome and we never had a need for it anyway.

We gave up on a sweepingly diverse day and returned to the hostel to tuck into our bunks for the night. As I lay there amongst the men, the hostel started to settle down to its own nightly quiet. The only remaining sound was the voice of the poor, elderly woman in the other dorm going on and on in a low, background scorn of someone or something. She wouldn't cease.

Another woman had had enough and shouted out, "Shhhhhhh!" loud so that we all could hear.

"Don't you Shhhhhhh me!" the older woman immediately snapped back in a louder voice. "I will talk as long and as loud as I want, anytime I want…" Her tone gradually faded off as she went on and on. There was chuckled laughter from bunks in both dorms as we'd all pretty much accepted that she couldn't help herself. Soon after we were all warm, safe and asleep.

The hostel offered a great night's rest but little else and we were anxious to move on the following day to see what would come our way. Libby needed a jean jacket, a new set of bootlaces, and a pair of pants that fit her so we headed for the shops downtown. It was still early when we arrived and all the shops were closed, but we did find a small coffee shop open for business and ordered a light pastry.

While seated on a bench having our breakfast we noticed the older woman from the hostel walking across the street. Her head was again wrapped in a partial turban of sorts. It was still early in the morning and traffic was very light, but for the old woman it didn't matter. She yelled at and scorned in rage each and every car that drove by her, including the local police. We couldn't make out exactly what she was saying but it was obvious that she was uncontrollably angry with them all as they drove by. She seemed to be completely consumed with anger by their not acknowledging her. We were afraid to make eye contact with her and ignored her as did everyone else which seemed to heighten her rage.

How sad was she and what on earth could ever bring on such a unique state of endless mental anguish? We both were thankful we had no such trouble in our lives. There she stood, all alone, genuinely hating each car and passenger that would pass by her. We were convinced that was how she would spend her entire day, angry with all and everyone for no apparent reason.

As soon as the stores opened we bought a snazzy pair of bright red and black bootlaces and a fitting pair of knickers. We also broke out a few extra bucks for a road atlas of North America inasmuch as we would head out of town without a clue or destination in mind. We talked of heading over to

Vancouver, which was another short-term goal. We still had only shortsighted vision and any long journeys from there had only been vaguely talked about.

A lifelong friend had told us at our wedding that he'd be in Vancouver after the Fourth of July competing in sailboat races. Gary Barbiers was the red-haired boy of our huge and extended adopted family. I'd grown up with him in Delran, New Jersey, since my childhood. His mom got cancer real bad and, just before she died, my mom promised her that she'd look after him. Gary had just returned from a couple of tours in Vietnam and had found a job selling sailboats. We were both pretty excited about maybe seeing another familiar face especially one from home so we set our day's sights for Vancouver.

We rode a ferry from Vancouver Island to the city of Vancouver on the mainland arriving there around noon. Vancouver was a huge city and we generally tried to avoid metropolitan areas as they could only bring us trouble. A crime-ridden town like Vancouver could chew us up and spit us out if we weren't careful and we knew it. Fortunately for us, we got a great, safe ride with an elderly gentleman from the city. We asked him if he knew about an international sailboat competition where we might be able to find our friend. He said that it was probably being held at the marina, but he so loved his town that he wanted to escort us around and show us all the sights of Vancouver first. He drove us through all the parks and gardens and even gave us a short cruise through Chinatown.

By mid-afternoon we were at the marina hosting the competition. Our new friend waited for us in his car as we checked the registry, but we sadly learned that our friend from back home hadn't entered any of the races. We figured it was unlikely that Gary would've made such a huge journey anyway. We were both saddened to accept that familiar faces were not likely from then on and the loneliness drew us even closer together.

We knew we had to get out of the city well before nightfall to be safe and had already agreed to never hitchhike at night.

Our new friend gave us a ride to a depot to catch a transit shuttle bus to the city's outskirts and the interstate leading north out of Vancouver. We gratefully thanked him for our tour as we hopped aboard the shuttle and headed out of town.

A few short rides led us further out of town and in no time at all we stood at a rural on ramp. To the east was a great, green field and a farmer who was bailing some hay for what looked like a dairy operation. I recalled the days of my not-so-distant youth when I helped the local farmers bail hay in Centre County. In the gleaming sun of that afternoon I told Libby how I worked all day in summer heat for a full meal and a few bucks. It was such honest, hard work. I told her one time a farmer gave me a suckling pig for my efforts, which we raised to eventually butcher. I told her how there was nothing like the taste of homegrown pork, especially the sausage. In my daydream as I watched those bales kick out into the wagon I thought, *perhaps that farmer would like a hand.* My boyhood daydream was interrupted by a car which had stopped to give us a ride.

The countryside opened up fast as we traveled north as towns and people became sparse. We were headed to nowhere. The last couple of weeks with all the ups and downs had offered some things we really enjoyed, the mountains and the smoked fish. We knew that we enjoyed serenity as opposed to urban settings and so we set a long distance goal late that afternoon. We took out our new road atlas and agreed to head for Alaska. We shook hands on it. Alaska from Vancouver is not much farther than Alaska is from Pennsylvania. In other words, Alaska was still a long, long way and we had no idea just how far it was.

By late afternoon we were pretty much stranded in a town with no name. We found a bus station and opted to lay down some big time miles by Greyhound. The bus didn't go the whole way to Alaska and so we bought tickets for the bus line's end at Dawson Creek. The bus wasn't scheduled to arrive until seven o'clock so we found some time to play billiards. Things were different in Canada than in the States. For one, they didn't play eight ball on pool tables. Rather, they shot snooker, which we never really figured out. The tables were long and because the balls were so small we struggled to even sink a single one. We gave up on the game and opted instead to hang out at the depot waiting for our ride.

As we met new folks at the depot we told them that we were heading for Alaska. Many warned us that going to Alaska was a commitment. Their stories about grizzly bears were true accounts and they also warned us that going to Alaska without known employment was certainly risky business. Most gave us strange return looks of skepticism, knowing that so many before us had tried the same and failed. Alaska, after all, was a journey. It sounded more and more like Alaska, with its mountains and fish, would not be our final destination.

The bus arrived on time. We tried to find some comfortable seats as we'd be aboard all night. The distances between towns in British Columbia were much greater than in the States and there was virtually no stop and go traveling. Nevertheless, sleeping on a bus was just about impossible when standing six foot three and weighing 210 pounds. Even Libby went sleepless. It was something about those seats; they weren't designed for sleeping.

The bus rolled north all night long through hundreds of miles of massive stands of trees but little of anything else in the way of interesting landscapes. By midmorning the next day we were both irritable and couldn't wait to reach our purchased afternoon destination of Dawson Creek where and when we could resume hitchhiking. There was very little excitement riding that bus. At a stopover town we met up with a short, friendly guy who was a few years older. He was a roadie for the band Queen and worked on their lighting, or so he said anyway. Neither of us really believed him but he was jovial and his conversation broke our boredom.

By the time we arrived in Dawson Creek we were ready to give up on our Alaskan push and thought it best to head east instead. Our decision to abandon a northern route to Alaska was rewarded by a full, spanning rainbow. Being so far north, more north than either of us had ever been, was unusually discomforting. Evening in Dawson Creek was strangely bright as the sun set so very late in the day. Our fatigue from the sleepless previous night on the bus led us to roll out our tent and bags in a quiet municipal park.

I found myself admiring Canadian highways the next morning. Though they were two lanes they might as well have been four and the shoulder of the highway was just as wide as each lane. The grades and curves were perfectly sloped and each was freshly painted with white and yellow lines. They were so much better kept than those in the States and were much less traveled.

At noon we found a roadside cafe where Canadian weirdness continued. That far north in Canada most roadside cafes weren't really cafes. They were more like roadside cafeterias where you grabbed a tray, walked through a serving line though no one else was there and paid an arbitrary amount for some assortment of grub you selected as you served yourself along the way. You then seated yourself. There were no waitresses and no tips. I never could get used to vinegar instead of ketchup on my French fries either. Anyway, there were a lot of subtle differences both good and bad about Canada that made us feel out of place, alien in a true sense.

We ended up nearing a city in Alberta called Edmonton late that afternoon. We didn't want to end up there for the night and luckily a guy in a pickup truck heading southwest gave us a ride. He was excited to give us a ride into Jasper National Park, which was the northern Canadian stretch of the Rockies. He told us of wildlife, glaciers, Lake Louise, and the Calgary Stampede. The more we talked about it the more excited we became. We figured that maybe a southern traverse of the entire Rocky Mountains might give us another chance to find the mountain we sought at the onset of our travels. We barely got into the park when night fell and found a quick and rough campsite just south of the park's north entrance.

The next morning we caught an immediate ride to the heart of the park at a huge glacier. Along the way we saw many elk, bighorn sheep, and a couple of large, brown bears. All the wildlife seemed to be tame and unafraid, which amazed us. Stories of Lake Louise came up again and we were told it was a must stop on our route south. There was a chateau at the glacier that served food, again cafeteria style. The entire stop was pretty busy with traffic and commerce. You could catch a bus tour of the glacier for ten bucks each, but we passed on it because we could see the glacier perfectly at our distance and twenty bucks was a little steep, we figured. The whole park, despite its beauty, had a creepy type of feel to it, kind of like we were out of place or maybe even intruders.

We opted to continue on our trek south and joined up with a fairly large band of other hitchhikers at the glacier stop. We talked with them all, one by one, two by two, as the hitchhiking had slowed to a screeching halt anyway.

We learned that Jasper and Banff were adjacent northern and southern national parks in Alberta. We learned that one passed right on into the other and that the town of Banff was the southern exit town of the park complex. The town of Banff was another 110 miles of absolute wilderness south. We also learned that we'd better keep a clean camp without food and not to stray from designated campsites or else chance being eaten by one of the many large, fearlessly carnivorous grizzly bears. We definitely got the message and waited patiently roadside with perhaps twenty other hitchhikers for a much needed long ride. Fortunately for us, there was a designated and patrolled camp ground within walking distance of the glacier stop and cafeteria. By evening we gave up on hitchhiking and headed over to the campground for the night. We built a small fire and cooked some canned beans and mixed veggies for supper. We had no other food with us except canned food so we felt safe as far as bears were concerned.

The next morning we again joined other hitchhikers at the glacier stop to catch a ride out. Once in a great while a vehicle would stop, but in a mad rush to get out of there only those seemingly having been there the longest got to ride by unspoken default. By the evening of the second full day, I realized that we were in trouble. We hadn't traveled one inch all day. We returned to the very same campsite for a second consecutive night. Never before had we slept in the very same spot, pitched our tent in the exact, same site, two nights in a row.

We started earlier the next morning than we had the previous day. There were lots of stranded hitchhikers and no willing traffic. By noon we got completely frustrated and bored and headed for the chateau cafeteria to hopefully change our luck. We talked about our predicament while going through the chow line and concluded that it was way easier for hitchhikers to get a ride into the park than it was to get a ride out. We also figured that most tourists had come from afar, say Toronto, for example. We also surmised that most auto tourists, perhaps with a son or daughter in the back seat, were thoroughly enjoying the scenery of their Rocky Mountain vacation out west. *Why should they risk picking up any hitchhikers who might spoil their whole vacation by killing them all, taking all their money, and stealing their car? Of course!* We finally understood their motivation and the first impression that we were presenting was definitely not working for us.

When we went to pay for our tray of food at the end of the chow line, the cashier asked us, "Are you guys hitchhiking?"

"Yeah," I replied.

She was familiar with our predicament. "You know, sometimes people will make a sign that helps them get out of here," she offered.

I kind of nodded my head to acknowledge her helping suggestion. My knee jerk thought was, *Ah, what does she know? We've never had luck with signs before.* But I knew that we hadn't really used signs much. For one thing we never really knew where we were headed to even post a sign. For another, sign materials were just hard to come by roadside. You needed a good piece of cardboard and a magic marker and we carried neither, ever. As we ate our lunch we imagined an idea; perhaps she was right after all. *What the heck, we appear to have plenty of time to give it a go.*

We changed our clothes to match. Libby put on her United States Navy green issued turtleneck sweater and I pulled on my United States Navy green issued rain jacket to match. I also changed into my brown khaki pants, like the ones she also wore. Our colors were green and brown. I combed out my hair and beard a bit and tucked my hair up into my baseball cap so as not to appear to be so rough. We asked the cashier if we could borrow a magic marker and some cardboard to which she gladly obliged. We cut the cardboard with a pocketknife so that it was perfectly square, not torn on edge. On the cardboard we wrote in almost perfect block lettering, "EMERGENCY STATION #14."

When we returned to the cluster of stranded hitchhikers we decided it might work best if we got some separation from them so we walked south. We got about one quarter mile from them when we turned to face the sound of our first passersby. On a whim I proudly held out our sign. We stood proud but without smiles, expressionless. Our very first attempt was successful! A small, four-door passenger car pulled to stop just past us. We walked to the car, opened the back seat door, and piled in, packs and all. We had no story together whatsoever and had figured on working that out while standing on the side of the road waiting for a ride. Little did we know our plan would be so immediately successful. Yes, and as it turned out, we had piled into the back seat of a car with the young daughter of a married couple seated in the front. They were all from Toronto and were enjoying the scenery of their Rocky Mountain vacation out west.

The husband was driving and he immediately pulled back out onto the highway south as his wife asked curiously about the emergency. They had stopped to pick us up because they wanted to help us park rangers with the emergency. Needless to say we both started fumbling through an increasingly unbelievable fable. Somehow we landed on the idea that a girl from our hometown had fallen from a cliff and may have been killed, kind of like what maybe happened at the rainbow gathering. But we could tell that they weren't buying our story, not one bit.

The mother asked the most obvious of questions. "Did you know her?" referring to the woman who had maybe died falling from a cliff.

Libby answered, "Yes," and I answered, "No," at the exact same time. We looked at each other in befuddlement.

Well, that was their cue, their dead giveaway that we were lying. The worried husband permanently fixed his rearview mirror on me. The mother completely turned around in the front seat and wasn't about to take her eyes off either of us in the back seat with their only daughter. We both heard her thoughts, that we would kill them all, take all their money, and steal their car. The unspoken tension building in that little car was nerve wracking, but hey, at least we were covering some miles. We tried to change the subject several times but all other attempts at conversation failed.

Suddenly the husband frantically started flashing his lights and blaring his horn at the Royal Canadian Mounted Policeman who had just passed us in his patrol car. He pulled us over immediately to investigate. We were all in the middle of nowhere.

Rats! It's for sure. We'll be calling Libby's parents from prison tonight. No doubt about it this time.

As we slowed to a stop, I had hoped to beat the mother to the cop but no way. She flew open her door and ran over to the officer in a full-blown conniption fit. She totally lost control begging for help from the officer and rambled on and on with him while pointing back at me in absolute hysteria. Meanwhile, I struggled to get our packs out of the little car and prepared for the hoosegow. As I approached the Mountie he told the woman to return to her car and for them to move on, as he would take control of the situation.

As she ran past us her eyes stayed fixed on me until she got safely back inside their little car. I told her, "Thank you for the ride," as she stumbled past. Though she said nothing, her bloodshot eyes were wrought with anger, fear, and vindication.

The Mountie's car was spit polished, as was he. He looked like an older version of Dudley Do-Right with glasses but no cleft chin. He looked me straight in the eye and squinted. "Now, young man, what's all this about emergency station #14?" he asked.

Now maybe not a great story, maybe not even a good story, but we had a story, the story we'd worked out from the back seat of the Toronto family's little sedan.

"Officer, look, here's all we know," I said as I looked down to the gravel and raised both my hands open palmed. "We're on our honeymoon and we learned at the glacier cafeteria that a woman from our home town was injured in a climbing accident. That's all we know. They said that she was taken to emergency station #14. We don't know where that is, but we'd sure like to find out where she is and if we may be of some assistance."

The Mountie rubbed his chin with his hand as I spoke. His lips were tight and his squinting, unblinking eyes were fixed on mine. In a flash, he reminded me of my mother who could always tell when I was fibbing. Surely, we both thought his very next words would be, "You are under arrest."

That eternal, silent moment was broken with his spoken relief. He said, "Well, I don't know anything about an emergency station #14. But if anything like that really happened, the first thing they'd do is airlift your friend by helicopter to Banff Hospital, eh? It's at the southern end of the park. I'll tell you what. Why don't you guys hop in with me and I'll get you right down there?"

"Would you, sir? Could you, sir? We'd be forever grateful if you could help us out here," I said.

"Don't mention it. Glad to be of assistance," he said as turned to get back in his patrol car. We eagerly piled in too.

His patrol car was no longer intimidating. To us it was more like a NASCAR cruiser and the perfect Canadian highway became a motor speedway.

He turned on the emergency lights and cranked her up to one hundred miles per hour. As we sped south toward Banff we all loosened up and enjoyed the ride. He too became fascinated by our stories of the road. We could tell that he enjoyed driving fast and ours was just the perfect excuse to wind her up.

At one intersection we passed another cluster of stranded hitchhikers. I rolled down my window and yelled and waved at them all as we raced by with lights ablaze. We were all laughing when I got my head back in the car. The Mountie made a great tour guide and pointed out all of the park's highlights as we raced by them. Lake Louise was breathtakingly spectacular, especially at one hundred ten miles per hour.

We reached Banff in less than an hour! The Mountie no doubt by the time we got to Banff had put one and one together and said, "You guys probably need to get cleaned up a bit before you head over to the hospital, eh? How's about I drop you off at the youth hostel first? You can walk to the hospital from there, eh?"

I don't know when we had ever been so grateful. We thanked him over and over again as I shook his gentle hand. Libby gave him a long, grand hug. We both held up our hands as we walked away, knowing that God had blessed us on that day. *God forever bless the Royal Canadian Mounted Police.*

The hostel wasn't much. It was more like a MASH unit set in the woods. Our sleeping quarters were mobile army tents. The men's and women's quarters were separate again too, which neither of us was excited about. There were still a few hours of daylight left so we decided to take advantage of the hostel's cold showers and then move on to Calgary instead. We'd been hearing a lot about the Calgary Stampede and weren't so sure about the "stampede" part, but otherwise it sounded like a fun celebration.

There was a renewal about bathing that cleansed the soul as well and as I showered, I thought back on the events of our day. We weren't at all proud of having been deceitful to get out of the park. *Those poor folks from Toronto were just out to vacation in the West. They never really planned on that experience they got with us, but then again, neither did we. And after all, today's a day they'll certainly remember and talk about for many years to come. It may have made their trip west a bit wild. They're probably laughing about it right now,* I thought as I rinsed the soap from my hair. I remembered how unnerving our day with Mack had been. I shivered and shook the water from my hair and beard at the thought.

I met up with Libby at a picnic table just outside the women's shower. She was perky and clean and met me with a grin, a hug, and a kiss. We headed for the two-lane road to Calgary and hadn't been thumbing for more than a few minutes when a brown van pulled past to pick us up. We opened the cargo door and jumped in at the instruction of the dashing blonde Canadian woman in her early thirties in the passenger side bucket seat. The driver was a smiling, friendly fellow in his mid-thirties with a naturally curly, fuzzy kind-of-afro hairdo. Immediately as we rolled out they started in with a profusion of dialog and they spoke with a new and foreign intent. They asked us very few questions but really put themselves out there to us. We weren't used to that, but they seemed to be safe and very friendly.

Somehow we got onto the subject of Ian Anderson, the renowned flutist and lead singer of Jethro Tull, likely from Libby's flute playing. The driver couldn't keep his eyes on the road and kept turning around to look at us as he spoke. At one point he pulled his right leg up on the dashboard of the van and threw his head completely back so as to emulate Ian's posture he so often took while onstage. The driver did it over and over and though we were all laughing, I know I preferred that he keep his eyes on the road and the building two-lane traffic. There was something very distinct about those two because their behavior was so outward, direct, and exceedingly friendly. We hadn't met a couple yet that was quite so open. He spoke in an understandable but very unique, mumbling Canadian dialect. His name was Gordon Koval and hers was Sharon. She never gave her last name. They weren't husband and wife or an amorous couple. They were just friends but we could sense there was more to it than that.

By the time we got to Calgary, Gordon had invited us to stay at his house for the night and they both seemed more than eager for us to accept his offer.

"You're more than welcome to stay," Gordon said in an almost slurred and friendly mumble. We figured, *sure why not, another helping hand.* His was a really nice, clean, comfortable suburban home in a residential community.

As we walked inside I couldn't help but notice that Sharon was a full-blown knock out, maybe thirty-two with long, firm legs in tight, faded blue jeans and a voluptuously full flannel shirt unbuttoned somewhat to expose her cleavage. Her hair was long; her fingernails and toenails were painted. She walked on platform shoes and she was as overly friendly as she was stunning.

Gordon was a bit of a mismatch for her. He was a total nut case, a goof ball, but one heck of a nice guy. How those two fit together was a mystery but then again they really weren't a couple, so they said. Gordon showed us a place in his finished basement where we could stay the night. It was cozy and warm, complete with a pull-out sofa, thick, shag carpet, TV, fireplace, and a fancy chess table too.

All in all it looked like a rare night for us and again he said, "You're more than welcome to stay." It was clear that he wanted us to spend a night at his house so we accepted his generosity and thanked him. We said that we would rather roll out our bags than use his sofa.

They made us comfortable and their friendliness was so unique. They had been invited to dine at their friend's house and had to step out for a while but said they'd be back shortly. It seemed they would've rather stayed at home with us and visit but they'd made prior arrangements. Gordon and Sharon stepped out and we took the opportunity to calm down and talk about the day over a friendly game of chess. It had already been a very interesting day.

Later that evening we heard some scuffling around on the floor above as Gordon and Sharon had returned from their supper engagement, so we reunited in their kitchen. They'd come home with another gentleman who was perhaps in his late thirties. He was tall, casually well dressed, and handsome. Though friendly, he wasn't as outward as the rest of us. Gordon offered us a cold beer as both he and Sharon had already begun to imbibe. The other fellow abstained from drinking as he listened to our small talk conversation. As we stood about in the kitchen the conversation gradually turned toward us. It seemed a little like three on two with all their questions but we held our own. We noticed a curious shift in both Gordon's and Sharon's behavior as they started asking us a lot of questions instead of trying to impress us anymore. By their questions it seemed like they shared an undisclosed intention of some kind. The new guy just stood and mostly listened to us converse.

Sharon started asking a lot of questions. "How old are you two? Where are you from? How did you end up in Canada?" and stuff like that. We had already covered those details in the van on the way to their house but she wanted the other guy to hear it all too. They seemed really interested in our answers, which we figured were fairly boring background details about us. They were more intent on that information than any of our personal accounts or even our encounter with Mack.

Sharon then asked me, "Are you guys interested in anything like this?" She handed me a piece of paper. Libby was fully engaged in conversation with Gordon who was pulling out all the stops in his increasingly debonair style. The paper that Sharon handed me had some text on it.

As I started to read, I noticed in the background behind the text was a shadowed, resolute image of a naked woman on her knees performing fellatio on her shadowy male partner. As I stared at the page in disbelief I abandoned reading the text though it seemed completely unrelated to the graphic, sexual image set behind. I also realized that Sharon's and the other guy's eyes were completely set on me to see my reaction. Their intent was finally out in the open though Libby, still engaged in conversation with Gordon, had no idea what had just transpired. Libby had glanced over my shoulder when Sharon handed me the paper, but she never really got the whole picture.

Still staring at the paper I knew that I was at another decision point. I felt like I might as well have been holding Mack's loaded Colt .45 again. I wasn't really sure how to react. I mean, I was definitely not interested in anything like that but at the same time I didn't want to offend anyone once their intent was known. At the same time, I wanted to get out of there real fast and I was no doubt blushing bright red. It was not likely, however, that back east rumors of my quick, but very average member could have gotten all the way to Calgary so fast. And as scruffy as I had become, I thought it unlikely that Sharon could seriously have any interest in me.

That was when my light switch went on. Ding! *Nope, it's not me they're interested in. It's Libby.* And sure enough when I looked up at her talking with Gordon, I noticed just how stunning, how superb, a woman she had become. Yes, her features were everything that a man could want, her high cheekbones and perfect smile, her long, silky brunette hair, her rosy lips, her naturally colorful complexion and her absolutely perfect and tremendous physique. Yep, they all shared interest in her and looked to me for approval.

For all I knew, there could have been a fully equipped video production studio set up in one of Gordon's bedrooms just waiting to employ a young, vulnerable woman of legal age. I had the distinct impression that there was a business proposition lying in wait for my approval. Their offer never went beyond that, I would not let it. That crossroads of decision was easy for me. Libby was all mine and no one but no one was going to take her from me. Gene's plan was firm on my upright chest. *No need to worry about anything, money, work, nothing. Stay focused on Gene's plan, to lead us right at moments just like this.*

My embarrassment eased at the strength of the thought of Gene's words. I was brought back into the moment with the thought that Sharon was likely becoming well known for her willingness to perform an assortment of unmentionable sexual favors.

With a smirky smile and a bobble head gesture that morphed into absolute and pronounced horizontal refusal, I handed the porn back to Sharon and said to them both, "I don't think so."

Boy, the party ended right then and there, I'll tell you. They made no attempt to persuade me. The new guy and Sharon both politely left Gordon's house shortly thereafter. We told Gordon that we were both tired and were going to fold up for the night if he didn't mind. Gordon was a warm and friendly fellow and agreed that it had been a day. We went downstairs, climbed into our bags, and fell asleep. I said nothing to Libby about what was likely the proposition of a lifetime that had just occurred minutes before upstairs. Believe you me, I would forever wonder what would have become of us had I accepted their proposition. I had no doubt that our lives could have turned on that dime. I went to sleep knowing that they were all really good people but lived a lifestyle that we would only imagine.

We woke the next morning to the smell of fresh brewed coffee. We rolled up our bags then headed upstairs to the kitchen where we found Gordon who was just about to leave for work. He asked us how well our night's rest was, which had been comatose. He said to help ourselves to all that he had to eat, but admitted that he was a little hurried to get to work. We thanked him, Libby with a huge hug, and before leaving he said once more in that unforgettable Canadian mumble, "You're more than welcome to stay." He grabbed his briefcase and was off to face whatever was his day. We each drank a hot cup of coffee before setting out on ours. Gordon was a total gentleman and we were convinced that it would've been, eh, okay if we just settled right in on him indefinitely.

Picking up the day fresh we set out from Gordon's toward the familiar, rumbling sound of the freeway several blocks off in the distance. *Screw the stampede,* we thought. *Let's head back for the States.* It was a beautiful, sunny day and the walk gave me the opportunity to reflect on our newest acquaintances. I respected the courage it took to put forth such a spelled out and taboo request. I admittedly had a curiosity to know more, but they clammed up tight on all details once they learned that we were not players. I suspicioned that with such daring promiscuity would come an equally risqué and clandestine lifestyle. I was amazed that, for folks who were so open and verbose, how little they had to say once they learned that we were monogamous. Still my curiosity to have known more about them all was huge. We talked at length about them as we stood at the on ramp for parts south.

Libby was unaware of their proposal and when I explained to her the nature of things she said with a joking smile, "Hurry up, lets go back there." I knew she was kidding and we laughed out loud at the pure randomness of the outrageous events unfolding in our path. We agreed that Gordon and Sharon were genuine, fine folks who had extended to us a chance at something very unique from their heart-felt goodness within. We forever after would recall their memory with a fond, flattering and exhilarating chuckle.

A newer passenger car pulled up to give us a lift. It was a single man in his late forties. He had dark hair that was slicked back with some kind of brylcreem. There was plenty of room in his car, but we threw our bags in his trunk as he insisted. We were guarded about locking our gear in somebody's trunk because we'd lose immediate access to our transient little home. We weighed him up in minutes on the spot and felt comfortable that he posed no threat. His request was an open-handed gesture of assistance, nothing more. I rode in the passenger front seat and Libby rode in the seat behind.

We struck up conversation with our driver who soon learned that we were on our honeymoon. We talked of many things and focused in on employment. As small talk, I mentioned that I was somewhat disappointed with my inability to find suitable employment.

The little guy read me like a book when he stated, "You know you can do anything you want to do." He went on to tell us about his successes in life. Apparently he'd started up his own small trucking company that had grown to a fleet of six tractor-trailers. He was doing well, quite well, so he relayed. He then shared with us the most profound advice we would ever hear. He said, "You can become anybody you want to be and you and I both know that you can do anything."

His statement filled me with courage and self-esteem. After all, there he was, a little, stranger guy, a brand new acquaintance, who didn't know me from Adam, telling me, "You and I both know that you can do anything." He went on, "The key to success is knowing that you have to become your very best at it. If you decide you're going to become a professional road bum, then commit yourself to be the very best road bum you can possibly be.

"Or dishwasher," I jokingly offered.

"Or dishwasher," he said with confidence as though taking me seriously. His confidence snapped my attention to take him more seriously; he meant what he was saying. I sadly knew that a dishwashing job might well be the limit of my skills and capabilities.

He went on, "If that's what you want to be, then become the very best road bum or dishwasher that you can possibly be. Get up at the break of dawn to rummage through the trashcans or pick up cigarette butts. Let no one else clean dishes as spotless as you do. You know what it takes to be the very best road bum or dishwasher, no one else does, but you do. If you decide you want to become a trucker then commit to become the very best trucker that you can be. You know what it takes to be that very best trucker and no one else does." He paused as he could see his words sinking in to our attention. Libby had both arms draped over the front seat as she too listened in fascination.

He then tilted his head back slightly and lifted one eye brow as he said, "But if you decide to become a doctor or a lawyer, every day before you leave for work, look yourself in the mirror knowing that you are doing all that you possibly can to be that very best doctor or lawyer. If you live fully up to your own expectations, you will far surpass the expectations of most all others."

His words hit us like a ton of bricks because we knew that he spoke the truth. His words came so freely and he stated them so matter-of-factly. He was so obviously right and shared knowledge that we knew to be right; we just had never heard it like that before. It was so simple yet so profound. I acknowledged with open and true appreciation for his sharing. He'd armed us in a sense with a very powerful thought. We admitted that neither did we know what we wanted to do nor did we have enough education or skills to be competitive in any field except maybe road bumming or washing dishes. But his words immediately took our fears away of trying to become more. He assured us that in time, we'd find work or a field that would best suit us. But, he reiterated that true success comes only from living up to higher self-expectations, not those imposed by others. All I could think was *where was this guy and his advice two years ago when perhaps I needed it most?* In all truth I needed it most right then and there as we drove south somewhere in southern Alberta, Canada, on a bright, summer's day.

He could see that his advice had been well received by us, and when he learned that we were far from, and out of touch with, home, he offered to share with us another of his most heartfelt values. He asked if we'd mind going off the interstate to his home where he said that he had something priceless to share with us. We were anxious to see what else he had to offer so we agreed.

We pulled up to a doublewide mobile home that sat by itself in a remote, open field. We felt the heat of day as we walked from the car to his front door. His trailer was dark, cool, and well-kept inside. We really didn't know what he had in store nor did he explain. He asked us to take a seat in his living room and offered us a drink. It was maybe eleven o'clock in the morning so we passed on his offer of alcohol but we each thanked him for a couple of ice cold cans of cola.

"Don't mind me if I have a snort do you?" he asked politely.

"Hey, you go right ahead, man," I said.

From our seats in the adjacent living room, we watched him mix a tall glass of cola and bourbon, make that bourbon and cola, on the kitchen countertop. As he finished preparing his drink he set out a shot glass, filled it to the brim then bolted it down tough. He chased it with his mixed drink, and then topped off his drink with straight bourbon. By the time he sat with us he was well on his way and the day was still young. Our guard went up because it was a strange turn from someone who otherwise appeared to be full of truth and unique wisdom. He started talking about all things that were dear to him and he sort of rambled on and on. He returned to the kitchen to refill his empty glass with mostly bourbon.

Libby asked him, "Hey, what is it that you wanted to show us?"

He talked as he prepared his turntable and thumbed through his vinyl stack of albums. His speech was slurring and his breath had an alcoholic sweetness to it. "When was the last time you spoke with your folks?" he asked.

We both drew blank faces as he fumbled to center the LP on the player. "It's been, well…over a month now," I replied as I realized that it had been that long.

He said, "I want to play for you my favorite song of all time," as he struggled to drop the needle onto the cut that he wanted us to hear. He couldn't find the dead space between songs so he set the needle down on the fade of the song preceding. He had a very sad look on his face as the song started to play. It had a ballad-like, country feel. We didn't recognize the voice or the tune and it might have been a song by Merle Haggard, but maybe not.

We don't really remember all the words but it was a song about "Mother." We caught a lot of verses like, "There is no other than your mother," and "Mom do you remember when..." and "Now you might love your father and your sister and your brother, but you'll never love another like your mother."

Between the classic country sound, lyrics, and the tears streaming down our new friend's face, well...we were humbly dumbfounded. Part of us was laughing inside, the other crying with love, compassion, and sympathy for that distraught and honest little fellow.

When the song finished he slammed his tall drink. We went over to him and we each put a hand on his shoulders to comfort him. We were reluctant to ask him for any details about his mother.

"Are you okay? It's all right," we reassured him.

All he said was, "Promise me that you'll call your mom sometime soon." He was clearly depressed and we assured him that we would.

We told him that it was time for us to move on and politely asked him to open the trunk of his car so that we could get our packs. He handed me his keys while slumped in his reclining chair. We went outside and grabbed our packs. I told Libby to wait for me by the car and alone I went back inside to return his keys. He stared blankly into the carpet with his head tilted down and away.

I thanked him for the ride, the cola, and his words of wisdom as I placed the keys on the coffee table. He acknowledged by raising his hand in a limp wave. He said nothing as I closed the door and returned to Libby who already had her pack on. We set out on foot on a lonely Great Plains country road. It was just afternoon.

We worked up a sweat getting back to the interstate, which was a few miles on a back track. The interstate was slow and relatively quiet, save for the occasional high- speed eighteen-wheeler. We'd hoped to make it Stateside by dark, but the spotty traffic and wide-open terrain made those prospects doubtful. The interstate eventually narrowed down to only two lanes and vehicles became even fewer and farther between.

By late that afternoon we realized and enjoyed that we were very much alone again. We were in the remotest of the Great Plains, well east of the Canadian Rockies somewhere. The mountains were no longer in sight on the horizon west and before long, late afternoon became evening. We got a ride to the edge of a very small town. The whole town was less than a quarter mile in length and the sun was within the hour of its setting. There were large grain silos and an adjacent train track to the southwest just a block from the main street. There were several other buildings in the town. The larger buildings were on the same side as the granaries. The smaller buildings were on the opposite side of an unusually wide main street. What was so different about that little town was that there was absolutely no one there, not one single soul. The buildings were all well kept. There were a few houses on the northeast side too, but there was strangely no one around. There was no gas station, no grocery store. There was not one business open. There was no noise of people or of their doings.

The sky was as enormous as the plains do offer. To the west were spectacular clouds of every color, cloaking hundreds of miles of both planted and wild earth. As we walked through the deserted little town we could tell that at times the place was busy with agricultural commerce. But on that evening, we were alone to enjoy the serenity. In a word everything and everybody were all "squenched" away as coined by James Whitcomb Riley for perhaps just such a setting.

At the other edge of town we made a solitary acquaintance. To our surprise, out of nowhere and from the silence of dusk, a small brown mutt waggled toward us sheepishly from behind. His approach was cautious and shy but by his tail we could see he was really happy to greet us.

Libby's loving voice broke the silence as she turned about and knelt down to scratch the head, then the belly of her newfound friend. "Hi. What's your name?" she squeaked as the little scruff rolled over in complete submission and utter delight. "Yeah, I never knew a doggie that didn't like his belly scratched," she said to him in a high then low pitched, baby-talk voice. "Yeessss, you're such a good doggie," she praised.

It all brought a grand smile to my face to see her in such joy. *Yes, animals will surely be an important part of our future,* I knew. Libby scratched and petted, then petted and scratched. When she stood back up, the little squirrel chaser scampered back to his recesses, seemingly back to nowhere. She turned to me with a corners-of-the-mouth-turned-down smile and with wet, winking eyes.

I hugged her and kissed the teary bone of her cheek. I told her that was what I loved about her most, her loving affection for all animals. She said she was briefly tempted to take him with us, but knew it wouldn't work out so well. I took her by the hand and we walked on and out of town, side-by-side, in the light of a grand and rising prairie full moon.

At twilight a large red Ford pickup truck pulled up to us and offered a ride. We threw our packs in the truck's bed and climbed up into the cab. The truck was taller than any pickup I had ever seen and we couldn't help but notice how high we sat above the road as we drove. As we rolled down the lonesome road we started in with our driver. He said that we were at the very headwaters of the Mississippi River. We were astonished because Mississippi was so far away. The thought was comforting, though, and brought us closer to home in mind. We told him that we originally were headed for Alaska but turned back because of the bear accounts we were hearing and reading about.

He said, "That was probly the right choice, eh? There's a lotta bear on the way too," he explained further.

The driver was an outfitter, a person who is paid to hunt and kill big game animals. His need for such an awesome pickup was fitting. As we traveled it turned into night and he started relaying hunting stories by the light of a great big moon and the dim glow of his dashboard. We were absolutely fascinated not only by his stories but that he was able to make a living, and a good one at that, hunting and outfitting others to do the same.

He recalled one hunt where he'd flown over a riverbed to spot moose for a hunt the following day. He said the next morning he found himself in thick willow brush on the flat of the river's flood plain. He said it was really hard to walk through let alone see game. Then he stumbled onto a short, open corridor in the willow to see an adult grizzly bear charging straight toward him. He instinctively raised his rifle and shot the bear repeatedly until it folded up, dying just a few yards from his feet.

He accounted in graphic detail how the bear would not die from one shot. It finally took a perfect shot to the bear's head to finally put it down. He said that he no more than gathered himself together only to look up and see her three hundred-pound cub appear, charging him as well. Within an instant he said the sow and her cub were dead within feet of each other. He said that he returned to the airplane, sat in the seat and started rolling a cigarette when the upwelling fear of what had just happened overtook him. He said he could not roll his cigarette because he was shaking so badly; the tobacco went flying everywhere. We knew that shaky, unnerving fear from our roadside encounter with Mack.

The outfitter told us that we'd soon be crossing the border and asked if we wanted to smoke some hashish. *Why not? What the heck,* we thought. The hash was strong and sweet and we got real high, real fast. We could see lights of buildings and such as we approached the border and as he put the hash pipe under the seat beneath him he assured us there would be no problem as we drove up to the customs agent.

The border was kind of like an official tollbooth and the attendant pretty much just waved us through. The outfitter wanted to stop and use the restroom of the customs office on the U.S. side. He rolled his great truck to a stop with absolute perfection and command as the large rimmed tires ever so gently nudged the curb. Neither of us needed relief so we sat alone in the warmth of his comfy cab with total amazement at our day. It was great being back in the States, though Canada we would surely miss. We expected the pace to pick up in the morning, as life in the States was faster and much busier for all. The outfitter returned to the cab and we headed down the road apiece. We asked him to let us out in the moonlight where we spent the night beneath a stand of large ponderosa pine in northern Montana.

STATESIDE

We woke the next morning to a gorgeous, sunny day. There was hardly any traffic, but we figured that getting a ride should be pretty easy. We enjoyed the quiet, especially the lack of interstate noise. In no time, an older white Ford van pulled to a stop to give us a lift. He was a scruffy, bearded fellow on his way to work. He was a welding inspector and traveled all around getting paid to inspect welds. He enjoyed his work because he really enjoyed traveling.

Now there's a job for you, John. If only we could find someone to hand us a legitimate paycheck twice a month for what we do now, we'd have her made, I thought. I remember sizing him up a bit wondering if he was being the best welding inspector he could be. *Who else really knows but he?*

We spent much of the rest of the day trying to reach Kalispell and had to skirt Glacier National Park the whole way. All rides encouraged us to trek the park but we really wanted to avoid that type of crowd. We wanted to avoid all national parks after our experiences in Canada, and local folks seemed to have more to share than vacationers anyway. They were certainly more willing to pick up hitchhikers. Montana has some beautifully scenic back roads and short of Interstate 90 there was really no other choice.

Leg by leg we finally found ourselves nearing Kalispell that evening in a ride with a Frenchman. He had offered us a night's rest at a commune farm just outside of town. The farm was fun with animals, sheep, goats, chickens, dogs, and cats. Libby loved it. There were a half-dozen French people living on the small farm. They struggled to be subsistence farmers and we could see they certainly had their hands full. They milked the goats, made cheese, and ate fresh eggs everyday, but just keeping the livestock out of the vegetable garden was almost a full-time job in itself. They let us sleep in their barn in a hayloft.

We walked to downtown Kalispell the next morning. It was a mile or so to town and the fresh mountain morning air made the walk that much more invigorating. We had ham and eggs with coffee for just a few dollars at an old cafe right on the town's main street.

After breakfast while walking out of town we came to a crossroads in our travels. That is, to travel east or west or north was terrain already known to us. It really appeared that a course south was the only real choice, but where would we go? We had to have a direction and a destination, at least as a goal; it gave our travel meaning, even if just a short-lived one. Long goals seemed to provide more adventure even though we might change our minds along the way. We might abandon it altogether but we still had to choose one. We stood roadside unable to choose a place, town, city or event we really wanted as a goal and at the same time we really didn't want to stay in Kalispell. Nothing against the town, we just wanted to travel and see new places, to meet new faces. We were still searching for our mountain but that goal was always background in mind and almost like finding the needle in a haystack. We talked about going to Mexico. I'd studied Spanish in depth, but the closest I ever really got to using it was with three Venezuelan girls in my high school lunchroom.

Surely it would be fun to converse in Spanish as we traveled through Mexico, I thought. *Then again, Mexico is a long, long way. And we would probably end up in prison down there. Maybe not, but what harm can come if we just head that way?*

We decided to pull out the road atlas and study it a while. *Perhaps there's a place of interest that we'll see.* After a fifteen-minute search we kind of got bored with all the options. We decided instead to have Libby close her eyes and with her right, index finger she pointed at a spot on the map of the United States. We laughed as we chanted and summoned the powers that be to lead her finger to that chosen spot, the spot of our enlightened path. The atlas became our real-life Ouija board and we committed to its destination no matter where her finger landed.

As it turned out she put the point of her index finger on Richfield, Utah. *Hmmm, never heard of it, don't know anything about it, let's go.*

The very next ride was headed south. It was a midnight blue Chevy Impala with a white ragtop. The driver was a light brown, frizzy-haired guy with no shirt. He had one glass eye that stared off and away. He also had no right arm, entirely gone at the shoulder. We never learned just what had happened to him and he offered no explanation. He introduced himself as, "Rex, the disco king from Kalispell," and seemed to be just as friendly and fun loving a fellow as we'd ever met. He asked where we were headed.

"Richfield, Utah," Libby answered.

"What's in Richfield?" he asked.

"We don't know. We're just going there because I just pointed to it on our atlas a few minutes ago."

The disco king from Kalispell gave us a big smile and said, "Hey, you guys wanna do some acid?"

Sure why not, we thought. He handed us two pieces of pure white paper about an inch square each, which we dropped right on the spot.

His Impala was a great car, big, comfortable, fast, and safe. He had the Bee Gees playing over a super-fine stereo and as we rolled down the road, he turned the stereo up to full blast. He liked to drive fast. "Saturday Night Fever" was big on the charts at the time and though I never really cared for disco before, that particular album was burned into fond memory as we blew over the Montana back roads.

Without giving it a thought, Libby took out her Swiss army knife to remove a thorn in her hand. Rex asked her politely to put it away as it made him very nervous, understandably so inasmuch as he had no arm to protect himself. She apologized and immediately put her knife away.

As it turned out Rex had a cabin on a big lake and invited us to go with him for a swim. We spent three entire days at the lake drinking beer. He turned out to be an outrageously fun fellow. We would occasionally leave the cabin for another beer run or just to take a drive. Everywhere we drove he'd open her up to one hundred miles per hour with the Bee Gees blasting away as loud as the stereo would go. Rex would often lift his left leg to steer the car and disco dance with his only left arm over his head as he sped down the highway. First thing in the morning he'd come out of the cabin and announce, "Breakfast is ready," while holding up a just-opened, ice cold beer. We had never drunk so much beer before or ever after our weekend with Rex. However stupid, we were fearless.

He had business to tend to on Saturday morning so we rode with him to his home in Kalispell where he lived in a small, residential area. Rex's presence had somewhat interrupted other matters of priority. He'd already gone inside his home when Libby was hit with a powerful sexual urge. She pulled me into the huge back seat of the curbside Impala for a wild, passionate, and impulsive go. We then gathered ourselves, went inside, and bid Rex a fond and sad farewell. It was dark when we finally left his home.

Our bender with Rex had taken its toll and somehow we found our way to the interstate south out of town. We chose to stay off the interstate taking a route more directly south. Besides, we were back in Mack's territory and weren't really up to another dose of him. We traveled a bit more at night since getting back to the States. We knew that Mack was a morning person, but when he did "work" it was usually very late at night. The odds of running into him were beyond remote. Nonetheless, the thought of him made our bones rattle with fear and so nighttime back road travel was our preferred means. We found sleep that night just off road, God only knows where.

We made the commitment the next day to push south and no matter what would come our way we figured we'd pass on unless it meant going south, fast and far. Interstate travel put us to Ogden, Utah, late that night where we gave up on any further trek south because urban congestion was building fast. Like other cities throughout the West, Ogden was a clear indication that humanity was rapidly wearing out its welcome on old planet earth. We thought of hitting the Great Salt Lake but figured we'd settle that in the morning. We slept just off the ramp of the intersection of two major interstate highways. It's funny how you can find a small depression in the ground behind a shrub in a place so incredibly busy and no one else would ever know that you're even there.

We rose early the next morning because the sound of traffic was alarming. We pulled out our atlas and in the morning sun we started weighing our direction and goal. Neither cities nor national parks were worth a damn for hitchhiking. *How will we get all that salt off of us from a bath in the lake?* To push south toward Richfield, Libby's finger-pointed destination of last week, meant a hot, hard lug through a major metropolis. We remembered how Mack felt about Salt Lake City. He hated the place and said that if we ever heard of the angel on top of the big church being blown off, we could rest assured that he'd be the one responsible.

If we continued south of Salt Lake City our choices would've narrowed considerably. We'd have had to deal with endless national park travel or end up in Las Vegas. We ruled out the national parks because we figured we'd probably die there of starvation. We had to think and talk a bit about Las Vegas knowing nothing about it except that gambling and prostitution were legal there. I figured that if they got one glimpse of Libby, in no time she would become a showgirl. One week after that I figured she'd meet Mr. Big and the dream of finding our mountain would forever vanish in the Nevada desert. We'd never been through a desert before and those old black and white TV images of crawling across sand dunes through cactus toward a mirage with blisters all over our faces and vultures overhead all pointed us east instead.

East of Ogden the atlas promised only Wyoming. *Hey Wyoming,* we thought. *Never been there. Let's go check it out.*

The atlas had little green dots along the most scenic routes, but Interstate 80 from Wyoming's west to the east state lines didn't have one single green dot. Even where we again crossed the Continental Divide, there wasn't one landscape feature worthy of a single green dot. Its desolation was unique and we'd have liked to maybe even stay there for a while. But we didn't want to stand out in the middle of nowhere behind a clump of sage brush for the rest of our lives and what we saw of Wyoming promised little else. We camped that night just off road at the intersection of Interstate 80 and Interstate 25 at Cheyenne. Though they were two major interstate highways there was very little traffic all night long.

We woke the next morning admitting that we were really wandering aimlessly. We were disappointed that there weren't any Native Americans in or around a town called Cheyenne and decided to move on. On the other hand it felt great living to the fulfillment of Gene's plan, without a care or worry in the world. Our direction had to turn south because north was known and east meant the Great Plains, to the Mississippi and beyond, to back east. We still had an inner desire to see some friendly and familiar faces but we knew no one. We recalled that one of our college friends had transferred to a school called "Boulder." Boulder really wasn't the name of the school but that's all we knew because that's how he referred to it. We decided one more time to seek an old, friendly face, one from Bucknell. Mike was one of our greatest friends from college and had transferred to Boulder for a fresh start as a sophomore. Boulder was only a few hours away and I figured that finding Mike could well take the rest of the day, so we headed for Boulder.

After noon we were going through the phone book in Boulder. We found Mike's number and gave it a call, but his line had been disconnected. We searched and found his listed address but, as most college students do, he had moved on and no one knew anything of him. We sat in the town square for a while and were approached by a scraggly looking character selling mushrooms.

The price was right so we bought them and as we were eating them he said, "Things will start getting real weird in about an hour." The mushrooms were small, dried, and a rip off. We grabbed a bite of food in Boulder but agreed a night in town meant us no good at all.

We had spent an entire day in another failed and futile attempt to see any familiar face so we pondered hiking over to Denver to see my great-aunt Kathyrn who lived in east Denver. My parents grew up in east Denver. I first met Aunt Kathyrn when I was seventeen in the summer of '75. She lived alone in my grandmother's house. My grandmother had passed away and her '54 Chevy was mine for the taking if only I had the gumption to drive it back to Pennsylvania. I recalled the morning I prepared to depart from Denver in that old car. I was replacing the car's battery when old Aunt Kathyrn and I discussed my travel plans.

"What are the roads like in the mountains?" I asked her.

"You're not thinking about heading up there are you?" she asked with a shocked look on her face. "You don't want to go into the mountains. Those roads are steep. There are rockslides and mudslides. Avalanches take out entire roads in places too. No, you'd be better off to just take the interstate straight home," she advised.

I came out from under the hood of the car and set down the wrench. I looked at her and could see a scared look on her face. "But don't you go up to the mountains from time to time?" I asked.

"I've only been up there a few times," she replied. "It's not worth it, John. There's nothing but trouble up there. What on earth will you do if you break down or even crash? No, John. You have enough of a drive just getting back to Pennsylvania."

I could tell that she had lived her whole life in Denver, terrified of the mountains, that she had no interest in fishing, hunting, skiing, hiking or camping. She had no interest in life west of Denver. She was purely a city lady. But she knew things that I didn't and I adopted her fear. She convinced me and I gave up on taking even a short ride to see the mountains that day and headed, as she had advised, straight home for Pennsylvania instead.

But as we sat in Boulder's town square, we knew that seeing old Aunt Kathyrn meant an enormous city on foot. I loved my aunt Kathyrn, but not enough to brave the monster of Denver. We were more afraid of that notion than walking through the Rockies. At that instant, we gave up on ever again trying to chase another familiar face. We gave up on seeing our friend and started walking, then hitchhiking north out of Boulder.

The mountains provided safety and excitement and we planned to just get clear of Boulder and find a safe campsite. By dark we were headed up a creek called the Big Thompson. There were many signs posting flash flood warnings, advising to seek high ground in the event of a deluge. I recalled hearing about a catastrophic flood on that drainage the previous summer.

This is what Aunt Kathyrn was talking about, I thought. We heeded caution and climbed a short distance to a flat spot, to roll out our bags for the night. As we climbed we wondered just how high we would have to go to be safe if it rained. Ironically, the ground at our feet was rock-hard, bone-dry dirt that didn't seem to have a single drop of water in it, whatsoever. The rocky canyon walls twisted and turned about and we could tell that water would have to come fast and from afar to create a flash flood. The excitement of danger in new terrain was what we wanted and we were anxious for morning when we turned in. We slept fairly light, listening for any sudden roar or rush of floodwaters in the creek gently passing by below.

We woke the next morning to an overcast sky and a light rain so we donned our blue jean jackets instead of our rain gear. Jeans had a more western, mountain feel and made a better first impression to other travelers. We got a ride with a guy in a jeep with the top down. He was headed for a place called

Nederland. *An unusual name for a western town,* we thought. He learned that we were on our way back from Alaska on our honeymoon. The length and direction of our journey made him curious and gave us an advantage. He asked if we'd ever been four wheeling.

"Four wheeling? No. What do you mean?" Libby asked.

"I'll show you," he replied with a bit of a chuckle and a grin.

On the way to wherever he was headed he pulled off of the small two-lane paved road onto a gravel road and headed for some hills. In minutes, we were climbing straight uphill. I mean, straight uphill in his little jeep. We couldn't see the dirt road ahead of us every time we'd crest out on a hill. Hill after hill we drove and laughed. The surrounding mountains were cloaked in fog but every now and then we could see great peaks in the distance. The fog as it turned out was actually a cloud. We were four wheeling over mountains in the clouds and it was all too fascinating and fun. *Still,* I thought, *Great-Aunt Kathyrn would be terrified.*

Our jeep driver had to get about his business and dropped us off at an intersection. We couldn't decide which way to go so I hitched north and Libby hitched south to see who could get a ride first. A newlywed young couple stopped for Libby's thumb. "Which way are you going?" she asked.

"Either way," Libby replied.

They told us to get in. He was a handsome, dark-haired man and she a sweet-talking, petite blonde. At first they wanted to know all about us. The conversation soon shifted to them and stayed there. They sold wood stoves for a living and were very open and friendly, but then they began to bicker and though neither was particularly angry, they simply could not agree. We listened at first while they discussed everything from food to who was going to do the dishes. It seemed like they resumed their complaining which was already underway when they picked us up. In minutes it seemed as though we weren't there at all. We grew bored and tuned them out to view the foggy countryside, which was far more interesting.

They turned into their drive and asked if we'd like to stay for supper and the night. Their house was lovely but their arguing was overpowering so we opted to keep moving instead as the day was still young anyway. We took it as a sign of how confusing and pointless arguing can be. They told us of a good place to eat in Nederland, which was just a short ride away.

East was Denver and so we headed west on the interstate. A wet drizzle had turned into intermittent rain but we stayed with our jean jackets. At an on ramp we met another hitchhiker. He was a tall young man perhaps a year older and we talked as we waited for a ride. We all ended up in a van headed west. A short ride put us at another on ramp where we all continued on. Our companion hitchhiker was from Vail and was a real nice guy.

The foggy clouds of morning had lifted to disclose the mightiest of the Rocky Mountains. Our new friend was from Denver and had moved to Vail earlier that summer. He was familiar with the names of many of the sites along the way and pointed out the Eisenhower Tunnel, the Gore Range, and Vail Pass. It was all remarkably breathtaking, even in the rain. As the weather worsened we all got a ride in the bed of a pickup truck and huddled up against the cab.

By the time we got to Vail it was getting late in the day and he offered to let us stay at his condo with his other two roommates for the night. We gladly accepted his offer particularly in view of the thickening weather. As we walked to his condo he continued talking about the town of Vail, how fun it was living there, and how incredibly deep were the snows of winter, and of course, the skiing. He said there were a lot of jobs to be had too, everything from bar tending to lift operating. He said the papers were full of unskilled jobs that seemed to pay much better than minimum wage. Vail was actually a small town and he got along just fine without a car by walking.

As we entered the condo, we noticed it was very much a bachelor's pad, complete with a foosball table. His roommates weren't home and he assured us they wouldn't mind us crashing there. We found a comfortable spot out of the way on the shag carpet to spend the night. He said that he had to go to town and meet with friends at a bar so we stayed behind and enjoyed each other's company rather than shadow his night's plans. He handed us a local newspaper and encouraged us to check the want ads. Before he left for the night, he called one of his roommates and told him that we were staying the night. He said not to worry because his other roomy would be staying at his girlfriend's.

As we read through the paper we couldn't help but notice the number of work opportunities. Vail was screaming for labor and almost every ad offered additional incentives above an elevated wage. There was one ad for the Vail Athletic Club that said, "Pianist wanted for Wednesday through Saturday evenings and Sunday brunch."

"You know," I told Libby, "I think we ought to go talk to them about getting a gig." After all, I could play piano and already had somewhat of a professional start playing greaser tunes in a band back east called Stevie and the Six Pack. Truthfully, I wasn't much of a pianist, but thought it might be fun to give it a try. I had no other skills except for baling hay and some assembly line experience. Neither were useful skills in Vail. We decided to run it by our new friend when he returned home.

The night got late as we talked about the day while sitting on our bags. The excitement of Vail we hoped would continue to unfold for us in the morning. Libby was a slalom ski racer in prep school and she was upbeat about trying out some Vail champagne powder the coming winter. Wishful thinking, perhaps, but we knew that our cash was winding down and that road life, Gene's plan, would soon be coming to a halt. *Why not Vail*, we thought as we went to sleep with anxious anticipation and hope.

Our friend had come in very late but had risen early the next morning. The bachelors didn't eat at home. In fact, they didn't cook at all and preferred to eat in town at restaurants or on the go. Neither of the other two roomies even came home the previous night. Our friend told us how much fun he and others had the previous night at such and such bar. I showed him the ad for the pianist and he said they'd been looking for a pianist at the club for quite some time. He said that a guitarist played at night on occasion but he knew they really wanted to get a pianist in the lounge on a regular basis. He thought it would be worth looking into and pointed us in the direction of the club. He was excited about the opportunity and said we could stay at his condo as long as we needed. He said the rent was all paid up and his other roomies were seldom around anyway. We gladly thanked him for his offer as he set out on his day.

We met with the lounge manager that morning. He asked me to play some piano and just like that he offered me fifty dollars a night plus the Sunday brunch gig. He said I could start on Friday as their house guitarist was already set to play that evening. Fifty dollars a night was the going rate and we could seriously take advantage of the quick cash. We bought some street clothes to take the rough edge off of our appearance and partied at the lounge that night with the guitarist and new friends. I played through Sunday, and all the while Libby sat right beside me as I played. She was so proud of me and we'd talk and chat between each song. She'd lean over to me and whisper little things as I played. You see we always so enjoyed each other's company.

We'd pocketed enough cash to cover our expenses and netted a nice profit, but by Sunday afternoon the little town of Vail had gotten too big for us. We knew that fitting in would be a long uphill struggle though most folks we met were friendly and we had a great time. But Vail had somewhat of a preppy feel to it and it was filling up with professionals like doctors, lawyers, and politicians. There was virtually no riffraff; it wasn't really our kind of crowd. It was lacking the salt of the earth so to speak and we decided to resume Gene's plan by thumbing west. We were sure we could return to find employment and opportunity after our honeymoon.

About an hour west of Vail, the road literally turned into a gorgeous canyon. We'd never actually seen a real canyon before. It gave me that same, small feeling I got way back in the redwoods. You know that feeling when the span of your lifetime becomes insignificant in the face of so much greater creation. For its entire length each rounding turn in the two-lane road disclosed formidable and spectacular views while paralleling a grand river in the very bottom of the canyon. We talked little with our driver except to gasp at the beauty as it unfolded on our way.

By evening we ended up in a small, western town called Glenwood Springs. The hitchhiking slowed and so we stopped to eat supper at a Village Inn restaurant at the exit. We tried again to catch a ride after supper but the interstate was virtually at a standstill. At dusk we called it a day. The mountains and canyons had become breathtakingly beautiful and we didn't want to miss any of the scenery by traveling at night. We walked up onto the interstate a hundred yards or so and found a break in a chain-link fence just beyond an overpass. We rolled out our bags under a small cluster of trees and slept well to virtually no night interstate traffic either east or west bound.

We woke early the next morning from a good night's rest and were anxious to see more of the landscape of western Colorado. We caught a ride immediately with a recruiter from a nearby job service office located in a town called "Rifle," some twenty-five miles west.

She told us there was a shortage of unskilled labor in the area. She said that oil shale development was a booming industry and that the wages were starting at seven dollars an hour. Additionally, she said that transportation to and from the work site was provided. Seven dollars an hour was top scale wage, equivalent to what bricklayers were making back east. We asked to know more and she went on and on about the local prospects. She called the job site the CB tract and advised that we not hitchhike out there because it was a very remote job site and they probably wouldn't let us even approach the project anyway. It was a very large-scale construction site and she thought it would be a great place to learn basic construction skills.

It all sounded too good. We'd traveled many thousands of miles and employment prospects other than fast food were pretty slim. We rode with her to the job service office where she convinced us to fill out two applications. In less than an hour she'd found us each jobs working a graveyard shift.

"All you have to do is be at the City Market parking lot at quarter to eleven tonight and the bus will take you to and from work," she said. She was much more excited about us getting jobs than we were.

Just like that, in the course of one ride, the honeymoon was over and Gene's plan was finished. We had succumbed to the pressure and worry about money, work, and life. We walked outside and talked a while. We had all day to mull it over, as the bus ride to work was a nighttime commitment. We ate lunch in a local bar/restaurant and talked over the pros and cons.

Hey, what's the rush? If the work was that good there should be plenty of work here after the honeymoon is over, we thought. It was almost as though big Gene was speaking to and through us. In the distant west we could see the great cliffs that called for a closer look. We weren't ready to give up. *That's it,* we decided, and gave up on the opportunity of the day, maybe the opportunity of the summer. Besides, we hadn't found the mountain we were seeking and there were a lot of mountains yet to see.

We went back in her office and explained that we had a little cash and weren't quite finished with our honeymoon. We told her that we'd likely circle back in if we needed to.

"Where are you going then?" she asked.

For lack of any destination in mind I blurted out, "Mexico. We're on our way down to Mexico."

Libby tilted her head back and gave me an astonished look of excitement. Until that moment we hadn't ever really nailed down Mexico as a destination. It was always just a fleeting thought.

The job recruiter gave me a look of caution. "Mexico!" she warned. "You guys don't want to go down there. There is absolutely nothing down there but poverty and desert," she went on.

"I know," I explained, having no idea at all what it was really like in Mexico. "We'll probably come back after our honeymoon. Will there still be work here then do you think?" I asked.

She said that employment prospects in Rifle were infinite. We walked away from her office feeling good but knowing that her offer was a rare and unique opportunity.

"Do you really want to go to Mexico?" Libby asked as we trudged back to the interstate. I could tell she was excited about the idea.

"Sure. Why not?" I replied. There was no turning back. No matter what, we were going to Mexico. We knew that others along the way would try to dissuade us but we were going to go to Mexico.

We had turned back from Alaska largely from fear. We knew that we'd probably hear stories about crime and poverty but we were set to go to Mexico despite any and all apprehensions. We'd talked about going to Mexico many times along the way but always chickened out. This time it was different. We were going to Mexico. Our money would stretch farther down there too because it was so much cheaper there we'd heard and having immediate employment opportunities in Rifle gave us something to fall back on.

Our job hunt in Rifle had taken a big chunk out of our day. We reached the interstate in mid-afternoon and caught a ride with a guy in a work pickup truck. He was in the drilling business and talked too about energy development of what he called the "west slope." We knew that the "north slope" generally referred to the energy developing regions of northern Alaska. It was interesting to find the word "slope" having the same connotation in western Colorado. He drove us through another spectacular canyon on his way to "Junction" as he called the town. It turned out to be the bustling city formally and appropriately named Grand Junction.

He let us off at the last of a couple of city exits. Any further travel west would surely lead to national parks or eventually Las Vegas. There were no skyscrapers and the air was as clean as the day was clear. Junction wasn't very well laid out and we struggled to get across town but between short rides and walking we managed to pick and poke our way to a road headed south.

It was early in the evening when we thumbed a ride with a husband and wife in an old, well-kept pickup truck. They were Native Americans. They let Libby ride up front between them as I rode alone in the back of the truck. My separation from Libby made me more conscious of my surroundings and as we drove south from Grand Junction, I was so impressed with the type and color of the terrain. In the distance was a great, flat-top mountain surrounded by some enormous water-shaped dunes. It looked like aliens had severed the top of the great mountain with twin lasers from coordinated spacecraft, and then sifted the tailings for some precious elements for fuel, or so I imagined. The dunes had an almost Jurassic feel about them. They looked like great dinosaurs were buried beneath them almost. Some of the largest dunes covered many miles and had perfectly flat tops of their own.

What a great place for an amusement park, I thought. Then I realized what an absolutely dumb idea that would be. Any notion of spoiling the natural setting of the landscape was just downright wrong. The sun was peering through scant cumulus clouds, casting sparse but lengthy shadows that streaked across the western evening sky. The cloud shadows were like heaven rays sweeping at angles to the sun making shadowy footprints across the landscape, on the side of the dunes and great, flat-top mountain. I had never seen anything like it and in a rare moment of solitude, while bouncing about in the back of that pickup truck, I felt a sense of peace.

We rumbled south to another quaint western town called Delta; it was evening when we arrived. There happened to be a small, main street cafe right where we hopped out so we stopped for supper. Libby started telling me that the folks of our last ride were really scary. The woman had a huge wound on her face and bandages all over her head and hands too. Libby said that neither spoke to her nor each other as they rumbled down the road. The woman pulled down the window shade to protect her face from the extreme, piercing sunlight. Libby couldn't imagine what may have happened to her, but said that she felt safe because he kept both his hands on the steering wheel.

All's well that ends well, we figured.

We had our fill of great western cafe food then walked a long mile across town to get another ride that took us to dark. It had been a very interesting day of opportunity and wonder. The landscapes were unlike any we'd ever seen. The heat of the day was challenging but it felt great to be out west. We climbed over a barbwire fence and topped a knoll to sleep under a starry night sky.

Our alarm clock went off early the next morning in the sound of a buzzing airplane. Over and over the sound would build, fly right overhead then fade out, time and time again. From inside my warm sleeping bag, I looked out to the light of clear day to see the crop duster spraying the field just across the two-lane. You know, there is a safety that you feel from inside the warmth of your bag, but that morning's wake-up call from the crop duster was a reminder of our predicament, kind of like being doused with a cold bucket of water.

Oh that's right. We're headin' for Mexico, no matter what, I remembered. That was my leading thought for the day and I can't honestly say that I was thrilled about it. Going to Mexico was more like something we *had* to do as opposed to something we loved to do. Waking up on the side of the road was getting old too. We'd gotten used to unfamiliar faces and had become calloused a bit from road travel. The heat of the western sun drove us from our bags, though we wanted to sleep late. We picked ourselves up and continued south with a brightened outlook from the sight of huge, craggy mountains in the distance.

We got a ride to a nestled mountain town with a strange name, Ouray. We found coffee and a biscuit for a late breakfast and took some time to prepare for another day. Restrooms had become cleaning stations, to wash our faces and hands, brush our teeth, and take care of any and all other essential functions. The road out of Ouray pulled upward, hard and fast, so we chose to wait for a ride rather than hike. We called it hitching instead of hiking. We still struggled to get a ride probably because I was starting to look a little coarse. My hair and beard were scruffy and our clothes were seldom laundered, only when the opportunity was there. The road kind of wore me down and others could see it on my face, in my eyes, and in my speech. We eventually caught a ride with a cowboy pulling a four-horse trailer.

He called it the "million dollar highway" because that's what it cost to build way back when. When it was built a million dollars was a whole lot of money. We could appreciate how much more costly it would've been to build in the modern economy. The road was clearly the most spectacular stretch of rugged mountain scenery either of us had ever seen. He called the mountain ranges by their names. They were all Spanish names: the San Juan, San Miguel, and La Plata mountains. As we rounded turn after gasping turn, the narrow, two-lane road virtually cut through rock on an unbelievable path to Silverton, then on to Durango.

His trailer was full of horses, racing horses, in fact. His weren't really racing horses in that they weren't thoroughbreds, but they were quarter horses used in barrel races, calf roping, and other rodeo type events. He was headed to Durango to enter the races the following day. It took all that his little three-quarter ton pickup could muster pulling pass after pass, and braking was an even bigger problem. We knew that his brakes were sizzling from the smell, though we never did stop to let them cool. He said they would cool down once he started to pull the next pass.

He tried to discourage us from going to Mexico, as the white American slave trade and prostitution were rampant. By the time we got to Durango he knew us well and as a friendly gesture he bought us lunch at a Mexican restaurant north of town. Lunch was his way of honoring our "nearly-two-month-anniversary-honeymoon treat," as he put it. We ate our fill of great American Mexican food. Though the rodeo had caught our fascination we chose to push on. We thanked him for the ride and walked south across town still headed for Mexico.

At the southern end of town the road kind of went east and west. We chose the eastern route because the western route would put us smack dab in the heart of the Native American reservations. Libby had actually worked as a schoolteacher in training on the Navajo reservation in Chinle the previous January. It was her last academic act before dropping out of school. We weren't really sure how they'd take to strangers hitchhiking across their land, and to hike across the reservation meant certain death from dehydration and heat prostration, we thought.

We had no luck at all getting a ride on our eastern path and by nightfall we gave up entirely. We noticed a lot of Texas license plates so we figured the vacationers were about as they were in the Canadian Rockies. Our chances of getting to Mexico through the reservations were better than getting a ride east, so we figured. We doubled back for a western route and settled on a flat, grassy area next to the river for the night.

The day broke with full sunshine and we gathered up early for what we figured would be another interesting day. Before our first ride, a state policeman, or "state bull" as they were called locally, pulled up to check us out. He asked us for our identification and when Libby showed him our marriage license and mentioned our honeymoon he was little impressed. I knew that he could see the wear and tear that road life was having on me. He dismissed us as fairly worthless, homeless road trash and sped off. Though we were almost completely legal about our affairs, we were targets of his investigation just by nature of our being transient.

Surely someday hitchhiking will be illegal.   I recalled that it already was illegal in some states. We'd heard that you didn't dare hitchhike across Kansas unless you wanted to go to jail and other southern states had a reputation for being downright dangerous places to hitchhike. Though we rarely felt threatened we understood that our journey was a little edgy in a sense, though we certainly never, ever meant anyone harm.

We snagged a ride to Cortez, which was really the last stop in the Four Corners region before the reservations. It was called the Four Corners because it was where the four corners of Arizona, Colorado, New Mexico, and Utah all joined. It was the only place in the U.S. where four states bordered.

As we drove across Cortez, we noticed a number of people sleeping right on the side of the road without any bags or other road gear. Our driver told us they were Native Americans sleeping off a hard night in town; there were many. The driver also pointed out the Mountain of the Sleeping Ute in the distance. It was a great mountain that appeared somewhat like a Native American asleep on the desert. He said there was legend behind the mountain's name but couldn't recall exactly what it was.

We thumbed over a flashy blue pickup truck with huge, gummy tires on the other side of Cortez. A young Native American fellow in a cowboy hat was at the wheel. He told us we could ride with him, but that we'd both have to climb in the back even though no one else was with him in the front seat. Glad for the ride, we piled in the back. We noticed he was driving particularly fast.

The landscapes change almost hourly in the west. Before long we were traveling through the great red cliff valleys and "monuments," as they were called. They were massive red sandstone buttes that jutted straight up to the sky. Their geological formation was a mystery but similar in origin we thought to so many others of the west. Much of the west looked like it was once under water, perhaps a great ocean. Like some huge basin, it looked like somebody had pulled its plug and drained all the water out. The sky out west was an orbital, cobalt blue, bluer than anywhere else we had ever seen. The clouds cast streaking shadows of an even deeper blue and a distinctly unique light. The Southwest with all its canyons, valleys, mountains, and deserts opened up fast to some huge and mystical country.

There was nothing quite like riding in the back of a pickup truck especially on a beautiful day. We thought that riding in the back of a pickup truck would someday be outlawed too, however harmless an activity it was.

While making our way steadily across the reservation, a cop car pulled up fast behind us with lights and sirens ablaze. There were two cops, one man and one woman. Our driver pulled over and they proceeded to check all of our IDs. One cop stayed with us while the other returned to the patrol car. We could hear various radio mumblings and soon after, without any pomp or circumstance, they arrested our driver on the spot. We never heard them read his Miranda rights. *Maybe they don't apply on the reservation,* we thought. They put him in handcuffs right then and there. The driver was pretty complacent and didn't say a word or contest the situation at all. They put him in the back seat of their patrol car and just like that, they drove off. There we were, still sitting in the back of this great, blue pickup truck, smack dab in the heart of the Native American reservation, two hours west of Nowhere, Arizona, on an absolutely beautiful summer day.

Getting a ride from there was easy because it looked like our blue pickup was broken down. By evening we'd made our way to Flagstaff. We recalled my brother Charlie talking about his trip to Flagstaff some years before and were excited about being there too as the name alone spurred our curiosity. Our pass through Flagstaff was fairly uneventful save for yet another check by the state police as we started south out of town. Two young men who were hitchhiking cross-country together were checked with us as well. They used the word "res" as a shortened way of saying "reservation".

What were the odds of being checked three times in one day by cops from two different states and two distinct nations? There was a prison break in the area and they were trying to round them all back up. Unlike the law from the north, those cops were completely unimpressed with anything we had to share. Our honeymoon, Alaska, nothing would rouse any semblance of interest, curiosity, compassion or personal understanding. They were interested in one and only one thing: if there were any warrants out for our arrest. Once we checked out, they let us move on to find an interstate camp just off a busy cloverleaf.

We woke early the next morning with Mexico in sight. I lost my Chevrolet baseball cap on that day and the desert without a brim hat was surely a bummer. Sunglasses were a little expensive for our budget too so we traveled on up tough. The Arizona sun in July was worthy of respect and we were hopeful to catch a long ride early in the morning since the intensity of the heat by high noon was debilitating.

We were lucky and caught a long ride with a cowboy dude on his way to Tucson in a beater, rice-burner pickup truck. He had a cooler full of beer and ice. He wasn't really a cowboy and probably never touched a cow or horse in his life, but his cowboy hat provided him some shade though. He was like some kind of desert cowboy dude. He was used to picking up hitchhikers and made no bones about offering us a ride to Tucson if we'd pay for half the gas. It was fine by us and certainly beat the heck out of standing in the hot sun on burning pavement.

When he learned that we were headed for Mexico his voice became cautious. He called us "gringos." I told both him and Libby what my high school Spanish teacher had taught me about the origin of the word "gringo." According to her, the American soldiers used to sing, "Green Grow the Lilacs" as they marched into battle against Mexicans during the Spanish-

American War. Ever since, people from the north were known by Mexicans as "gringos."

The cowboy dude spoke of known accounts of Americans who'd been abducted in Mexico by some type of slave trade of the drug cartels. His accounts were frightening and convinced us that there were known risks to gringos hitchhiking through Mexico.

As we drove further south, the landscape morphed into a saguaro cactus desert not really fit for human beings. And then, like some type of daydream, the air-conditioned city of Phoenix, with all of its own air-conditioned cities, appeared like a mirage in the middle of a place so inhospitable.

"Where do they get all the water to keep Phoenix alive?" I asked.

"You'd never know it, but there's a great aquifer beneath that desert," he said as he nodded the brim of his cowboy hat outward to the passing desert. "It's kind of like a hidden underground river."

Looking out over the desolate landscape we found his explanation to be virtually unbelievable. Between the smog, traffic, and the overall Phoenix rat race we couldn't help but fear all its inhabitants were just one good old-fashioned blackout away from complete and total devastation. We had growing anxiety from being amongst so many sharing such vast and fragile technology. Pheonix, we figured, would be among the first of cities to fold if and when times ever again got tough. Mexico, we knew, would only be worse. Nonetheless, we were headed for Mexico come hell or no water.

Hell came as we punched further south for Tucson; the heat was absolutely unbearable. We bought the half-tank we agreed to and bid "adios" to the desert cowboy dude at the filling station. He had instructed us to continue south and to cross the border at...

OLD MEXICO

We made Nogales by late afternoon without a clue as to what we were doing there and crossed the border on foot. Not everyone was bilingual and we were obviously in a foreign country even though we were just barely over the border. We mustered the courage to try to push our way further down into Mexico on the spot.

Mexico had no real definition on our road atlas. We learned that a train ran out of Nogales for southern Mexico a couple of times each week and rather than hitchhike to the heart of Mexico we thought train travel might be more touristy. Mexico hosted a lot of unknowns so we figured *better to be safe than sorry*. Our chosen destination in Mexico was a place called Mazatlán. We knew absolutely nothing about it or where it was except that it was the end of the train line south. We also knew the train would travel nonstop, all night long to arrive there sometime the next day. We planned to get to Mazatlán, see how things were going then make a call about further travel. We were hoping that our diminishing cash could stretch out considerably longer in Mexico than in the states. *Who knows, maybe we'll be able to push down to South America,* as we once dreamt. We planned an open-ended journey that we'd begin by train and last as long as our money would hold out.

We headed straight for the train depot, which was pretty beat up, and found a lone person at the ticket booth. We learned from him that the train wouldn't depart until the following afternoon if all went well. It wasn't that the train might run late, it sounded like sometimes it didn't run at all. Things in Mexico were different, but so were they in Canada, eh? We felt disappointed, kind of like Dorothy and Toto standing at the steps to see the great wizard of Oz only to learn that we'd have to come back tomorrow; after all we'd traveled so far and worked so hard to get there.

We got a sleazy room for the night in a back alley hotel that was more like a ram-shackled apartment. Then we had supper at a small mom and pop restaurant. Passing on any other nightlife, we went to bed early that evening to the street sounds of Mexico.

We hit the streets early the next morning and began to make preparations for our journey south. Nogales was a typical border town, so it seemed. There were lots of shops called *tiendas* to purchase anything, and almost all things were for sale at a haggled, bargain price. Nothing for sale had a price tag. We cut a deal on a couple of cactus-cloth hooded pullovers and a neat leather shoulder bag for pittance. We came up with a plan to travel light and condensed our belongings to all that would fit in the new shoulder bag.

We decided to ditch our backpacks for a while, but where? Believe you me, the thought of returning to the States broke, to find that our stashed packs might be gone as well, was a little scary. Knowing that we had something, if nothing other than sleeping bags and a change of clothes upon our return, was reassuring.

We figured that the only safe place to leave our packs would be a church and though we couldn't find one, we found a convent that was on the U.S. side of Nogales. We knocked on the convent door expecting one of the nuns to answer. We were surprised to see a woman in street clothes open the door to greet us. At first we thought maybe we were mistaken, that it wasn't a convent at all though the woman assured us that it was indeed. She further explained that though she didn't wear a habit that she was a nun.

We explained ourselves and our truthful intentions and the nun compassionately heard our plea. She assured us that our belongings would be safe with her until our return. We could see in her eyes that she was sincerely trustworthy. She had us place them just inside an entry way to the convent.

I asked if she would rather we put them somewhere more out of the way but she said, "No, they'll be fine right there."

We stuffed as much clothing into the leather shoulder bag that we could and donned our new Mexican cactus-cloth hooded pullovers. We thanked her and headed back for the border to prepare further.

It was unusual for us to walk about free of the weight and burden of our backpacks. We felt relieved but quite insecure, almost naked in a sense. We stopped at a bank and exchanged some of our cash for pesos. We got fourteen pesos for each dollar and having pesos on hand was easier than trying to figure out the correct change all the time.

Though the heat of the Sonora Desert was indescribable, we'd abandoned drinking water because there was no mass public-health campaign in Mexico. Drinking water in Mexico meant certain trouble, so we'd been repeatedly warned. Cola and *cerveza* were our beverages of choice for the duration of our stay.

We learned that we needed to have a local Mexican judge sign off on travel papers inasmuch as we had no passports or visas. The judge would issue a short-term visa so long as we provided him with U.S. identification including birth certificates. Whatever inspired Libby to include those birth certificates when we left Pennsylvania I'll never know but without them we wouldn't be going to Mexico for more than a day by foot in Nogales. I guess just before our wedding, we had talked about heading maybe even to South America and she knew that without birth certificates it might be hard to get back into the States.

The judge's office was closed and he had to be reached by phone. We got him at home and explained in Spanish that we wanted to catch the train south the next day and needed a visa signed before they'd let us board the train. He agreed to meet us at his office at four o'clock.

When he arrived there were six others needing his signature as well and though he never opened his office, he signed for each of us a slip of paper on the hood of his car. Then he charged us all ten dollars each before handing us our "visas." Ten dollars was outrageous but it was either that or face the desert in all directions on foot. We all paid him grudgingly. In less than five minutes he was gone and we all questioned whether or not he was even a real judge.

Time was running out on us in Nogales so we scurried across town and headed straight for the train depot hoping and praying the train hadn't departed without us. Another night in Nogales was absolutely out of the question. We argued that if we missed the train, we'd return to the convent, grab our full packs, and take our chances on foot to South America.

We got to the depot about forty-five minutes late of the scheduled departure time. There were more people about than on the previous afternoon, but it appeared that we'd missed our ride. Fortunately for us the train was just running late. Everything about the depot was more laid back than we expected. Mexico had a uniquely different pace altogether.

The ticket booth opened and we purchased an overnight travel package for only three hundred forty-five pesos. That was the deluxe package, which meant an air-conditioned Pullman and a good night's rest. The only other options were coach, which meant open air, school bus seating, or "freight." Freight was the cheapest but the Lord only knew just exactly what that meant. After all, we were on our honeymoon. *Nothing but first class,* we figured.

About an hour later people just started coming out of nowhere and in no time at all the depot was alive with activity. It was almost as if everybody except us knew the train would arrive at a precisely late time. Excitement started to build as we could all hear the train blast its horn a mile or so out of town. A minute later it burst into the depot and came to a screeching halt.

We found our way to one of just a few air-conditioned cars and boarded the train. Our Pullman was perfect, small, clean, and cool. We kind of had expectations that it'd be a night like one of those train sleeping episodes on the Three Stooges with the hilarity of people falling into the sleeper births of others. We appeared to be the only ones on the air-conditioned car though.

How can they possibly afford to pull this entire train car to southern Mexico when we paid only three hundred forty-five pesos and still turn a profit? Things are different in Mexico, we thought.

The train blared its great horn again and we started to rumble out of town. *We're off to see the wizard!* In no time we were headed across the great Sonora Desert. Our quarters had a huge window through which we could see the full landscape pass by. We also had a bathroom with a toilet and sink. The seats faced each other and were kind of like bus seats. We found them to be pretty uncomfortable so we folded down the bed across the seats. We reclined on the bed in each other's arms viewing the great landscape from our picture window as we rested a while from the day's bustle. That had been the busiest day of our summer and though we hadn't moved more than a couple of miles by foot we were completely exhausted. As we laid there thinking and talking of the day, we felt the comfort of the train's vibration. The rhythm of the sound of the steel wheels on the track was uniquely comforting as well. We sighed with relief.

With the approach of evening we decided to go find the dining car. We actually weren't as hungry as much as we were thirsty. We left our canteen (one of our wedding gifts) at the convent and the need of just a sip of fresh water was on our tongues.

The train cars had kind of a hallway down the center. Where each train car coupled you could actually get some fresh air and look out over the terrain as well. There were usually a lot of folks standing at the coupling because it was often cooler than the seating in coach. Now mind you that my Spanish was pretty good but a little rusty. It was kind of like riding a bike in that I never forgot and it came back quickly. Mine was a rusty old bike. Libby spoke none at all and few spoke English in rural Mexico.

We inquired about the dining car and were directed to walk several cars toward the caboose. Several cars turned into many, then many, many cars of very crowded coach passengers. There were people, families, kids, and the like kind of haphazardly sitting and standing about. There was no assigned seating nor were there any safety belts. Each car was like a really crowded school bus. All of the small windows were opened as wide as they could be. Some children stood on the backs of seats with their heads and arms dangling out the windows to get fresh air.

Not only was each car packed with passengers, their luggage was with them. Most carried string-tied, cardboard boxes and such. Very few folks had actual suitcases. In addition to the passengers and their luggage, each car was loaded with their animals. Some had pets like dogs and birds, large and small; others had crates of livestock like chickens, goats, and small pigs. That was how they regularly traveled from northern to southern Mexico. Each car had the interesting fragrance of sweaty human bodies and animal odors. Where they went to relieve themselves we pondered but really didn't want to know.

We felt the train slowing down and rather quickly it had come to a full stop in a small, rural pueblo. Folks started to approach the train from all directions, to sell food and drink to the passengers through the little windows. A lot of folks were getting off the train while others were piling on. It wasn't really a depot; it was just a stop on the tracks in the pueblo. It actually got frantically busy with the trade of goods and money back and forth from person to person on the train car and we were in their way.

In the shuffle, we decided that we'd better skedaddle to our Pullman. When we got to the first train car coupler we stood in speechless awe to see that the train had broken its coupler right before us. We watched as the segment of train attached to our engine and our Pullman sped off to the Mexican horizon without us. All of our belongings, our money, and our identification were on that other train. It rolled right straight away from us. There we were, on the end of that motionless train car with hordes of other destitute, Third World *campesinos*. We watched in total horror as our train car sped off without us.

There was a lot of confusion as we tried to walk around passengers who themselves were stirring about. We had only passed through a couple of cars when we heard a loud "clomp, thud, kabang" type of sound. The whole train shuddered momentarily then stopped dead again.

We went into absolute panic mode! We thought if we jumped off the train and ran fast enough we could maybe catch up to our train and hop on board like we remembered from one of those western movies. No way, the train sped off out of our sight with all our things, the whole kitten caboodle, gone. There we stood, Libby in her bare feet, with only the clothes on our backs with only pesos in our pockets and absolutely no identification whatsoever. We were pissed off, frustrated, but mostly downright scared.

We ran back to the train cars that had been uncoupled and left behind to get some damn answers, but in our frantic search we found no one officially accountable from the train. I got so mad that I couldn't even spit out anything of meaning in English let alone blat out something, anything comprehensive in Spanish to all who otherwise seemed to be joyfully apathetic of our plight. We realized that we were doomed and stood there looking into each other's eyes in absolute, unspoken horror. I would certainly end up in the Mexican-American slave trade and Libby was destined for prostitution to somehow make our way back to the States. All the forewarnings of others would come true. We'd ignored their warnings and their fears, all against our better judgment pursuing some stupid dream and Gene's plan. To hell with it all, we were in trouble. We were in very serious trouble, and we both knew it.

We were distraught and in our despair we sat down right on the tracks, shaking our heads and cursing. There were several sets of tracks and Libby got up to walk about. I was stuck in denial and told her that it didn't add up because we had no warning. It all just didn't seem right. We walked back over to the several train cars that had been left behind and I struggled to get some answers but we were clearly so shaken that no one understood our questions nor did we understand their answers. We noticed that some folks had stayed on the train and many others were returning to it.

From behind we turned to see a single train engine pushing a long, gray car toward us and watched as the engine and gray car coupled to the coach cars that had been left behind. We figured we might as well board because maybe the short train would catch up to the other that had left with our belongings. Minutes later we heard another "kathunk" and the new engine rolled off and away.

We could not figure out what the heck was going on and no one could tell us. In the distance we saw yet another longer train approaching us on the same track. The closer it got the better we could see that it was our train! It was in reverse. We jumped off the coach car and watched as our train coupled up to the gray car left behind by the engine minutes before. We realized that the train was again whole. We boarded just ahead of the new gray car. It was the dining car and apparently had been parked out of sight in that little, rural town. The train had uncoupled to insert the dining car between the first class and coach cars.

We dashed through the aisle on a number of cars until we finally found our air-conditioned Pullman with all our belongings safe inside. We laughed until we cried. As I said earlier, things were different in Mexico.

We heard the great horn of our train's engine and slowly but steadily we started to rumble out again. The train got up to full speed and in no time at all we were again safe on our way to southern Mexico. We decided to go hang out at the first open coupler to watch the setting sun and the beautiful Mexican landscape roll by. The sun had set entirely but in the western twilight were a crescent moon and a perfectly tangent star. Most likely a planet, Venus or Mercury, the bright star was adjacent to the very bottom of the moon's fingernail tip.

There was an old man, *un viejo,* standing next to us as we stood arm in arm taking in such a rare sight. Neither of us had ever seen a sunset like it and there was a calm that came over the entire desert with the setting of its otherwise relentless daytime punishment.

The old man turned to us and said something. His voice was masked by the sound of the train's steel wheels and we couldn't quite understand what he said so we asked him to repeat himself.

"Que romántica la noche," he said again.

Libby asked if I understood him. I told her he said, "This is the most romantic constellation two lovers will ever see in their lifetime." Though I stretched the truth a bit, it couldn't have been more fitting. Little did we know that we'd never, ever again in our lives witness that very same celestial alignment. My translation, given that day and that night, couldn't have been more appropriate. The old man left us to ourselves and so we held and kissed long, our hair flowing in the soothing breeze of the desert night air.

The dining car that had brought us so much consternation turned out to be quite fun after all. Each table had a pure white tablecloth and fine silverware and our waiter wore a pure white uniform. We each had a couple of colas. Libby ordered a pair of quesadillas while I had white corn flautas. We each had flan for desert.

Soon after supper, it was time for bed, and we returned to our Pullman well after dark. The train hadn't stopped or even slowed and so our progress into Mexico was steady. Though our Pullman was air-conditioned it barely kept up with the pervasive heat of the desert. We usually slept partially clothed but in the desert heat and with the comfort of our bed we slept naked on the train. I was taller than the bed was long which kept me from stretching out which was a little bothersome, but infinitely better than sleeping on the ground, our usual fare. With all of its business the day had been a wild one and a good night's rest was needed to prepare for the following day.

I woke in the dead of night to hear the rumble of a train engine, but realized that the train had stopped moving. Oddly enough I realized that the rumble wasn't from our engine, it was from one that was slowly rolling past our picture window. Its headlight shone bright as it went on by. I tried to get back to sleep but the noise made it impossible. I lay awake for the longest time. Libby finally woke as well and we talked back and forth waiting for the sound to pass, the light to go out or for our train to move on. Imagine if you will the sound and vibration of a diesel locomotive engine just outside your bedroom window, let alone the light from the million-watt headlamp blinding everything and everyone in your room.

Libby raised her hand to shade her eyes from the light and saw the engine just feet away from our window. The engine had kind of a small deck or gunnel and rail. On the deck at eye level stood half a dozen Mexican, railroad workers sneaking a midnight peek at Libby's immaculate nudity in full view just feet away. They giggled and laughed, gawked and pointed as she pulled down the shade.

With the curtain closed, she sighed and said, "Oh brother!"

I told her that she ought to be flattered. After all, her lovely nakedness had stopped a midnight desert freight train dead in its tracks. Minutes later our train resumed its slow, lumbering roll then gained full speed, lulling us back to sleep.

The next morning was a white hot, sunny day. It's a good thing that our train arrived in Mazatlán around ten o'clock because the sweltering heat of the midday was testing the air conditioning of our Pullman. We got off the train to an overpowering heat. Mazatlán turned out to be an old town on the west coast about a hundred fifty miles south of Culiacán, considerably south of the Baja and the Sea of Cortez. We asked for directions and learned that there were seaside hotels within walking distance of the train station.

As soon as we left the depot, things went from bad to worse. Then things went from worse to in your face, downright Third

World, perhaps fourth. We weren't prepared for such poverty. The living conditions for so many were abysmal and we simply couldn't believe that people actually lived within the shanties and amidst such squalor. And there we were, two American tourists, with our leather shoulder bag and me with my blonde hair and blue eyes. We missed our backpacks and felt even more out of place without them.

Mazatlán was billed as a tourist destination; nonetheless we walked for miles among people and their shacks, their pets, and their trash. Everybody wanted to make eye contact with us but in my guilt I either looked away or just stared straight ahead. We turned heads everywhere we went. It wasn't fair to call them neighborhoods or city blocks. Life was laid out in a very random, almost arbitrary way. There were no street signs, no traffic signs, no pavement, no one had running water, there was obviously no trash collection because every here and there was another dump of garbage and detritus. Some domestic livestock ran free in the streets; chickens, pigs, goats, cattle here and there, dogs, none were tended to nor were they fenced. The livestock drank from open groundwater pits that were obviously contaminated with refuse. It had all the makings of an uncontrolled experiment in modern civilization gone awry. We stood out like sore thumbs to the beggars who appeared to have no other way to make a living.

We made our way to the heart of Mazatlán, which had an older, Mexican feel, but was still quite impoverished. We found an old restaurant where I ordered some eggs and a soda pop. We noticed a craving for pop in the morning even though that's all we'd been drinking for three days in a row. Neither of us really drank pop much, but made the switch for the days in Mexico. Funny though, once we started drinking soda pop, we couldn't quite stop. We found an insatiable taste for it and found not only could we not stop drinking it, but it had no real thirst quenching properties. As soon as you'd finish one, you were thirsty for yet another.

I ate my eggs and drank my pop on ice. The ice tasted so much better though. Libby didn't eat breakfast so I was prompt with mine and we headed on west looking for the ocean. The western shore had a touristy, seaside feel to it and we were in luck to find an open-air, seaside hotel. There was no real air conditioning anywhere in the town and shade of day was appreciably the only way to stay cool, that and a pop constantly in hand. We got a deluxe room with a bathroom for one hundred fifty pesos per night.

We changed into our cut-off jeans and headed for the beach across a fairly quiet, coastal road. We had no beach towels or beach chairs and there were no concessions for such. When we stepped onto the sand leading to the lapping surf, we thought our feet would blister from the heat. Of course we had no beach footwear and had to run to the water to keep the soles of our feet from burning in that white, hot sun.

The Pacific Ocean in Mazatlán was much warmer than it was in Oregon. We plunged head first into the surf and swam about each other, talking and laughing, then hugging and kissing. The ocean was such tremendous comfort. Any full-bodied immersion into water was a rebirth of spirit, especially in the desert sun.

We emerged from the surf and attempted to brave the hot sand one more time, but could not endure the piercing heat. It was no wonder why there was no one else on the beach that day. It was like trying to stand or lay down on a hot skillet. You could only leave one foot down for a second or so then switch to the other, then back and forth. There was no getting used to it so we retreated to the cool, tidal sand at the water's edge and dried there, but within minutes, the sun's brutal strength forced our full retreat back into the water.

By noon we realized we had to abandon our day at the beach. I soaked my tee shirt in water and every twenty feet or so we'd stand on it for temporary relief. We did that the whole way back to the hotel. To any onlooker we must have looked ridiculous.

We took a long, Mexican siesta to let the high heat of the day pass and our room was quiet and comfortable. We tried again to brave the hot sands that afternoon and though not as bad, we were able to make it out and back from the beach in much the same fashion as we did that morning. It was clearly the off-season, which meant that we were the only gringos in town.

We sat at a small, shorefront cafe for a pop and in the course of fifteen minutes were approached by several groups of beggars. A mother and her toddler son offered to sell us some individually wrapped Chiclets chewing gum, which we obliged. Though we'd become impatient with beggars by that afternoon, we always gave in to their needs. I wished we were millionaires, partly to help them out and equally to be rid of them without hurting our own diminishing cash. We figured we could recover those losses by buying a bottle of rough, unfinished opals in stone from a street vendor. Apparently, there were a lot of opals in Mexico so we bought a jar full for five bucks. We thought they'd be worth ten times that to a jeweler in the States.

We walked through the mercado on the way back to our hotel. It was kind of like an open-air flea market with lots of produce and other food for sale. We noticed that the *carnicería* offered a variety of meats but mostly beef. When someone wanted, say, a three-pound cut of meat, the butcher would pull down a huge chunk off a meat hook, raise his great meat cleaver and lop off a piece. The meat that hung was literally covered with blowflies. Neither the butcher nor the buyer seemed at all concerned about the flies laying eggs all over the meat, butcher block, and cleaver. Funny thing how in the States it was considered unhealthy to refreeze meat once it had thawed. Well, we got new perspective on all that. Again, things were different in Mexico.

We returned to our room late that afternoon and cleaned up to set out for supper. We learned that there was a seaside seafood restaurant a cab drive away. It turned out to be easily within our walking distance; after all, we were very accustomed to walking long distances. We arrived at the restaurant by cab at sunset. It was a quaint restaurant complete with a mariachi band and a solo violin serenade. We were their only customers so we hired them all for a song or two. *Now this is how a honeymoon should be,* we thought. We avoided any beef on the menu and ordered a delicious seafood platter that featured everything from jumbo prawns to sea turtle.

After supper it was dark when we got back out on the street. Rather than take the cab we chose to walk back to our hotel instead and as we walked we rationalized our situation. We could see that Mazatlán was struggling to become a tourist town and we could also see that it would certainly benefit an otherwise impoverished community. We also got the impression that in a few days our money would dissipate into a destitute populace; that we'd be living indefinitely among the poorest people on earth.

We turned in once we reached our hotel. We had no plan for the following day; life in Mexico appeared to be largely unplanned for most of its citizens. We soon fell peacefully asleep. I woke abruptly at midnight to an explosive bout of Montezuma's revenge. I'd gotten hold of something really bad. In so many ways it seemed like the same sickness that had overcome me twice before in the Northwest. I laid sleepless on my back, then on my side in high fever with persistent nausea. After each trip to the commode, I could find a few minutes for the misery to subside and get some rest only to be awakened by another need to rush to the bathroom. It felt quite literally like someone had jabbed a knife into my stomach and another in my back and about every minute or so they'd give them each a sharp twist of the wrist. I was completely incapacitated with a non-stop migraine headache. I spent the entire next day either in bed or naked in the fetal position on the tile floor of the bathroom in total pain and exhaustion. Diarrhea had set in for good. The strange thing was that the most nauseating thought was the ice cubes I'd eaten with eggs the previous morning. I'd never given it a thought but the water in those cubes was contaminated for sure. The thought of any food was imperceptible, but the memory of that ice was prominently bad. I was certain that was where I had picked that bug up. I could not function.

Libby had come and gone all day to try and find me some
relief, but aside from a bottle of aspirin, she had no luck at
all. She couldn't even find Pepto Bismol. She appeared to
be enjoying her trip to Mexico at least. I assured her that my
illness would pass as quickly as it had come on. I remembered
my high school Spanish teacher talking about getting sick in
Mexico. She recalled her experiences with a chuckle saying
that the first day was the worst and then its symptoms would
soon subside so that you could go on about your tour with
little trouble. I cautioned Libby to be careful of what she ate
for obvious reasons. By that evening my body was completely
purged of water and food. Except for the occasional sip of
warm pop I ate absolutely nothing, I couldn't.

The following day I got worse. I couldn't hold my head
upright for more than just a few moments and my energy
had dissipated completely. Libby had found another hotel
that was in town for eight pesos a night and somehow by late
that afternoon, I worked up the strength to make the move.
The new hotel was only blocks away, but it might as well
have been a death march for me. I couldn't get over Libby's
eating popsicles and barbecue from street vendors despite my
repeated warnings.

Libby said, "Since you're sick, I might as well be too. That
way we can lay sick in bed together." She was unaffected by any
and all things she ate. By the time we checked in I was deflated.
I immediately found the bathroom, and then collapsed on
the bed. I had broken out in a profuse sweat from the fever.
Whatever was in that damned ice was exuding from my pores
and never before had I felt so faint. The only moments of
happiness were seeing Libby's smiling face as she'd check in
from time to time and tell me of all the things she was doing
and folks she was meeting. She seemed to be completely happy
and content though walking about alone in the streets of a
foreign land and unable whatsoever to speak their language.
Her strength of heart, character, and body I envied.

How is it that we ended up down here in Mexico? We talked, she from her reclining Spanish chair and I in a fetal position on the bed. *A girl like her deserves and could do oh so much better. Had I drug her down here for some selfish, self-fulfilling need of my own? But she is so willing. She'd walk through a bed of coals had I the stupidity to do so first.*

As we talked, we learned that we both used to dress as bums for Halloween when we were kids. We figured that you could tell a lot about a person by their chosen Halloween costume. Beware a chosen bride of Frankenstein, we agreed. We also found that we each had run away from home at a young age. In fact, we each had run away for the very same reason; we were denied something that we really wanted to do by ourselves. I had watched my older brother extinguish the table candles with his licked fingers the night before and was promised that I could do the same after supper. I so wanted to be just like my big brother. Table candles were a very rare treat for us and were lit on that consecutive night solely for my right of passage.

I worked up the courage and excitement all through our meal to douse those flames with my licked fingers only to watch my brother steal the chance from me for just that purpose. I ran away from home that night and having nowhere to go I returned minutes later reluctantly, but hoping that everyone else was worried sick about me. My mom was waiting for me with another lit candle to douse, but it just wasn't the same. I received her act of consolation but I was still mad at my brother.

For Libby, apparently it was customary for a parent or older sibling to prepare her dinner plate, to cut her vegetables, to pour her drink or to slice her meat. Her family had a very close eye on her with knives, forks, hammers and such because at the age of three she, without a moment of hesitation, shattered the glass door of the sun room with a croquet mallet to escape the boogie man with whom she'd been entrapped intentionally by her brother.

Much to the dismay of her parents and their full house of dinner guests, Libby's impulsive courage was thereafter kept in check as all feared rightfully for her well being. But one night at the age of six or seven she'd had enough when denied once again the chance to prepare her own plate, like the grownups did, like all her siblings did, like everybody else did. We each recalled when we were young, setting our sights on running away from home for good and agreed that our young paths were very similar. For all we knew, we may have run away from home on the very same night, she at seven years of age and I at six. We must have shared the very same feelings then as we did in that old Mexican hotel room.

We were swept with a sense of something so much greater than we two, especially looking back over all the events leading up to our strange honeymoon. It seemed like at weddings and funerals when our families came together, sometimes an intense, jacked-up weirdness would overcome us all and the events leading up to our wedding were no exception. Libby's folks were certainly less than curious about me and for good reason. The first time I met them was to relay that we were going to drop out of school together, get married, and then who knows what, end of plan. I had no excuses either and made no attempt to explain myself; I couldn't because I really didn't know what I was doing. But Libby and I both knew well what was meant in taking a vow. It was an eternal oath that transcended life itself; we knew it and we were prepared for it. Considering that we hadn't ever really expected anyone to be witness to something so sacred to the two of us, we were delighted that on our wedding day, family and friends came together and forever set aside any and all apprehensions. A minute of peace came over us that evening.

Libby stepped out into the streets as I rolled over one more time from an endless stabbing in my stomach. I couldn't help but still wonder, *who is this woman that I've married?* After all we'd only known each other for eight months and I had so much to learn about her. All of the strange events that led up to our honeymoon started to flood my mind and all that lay ahead in our discovery of each other I knew would take time, years, a lifetime. But I couldn't have imagined a woman more compatible, or of greater courage. I knew those traits she'd gotten from her father and her optimism most likely she'd gotten from her mother, but then again, they all seemed to be genuinely hers and hers alone. She seemed to fit neither the mold of her parents nor her siblings and yet her core personality I was still just beginning to know. She was such a mystery in so many ways, but with every new unfolding of her character came renewed joy that I'd found my soul mate. *I am a very lucky man,* I thought.

As I lay there the thought of traveling to Central or South America or even deeper into Mexico started to wane. *What had happened to lead us to this point, to this old, beaten hotel in this poor desert waste of a town? This will have to be an end to many things.* So it seemed that a great Hand had again come down before us on our journey, to divert us from a place, direction or thing that was not to be ours. On that night we'd forever choose to acknowledge our fears and dismiss our inability to deal with them.

For some reason being sick again made me recall the worst of my memories and of myself. *For us all there's an inescapable hypocrisy written into life; it's a given human circumstance.* On that night I kind of likened it to sin, maybe even "original sin" as the nuns of my childhood put it. You know, that painted in a corner feeling you get when you find yourself guilty from an inadvertent act.

I remembered how awful I felt about what had happened to my little brother. When he was three, both tires of our '57 Chevy station wagon slowly rolled over his chest and head on the asphalt pavement of our sloped driveway in Delran. Minutes before I'd been playing taxi driver in the driver's seat and had gotten the transmission stuck in neutral. I thought I'd broken the car and fully feared my mother's spanking and chose to not tell anyone. Meanwhile, my elder brother and his friends were playing football on the front lawn. When one of the neighbor kids caught a touchdown, he bumped into the old Chevy which was just enough of a nudge to make it begin to roll. Little Hugh was sitting on the asphalt behind the car drawing with crayons when the car knocked him over and rolled over his head.

I didn't see it happen. I was inside our house but heard the horrible screams of others who witnessed it happen. They rushed Hugh off to the Hospital and he survived purely because his guardian angel was with him and also that he was one tough little customer. When my mom brought him home from the hospital that night, his head was fully wrapped in bandages. Everyday for weeks, she had to scour the pitted scar on his cheekbone daily with hot, soapy water. His painful cries were agonizing for me as well. He wore tire tread marks embedded on the skin of his face over his other cheekbone for more than a year.

When you inadvertently do something wrong, you feel guilty. When you intentionally do something wrong, you feel *very* guilty. I still harbored a sense of guilt making me reclusive, withdrawn, excluded from others from that whole experience. I remembered that night how shocked I was that no one asked me what I had done to the car just minutes before causing the accident. But I could hear them all blaming me in their whispers. I was shocked that I never got spanked for not warning anyone that I'd broken the car. I deserved a spanking but never got one. I didn't mean to hurt Hugh, it was an accident, but I had no way to get it off my chest because no one asked. I knew that as soon as my mom found out that I hadn't told anyone, that I'd broken the car, she would bestow her wrath. But she didn't ask me, nor did I ever tell her or anyone else the truth about it even though they all already knew. Though they all knew I was guilty, I never got what I deserved, and I held that frustration inside ever since. I was six years old at the time and learned right then and there that my actions, however intended, can and do affect others. I also learned to assume the responsibility for those actions, be they right or wrong, intended or incidental.

For some strange reason, being sick again reminded me of that responsibility, but didn't ease the burden of those painful memories. Perhaps from both our experiences it was harder to feel accepted, part of the group. *But it was certainly no-one else's fault that I lay here sick, in old Mexico, wishing it weren't so.*

I recalled the days of my youth and innocence. *Walking to church on Sunday in the cold, I could feel the wet dark of wee morning, with all the world asleep. As I look to my boots to see a mosaic of the fallen color of autumn leaves and a dripping rain beneath the streetlight, I realize for the very first time that I am alive. Then I walk into the sacristy with its ever-familiar smell of frankincense and don my altar robe. The priest dons his, then blesses me. We walk together to the altar where he begins the first mass of day. He speaks in Latin but somehow I know the meaning of each and every word. He delivers an impassioned sermon from the pulpit as though addressing a legion of the faithful, though there is only one, an old woman in the still dark of morning. The priest prepares for us, three holy Eucharist as I stare at my savior dying on the cross. The grey light of day starts to work through great panels of stained glass and morning finally fills the church. I feel for the first time that if God can forgive me, than I can certainly forgive myself and, most importantly, I can forgive others. All of the poorest people of the world, which now include me, God forgive us all,* I prayed.

Libby brought me a hot cup of tea from boiled water the next morning. *Surely, boiled tea water is safe to drink,* I thought. Food was still unthinkable but I knew I had to increase my fluids regardless. The nausea had gone and so had the headache, but I was weak and was willing to give moving on a try. Another further trek south meant Mexico City, the world's largest population with the lowest net per capita income. That could only spell trouble for us, we agreed. Also, our vacation to Mexico hadn't been as cheap as we had hoped so we figured we'd better head back north, one way or another. With any luck we'd get back stateside with just enough cash to get somewhere and start some kind of life back in the real world.

We learned that the train would depart for Nogales that afternoon so we decided to pack up and head for the train station. I wasn't so sure I could make it without a bathroom stop. When I stepped out into the sunny street from our hotel, everything went white on me. The sun in all its power I'd never felt like that before. I had to shade my eyes from the pain of its burning and leaned my back to the white stucco of the hotel to gather strength in the moment.

Libby asked if I was going to make it. I told her that we needed a cab to get us to the depot. She took me back into the hotel and sat me down on a bench in the shade. A while later, she came and helped me fall into a cab. Libby was on the accelerated, foreign language program and remembered the word *ferrocarril* as the driver nodded and drove us to the station.

Waiting for the train, we met an old woman and her son who were selling white corn tamales. We knew that I was behind on both food and water so we bought four of them. They were still very hot and wrapped in cornhusks. They were so sweet, as sweet as was the old woman. What would we have given for a tall glass of water, not pop, not beer, just water, fresh, cold, clear water? Our mouths and bodies were great big clumps of walking sugar. One more pop and we'd have certainly crystallized hard on the spot. Fresh drinking water was a precious and rare resource in Mexico.

Within minutes of eating a tamale, my stomach revolted with knife twisting pain, making me double over. I stayed crumpled up on the concrete floor of the depot until the train arrived for boarding that afternoon.

It felt good to be rolling north again. The train traveled all night and the familiar rumble of the steel wheels on the track was comforting. I decided to hole up for the night. Libby, in her restlessness, went about the train to get some fresh air. Late in the night she returned to our Pullman with two other gringos and a bottle of tequila. The other two were well on their way to a good time. They'd convinced us that straight Tequila would quench the fire in my stomach, especially if I swallowed the worm. The four of us kind of bounced around in our Pullman doing shots with salt and lime until the bottle was empty. I passed out downing the worm. It didn't really settle any of my gastric issues, but it was fun talking with other Americans and sharing experiences in English on that old, rusty, desert train.

We woke with alarm the next morning to a loud, insistent pounding on our Pullman door. A loud voice outside was saying over and over, "*Abierto! Federales!*"

I hopped out of bed and opened the door to find two men in suits that basically burst into our Pullman. Libby pulled the sheets over her and we both stared blankly for some sort of explanation. One of the two of them was obviously in charge. The two were searching our Pullman, looking underneath seat cushions, the commode, and going through all of our few belongings. They were obviously searching for drugs. The cop in charge had slick, black hair and sunglasses. He reached down under the bench seat and picked up a small plastic baggie that had a white crystalline powder in it.

"*Es* cocaine, no?" he said while looking me straight in the eye. Believe you me, my Spanish got real good, real fast. He wasn't laughing and neither were we when I told him that it was a bag of salt for the tequila we'd shared with others the night before.

He tasted the salt then broke into a great smile and said, "*Muy bien,*" as he gestured his partner to leave. They walked out our door almost as quickly as they had burst in.

We straightened up our car and collapsed the bed. I was still reeling from diarrhea, dehydration, and that endless, nagging, knife-piercing pain in my stomach and back. The tequila had done me no good and I was weak from exhaustion. The heat of the day alone was more than enough to deal with. Being sick only added a delirious component to our desert tour. We knew that our arrival in Nogales would mean throwing ourselves back out into the desert on foot and sick or not I had to ramp up the energy for the effort just hours ahead.

THE DESERT

The train pulled to a full stop in Nogales on time at two o'clock. We were excited about soon being stateside again and hustled to the checkpoint at the border. We walked back into the United States of America, the land of freedom, opportunity, and unlimited, potable drinking water. Our very first stop was a McDonald's restaurant where we virtually bloated on water, just plain, old, clear, clean water. Figuring it was safe to eat, we each had a burger too, but it didn't sit well in my stomach. I couldn't retain food in me for long. It seemed to just pass straight through, stabbing at my insides the entire way.

We went over to the convent to get our backpacks and what little of a life we'd left in the States was rewarding to come home to. We were looking forward to seeing the nun at the convent to tell her about our trip in Mexico. Perhaps we were more hoping to see any familiar face and hers was our only recent acquaintance. That too we were denied. An older priest answered the door. We explained that we'd left our packs earlier in the week and so on. As I spoke I could see our gear on the floor just behind him. He let us in to gather our packs, which hadn't been moved one inch from where we'd left them just as the nun had promised. We thanked him and asked him to thank the nun for us.

We belted down our packs and I, with temporarily renewed vigor, headed at high step for the interstate north.

"Now what?" Libby asked out loud as we walked.

"I don't know. Let's just get out of here," I said.

Our only choice out of Nogales was north to Tucson then the options included continuing north, or heading either east or west. As we got closer to the interstate we could see in the not-too-distant north some tremendous, building, anvil head clouds, black with rain and white with lightning.

We got a short ride perhaps an exit or two, but ended up at a rural exit in the middle of nowhere. A light rain started on us but we could see it was going to get worse. Rather than wait there on the ramp for few if any cars, we chose to continue walking on the interstate. With the storm's approach we figured surely someone would stop to help us out. Little did we know that the desert, with all of its unforgiving heat, sported a pretty violent afternoon thunderstorm almost daily during the monsoon. Well, we were soon smack dab in the middle of one and within minutes were soaked to the socks. Cars, trucks, vans...you name it, ripped right on past as we walked north with our thumbs out and our backs to the traffic. The sky went black with rain and clouds. We could see clear skies far to the west though the sun hadn't set for the day. The desert was an unforgiving place. We'd gone from the extreme heat of day to an absolutely pointless and overwhelming thunderstorm.

Finally, a guy in an old pickup truck pulled to a stop just past us to offer kind relief from the storm. As we rolled north for Tucson the storm worsened. Every here and there were bridges that spanned dry gulches or "arroyos" as they were called. We were astonished to see them fill in only minutes with a torrent of thick, muddy water from the thunderstorm. Our driver said you could easily get swept away in one and that people often did. He said that they dried up as fast as they appeared too.

As we approached Tucson we had to make a decision based entirely on our ability to avoid the storm, which had become ominous in all directions. We chose to head east on Interstate 10. The skies west were black so we figured that the storm was moving west. Perhaps by traveling east we could run under it, so we thought. We got out on the exit ramp and had a pretty lousy and lengthy hike to on-ramp traffic. It was raining damn hard and between the thunder and the lightning neither of us had any idea that it could rain so hard in the desert. We couldn't just stand there in the rain so we chose to walk along east bound, again with thumbs out and our backs to the traffic.

Many cars raced by with their headlights on, making a lot of splash, and every now and then Libby would turn around to face them. She was a sight. Her long, brunette hair was drenched in rainwater. I was not only sick, but I was embarrassed that once again I had let our luck completely run out on us.

Libby turned one more time to the traffic and our luck changed. A brand new white Ford Econoline van slammed to a stop. The bright red brake lights had never looked so good to us. We ran for the van and piled in. Libby sat on the cargo floor of the van on our packs and I hopped into the passenger bucket seat.

"Wow," I exclaimed to the driver. "Thanks so much for the lift." We were truly grateful. He was a quiet and reserved, older man. He didn't strike me as the kind of person that would volunteer a helping hand. *But hey, I could be wrong.* He obviously was just that. I couldn't help but notice that he had the air conditioning cranked up on high. We were already cold, but just being out of the rain was a blessing for the moment. I thought to ask him if he would blow up the heat for a few minutes but decided against any suggestion. We no longer could hear the direct sound of the pounding rain we'd been walking through. The acoustic quarters of his van were much quieter though we could still hear the muffled sound of rain pounding his van from outside over the blasting air conditioner.

We rolled eastbound as I watched for a break in the eastern sky though there was none; it only appeared to be darkening. Rainwater from my soaked head was dripping off my hair, nose, and beard as we drove. I again thanked the driver and apologized for getting his van a little wet. He said that it was a company van. As we continued east we could see that, like it or not, there was no chance of outrunning the storm eastbound. By then we'd gotten a bone chill from his air conditioning. We talked briefly about it and thought our chances westbound might be better. After all, the skies west showed a glimpse of clearing and there wasn't a respectable eastbound town from Tucson for many hundreds of miles.

I told the driver that we were going to have to take our chances westbound instead and thanked him for the ride. It was still raining, and raining hard outside. The driver said, "Well that's okay. I'll turn around too." Rather than let us out and continue east, he took the exit ramp and started driving westbound on the interstate.

I turned around and looked at Libby and she looked straight at me. *Whatever is going on with this guy is not good.* We both knew it. *Nobody, and I mean nobody, heads east out of Tucson on an interstate to turn around and head west just because some road bum hitchhikers want to try to outrun a storm. This guy has an intention of some sort.* At the speed limit heading westbound we were waiting for him to finally declare himself and believe you me, we were ready for just about anything.

And by the way could you please turn off the fucking air conditioning for just one God damned minute, I thought to myself.

Well, right about then he asked me, "Do you guys want to make some money tonight?"

My tongue immediately pushed to my cheek and my jaw stiffened as I looked to Libby who appeared confused. She couldn't hear what he'd said over the blowing air conditioner and the pounding rain. I looked straight at the driver. "Doing what kind of work?" I asked.

The driver hesitated a moment then said, "Going to a party."

"What kind of party?" I asked as I looked again to Libby who struggled to hear the details of his proposition.

The driver mumbled something barely audible.

"What did you just say?" I asked as I leaned toward him, my eyes still fixed on him.

"A sex party," the driver replied in a slightly louder voice.

My pupils closed tight, my jaw clamped, my fists clenched, and I felt a surge of anger rise in my spine stiffening my posture and raising the hair on my neck. "You pull this van over right now!" I immediately ordered him in a loud, direct voice as I pointed to the side of the road.

He nodded his head and continued on down the interstate toward an exit.

"You don't understand. I'm telling you, you stop this van right here, right now!" I ordered him again in a clear and firm tone.

"Okay, okay," he said. "Let me stop up here at the stop sign."

In the thirty seconds or so it took him to slow down and stop I had a rush of adrenaline. For just those few seconds, I forgot all about being sick, wet, cold, thirsty, hungry, and tired. *How dare this worthless son of a bitch try to take advantage of us when we are so down and out? Over my dead fuckin' body, pal,* I thought to myself. I was worried about getting Libby out of the van first. She still looked confused and didn't really catch the gist of the guy's despicable perversion nor did she understand why we were getting out of the van and back into the wet, cold night.

As the van slowed to stop, I got out of the bucket seat and grabbed her by the arm. I then opened the cargo door from the inside and basically pushed her out. Then I threw our packs out and finally, I jumped out. As I went to slam the door shut, Libby, the lady that she was, as politely as only she could be, thanked the driver.

"Thanks so much for the ride," she said with a smile, not knowing what had just happened.

I slammed the door shut and then buried my size eleven hiking boot into the side of the van's brand new door. I was pissed, yelling then screaming at that bastard as he drove away. I let out every little bit of anger and what little energy I had in reserve. We stood there on the side of the road in the rain.

We were both beaten. As I stared into her beautiful face, her hair was ringing wet and draped down, pasted to her rosy, welsh cheeks. She had a grin on her face when she asked, "What was that all about?"

I just looked to the ground and shook my head. I tried to explain but she could see I was wrung out. She knew it was a bummer ride but hugged me and kissed me. Her courage and compassion made me limp. I kissed her again and in the rain

I could see a flashing pink, neon reflection in her eye and on her face. I looked around in the night to see a small motor inn a hundred yards or so away on the frontage road. We decided to see what it would cost for a night.

We checked in and Libby brought me a cup of boiled rice water that the inn's owner assured her would cure my chronic stomach pain. She took a hot bath. Shortly after, we lay down to sleep in clean sheets with wet hair.

I was up and down all night with stomach pain and the runs. The rice water cure didn't seem to give me any relief at all. In fact, it seemed to make things worse. I showered the next morning as I figured it might be a while until my next chance at one. Libby was still cleaning up when I noticed a pay phone at a gas station next to the motor inn. I got an urge to call home and told her I was going to do just that as she showered.

The phone rang and I sat in patient apprehension for someone to answer. Dood was always home even if Mom had gone to a dog show for the weekend. Finally after a number of rings, Dood answered my call.

"Hey, Dood. This is John. How are you?" I asked with loving curiosity.

"John, it's great to hear from you. Where are you calling from?" he asked.

I had oh so much to share with him and struggled to even begin. I blurted out, "Well, right now we're just outside of Tucson."

Dood offered no more curiosity about how we'd gotten there, where we'd been or where we were heading. He just listened silently for my next prompt. In that moment I paused and hoped that he'd start in on some questions for me. I'd hoped that I could break through to a part of him that I'd never, ever known. In my hope was a need to hear his laughter, his pride in me, a sense of shared accomplishment and courage, or just an outward interest directed to our well-being. But there was none, nothing at all.

I broke the silence with another question. "So how are you doing Dood?" I asked.

"Well, okay I guess. I'm kind of anxious," he replied.

"What's wrong?" I asked.

"Oh, I don't know. I just have a lot of anxiety," he went on. We were all used to his depressions. For him they were typical.

"Is Mom home?" I asked.

"No. She and Dale are at a dog show. She won't be home until Sunday night," he explained.

"So what have you been doing, Dood?" I asked, prepared for little of an answer.

Dood spent the vast majority of his day either in bed, sitting on the stoop to the kennel or in his chair in the front yard. Within reach would certainly be his sweetened iced coffee and between his fingers was surely a lit cigarette. I already knew his days were routinely uneventful. His schizophrenia was debilitating and the caffeine and nicotine may have amplified his bouts with anxiety and depression.

"Oh, this morning Badness pissed in my shoe," he shared in sad frustration. I remembered how Badness, one of our several cats, would lick milk right from Dood's cereal bowl on the kitchen table as he ate breakfast each morning. It never really seemed to bother him, though.

"How about Charlie and Hugh and Ronnie? How are those guys doin'?" I asked hoping for some glimpse of fun or happiness from him.

"There doin' fine," he explained in short.

"Oh well, I thought I'd just touch base with you guys and see how things are goin'," I finished with little else to say.

"Okay John. Lovie," he said as we both hung up.

I was blank. With my hand still on the phone, I realized that he'd walk right straight back out to the stoop with his head down and light another smoke to return to the sad, worry-ridden world of his troubled, captive mind. Or perhaps he'd just resume pacing back and forth in the kitchen with his head low as he so often did to pass the time. I knew that he loved us but couldn't connect to our situation, travels or personalities. He was completely self-absorbed and couldn't connect to anyone. At least he wasn't worried about us which I dismissed was just as well.

I returned to our room to find Libby packing up for the day ahead. We did a survey of our cash and realized that we'd soon be flat broke. We needed to seek gainful employment on our way to nowhere we agreed. The morning was bright and clear and promised to be a cooker. Even the morning sun was hot in the desert and warned that we'd better have a plan for the midday heat. We filled the canteen to the brim and put a roll of toilet paper in my pack.

Resuming our path east for no real reason, we thumbed over a long, blue Cadillac hard top. The driver was a short, chubby, balding guy with a thin mustache. He wore wrap around sunglasses, the real dark kind; we couldn't see his eyes. He asked us if we wanted to make some money.

Oh no! Not another one of those guys.

We both looked at him as I asked, "Do you have a real job in mind because we're not interested in any other type of offers?"

He kind of tipped his head back and away to one side as he looked at us while driving on. "What do you mean?" he asked.

"No offense, it's just that we've had some very strange offers come our way. We're interested in making some money, but only in legitimate jobs," I added.

He kind of nodded his head in understanding and didn't ask for any details. "No, really. I could put you guys on as laborers at Old Tucson. We're gettin' ready to shoot a couple of scenes. One is for 'The Sacketts' and the other is for 'Centennial'," he went on. "It's an old western, movie set, kind of like an old western town but it's out in the middle of the desert and we need a couple of laborers. I could start you guys out at seven bucks an hour, cash," he said in a very direct and matter-of-fact tone, all the while glancing over at us through his dark shades. "I can't offer any real, long-term jobs but you guys could make enough money to help get you further down the road," he said.

Heck, I figured. *At those wages we could make enough money in just one day to travel a week or more.* We just about jumped out of our skins with elation. Libby started right in on him with the thousand questions and I started doing math in my head. In less than a minute we agreed to take him up on his offer having no idea at all what we were in for.

A few exits later he turned north on a dirt road. Maybe a couple of miles later he drove left into the heart of an old western town, I mean the kind of town you use to see on "Gun Smoke" or "Rio Bravo." There was a general store, a livery, various other storefront buildings and an old, grand, two-story hotel in the heart of town. It was fake but damn sure looked like a real town from the dirt road main street.

He pulled to a stop in a cloud of dust. There were already a few carpenters and such on-site shoring up braces behind the scenes. The driver pointed out that the buildings weren't buildings at all. They just looked like buildings from the camera's point of view, but were actually just facades. The old grand hotel was more of a real structure and had been used for some bar scenes in westerns. Otherwise, work was never ending and ongoing to keep the town from crumbling in the brutal heat and storms of the Tucson desert days.

The driver introduced us to another guy who turned out to be the job foreman. He was a husky guy with slick hair, shades, and wore nail bags around his waist. He shook our hands and said he could use some help for a day or two. On the west edge of town was a corral that was overgrown with live tumbleweed.

He said, "If you guys can tear all that up and make it look like cattle have been in there for fifty years, we'll pay you seven bucks an hour, cash."

"Boy, that we can do," we told him with eager smiles of excitement.

On our way to the makeshift tool shed for shovels and picks, we pulled our packs from the Cadillac and bid a two-thumbs-up farewell to the driver.

We headed for the corral and started digging, picking,
raking, and whatever to ready the set for the following week's
filming. Our boss let us work unsupervised so it was just we
two, out in the middle of the Arizona desert.

The midday Tucson sun was relentless in strength, and
working up a sweat helped me ignore the pain in my stomach.
Our boss came over to check our progress, which was steady.
We'd cleared the corral of a huge pile of waste lumber and
stacked it on a trailer. He brought us a cooler full of water to
keep us going. We'd just started ripping tumbleweeds when he
invited us to join him and the rest of his crew for lunch in the
shade on the porch of the old grand hotel.

As it turned out, they were all union carpenters, which
meant they were making more than twice the money that we
were. The requirements of becoming union workers sounded
a bit more complicated than we could deal with and labor jobs
were perfect for our situation. Their meals and lodging were
also provided. They ate a lot and they ate well and so we did
too. There were coolers full of water, pop, juices, lunchmeats,
cheeses, bread, mayonnaise, ketchup, mustard, pickles, chips,
cookies, and even cheesecake. With everything but beer, it was
an unlimited feast. It might as well have been Thanksgiving to
us. We had our fill and my stomach knew it as it spiked back
in refusal and forced me to take a quick trip to the porta potty.
We took a full hour lunch break then headed back to the old
Tucson corral to finish our day's work.

As we worked, we could see over the desert landscape
some mountains in the distance. Some were northeast, others
southwest and southeast. They gave the horizon character and
depth. It was a well-chosen site for a western movie town. There
was no air traffic either so it was quiet and serene except for the
pounding of nails and their echo off in the distance. I recalled
the snow-capped mountains further north in the Rockies, how
massive they were. Our mountain's search had gone by the
wayside but we still clung to that notion in our hearts.

The desert landscape is big too and will have to do for now, I
thought as sweat dripped from my brow and nose. There was

no way that we could drink enough water, but the cooler was large and the water was cold. The desert was so hot and dry that little sweat could swamp my clothes. Instead it evaporated as soon as it came out of my skin.

Late that afternoon, our boss came over to the corral and acknowledged the long, hard day's work we'd put in. He said that he didn't have the cash to pay us on the spot and mentioned that he had more work for us on Monday. After all, it was Friday and he and his crew were heading to Tucson for the weekend. Because they were union their employer compensated their weekend expenses. We, however, were not invited, as we were non-union labor. He did offer that if we wanted to stay at the old movie town for the weekend, they'd leave all the coolers and food for us to kind of just keep an eye on things. We really liked the offer and agreed to meet him Monday morning if for nothing else but to settle up.

They all piled into their pickup trucks and headed for Tucson in a cloud of dust. Within minutes the quiet of the old western town settled in. There was a slight howling noise just exactly like we'd heard on some old western movie. You know, where two gunfighters stood off with sprawled arms, ready to draw. Well, the wind noise came from a very small wire that had been strung across the dirt main street from building to building specifically for that purpose. The wire was almost invisible. It was so small, but in the slightest breeze it made that perfect "wooing" sound so familiar in those old westerns.

We rolled out our bags on the porch of the old grand hotel to settle in before sundown. The only moving things were occasional rolling tumbleweeds and a lone tarantula fighting his way against the breeze on his way up the dirt Main Street. Libby said that she could see him in a cowboy hat with six shooters strapped to his furry little waist.

Soon it was evening and we learned to again appreciate the sheer beauty of the desert at twilight. The sun could usually find a cloud or two; the shadows were long and cool to the eyes. The day released from its captive, torturing heat to peaceful landscape and sky. The distant mountains suggested a true curvature of the desert floor, which expanded in all directions to form but a small section of the earth's massive sphere. Finally the sun set and gave way to a rising, starry night sky. We were overcome by the peace of night that even put to rest the pain in my stomach. For the first time in many nights we fell asleep thankful for the day given us.

You know, it's funny how we were moved to seek shade the very instant that August sun poked its nose over the eastern desert horizon. It made no difference whether the sun hit our faces, our hands, our necks or just a part of our sleeping bag. That was our prompt to get up and start moving about in search of shade. Any shade provided momentary solace to appreciate the desert's morning beauty. In only minutes, though, we found that it would be a daylong struggle to stay alive from a threatening heat.

We sat with our backs propped against the wood of the old grand hotel with our sleeping bags draped across our legs. As we talked we realized that we had coolers full of beverages and food and that the day would be a good one. Our job was to find shade, eat, drink, and be merry.

Libby climbed out of her sack to prepare breakfast of a couple of cups of water and two chocolate chip cookies each.

Oh what a fine woman and cook she is that I've married, I thought to myself and then proclaimed out loud. She slapped me across the shoulder and we both laughed a bit. She was a fine cook, though, and her specialties were breads and deserts. She could also whip up a mean chicken paprika.

Someday we'll have a kitchen, a real nice kitchen, one that has the pots and pans drying on an overhead rack, and a garbage disposal too. We dreamed as we talked and watched the yawning of the Arizona sun across the desert.

Libby said, "Hey, who is that?" Her head turned to the east in the direction of the food coolers. As I fixed on an object, no a person, I realized it was a big person, a really big person walking our way. He was between us and the sun and his shadowed features cleared as he got closer. It was a man, a very large man with full-length hair and a long beard, perhaps ten years older than me. We could see he wore a tee shirt and shorts and that he was barefoot. If I didn't know any better I would've thought he was Big Foot. As he walked right, straight up to us, we felt a little more comfortable to see a smile on his face. He turned out to be a behemoth of a man, bigger than big, a true colossus.

Libby whispered to me as he approached, "You think you can whip 'im? We'd better hope he likes us."

He outstretched his enormous hand and I took a firm grip of him. His hand dwarfed mine but his shake was gentle. He stared straight at me with a great smile and still-water eyes.

"Hi, I'm Tree," he said with a smile.

"Tree, eh?" I replied. I figured he must have been a straggler from the rainbow family clan with a name like that.

"Yeah, Tree," he reiterated with a full and unwavering grin.

We felt a little humble to present ourselves as Libby and John. After all woodsy, native-like names weren't nicknames at all, but the declaration of new identity. They were the thing of the day back then and without one you weren't really anybody, especially when among many other West Coasters with adopted, nature loving surnames.

Tree walked right over to the food coolers and started to help himself to some breakfast. He apparently had an inside scoop on the affairs of the movie town haven. He'd come out of nowhere but neither of us felt at all threatened by him save perhaps his enormity and his equivalent need for food and drink.

This guy could empty both coolers in one good sitting, we thought as he sat and started in on a pop and some cheesecake.

Tree was a great big friendly fellow with a mysterious background, which he was reluctant to share. We learned that he lived on the outskirts of the movie town, at least for the time being. He had a camp trailer that was parked without a vehicle to tow it around. We also learned that he'd been there for some time. We could see that the desert was taking its toll on him; he wore a big smile, but his hair, face, and skin were as weathered as were the lapboards of the old grand hotel. Apparently, Tree had gotten into trouble with the authorities and was acting as a recluse in the old movie town as an evasive measure. He never really went into detail with what we didn't really want to know anyway. Like us, he'd been able to survive as a scavenger, living off the leftover cold cuts and such remnants of the union carpenters who worked through the week.

Tree had a wife and kid who lived in Tucson. "Would you like to meet them? My wife and son?" he asked.

"Sure," we said, though we couldn't quite get just how that was going to happen.

"They'll be out here this evening," he said. "They always come out on Saturdays," he added.

Tree filled us in on a lot of things. He knew the desert well and warned us of straying too far from the town in the heat of day. He said the best time to walk about was at night. He also shared a lot of history about the town.

"Nobody, not even the locals know it's here," he said. "If they did, it would surely get vandalized or burnt down. Most folks know old Tucson as the one that's in town. It burnt down a few years back so they built this one to replace it, but no one really knows about it. You're really lucky they even let you guys come out here," he said. Tree gathered up a couple more cans of soda, an enormous fistful of grub, then headed back for his camp trailer. He said that we would see him off and on.

We took Tree's advice and snoozed late in the shade of the old grand hotel. "High noon" is aptly named as when the sun is so directly overhead that shade is scarcely a premium. We waited out the midday inside the old grand hotel. It was like an old bar with swinging front doors. The carpentry was rough and though it all looked authentic, it was structurally a hazard. Stairs were impassible and just a touch in the wrong place could bring down an entire wall. There was no real intent to build a safe structure. *Just make it look good,* we figured. Then again, that's how they built things way back when anyway. We could imagine a John Wayne bar fight scene where people and bodies were flying about, smashing into stairs that collapsed, chairs being thrown around, and bottles being bashed over drunkards' heads. We could tell that it was certainly a place where a lot of fun things had happened over the years. But on that day it was dead quiet except for the whirring sound of the desert breeze across the movie town wire spanning the main street outside.

With evening came the desert's reprieve so we walked about as Tree had advised. There was really nothing of the town. The cool desert air settled over us as we saw Tree walking our way, his wife with him and she held in her arms their toddler son. We all introduced then retreated to the porch of the old grand hotel for a sunset supper out of the coolers. Tree's wife was a beautiful and friendly woman and their son was a curious little fellow who'd always retreat to the safety and comfort of his mother's arms. He'd quietly listen as we all chatted.

We talked of our wedding, and of school, and such. We told them some of our travel stories. We told them about Mack and how we so narrowly escaped him and his dealings and how we hoped we'd never, ever see him again. We all shared so much in common. Most importantly, we were all struggling to keep from falling through the cracks of society. But surely we were happy and at peace with ourselves we agreed. Their little family had been fractured by the questionable legitimacy of the law and theirs seemed to be a hefty price to pay to avoid an even stiffer penalty should the law catch up with them. For now, though, on that evening we were all happy and laughing over the spectacular setting of another desert day.

Tree always was barefoot but walked about so sure-footedly. "How can you walk around in this heat in your bare feet, Tree?" Libby asked him.

He said he was well used to it as he lifted his huge left foot and rested it on his right knee. We both gasped with astonishment, then laughter to see the sole of his foot was as hard as concrete from stem to stern. We had no idea that one's feet could become so hardened. The August beach of Mazatlán would've been a walk in the park for Tree.

He told Libby, "Go ahead. Touch it."

She ran her fingers across his hardened sole then knocked on it as though it was a wooden barn door. It made us all chuckle.

The next morning had the feel of a Sunday and by the time we woke the sun was well on its way to record-breaking heat. We retreated to the shadows and talked long about our situation. The charm of the old western town, which was superficial at best, was fading. The desert called us out so we ventured about to find only prickly, dry plants and lots of lizards. There were no birds or other animals to speak of and by noon the desert had fully expressed its ruthless heat.

We ran into Tree at the food coolers. He offered to show us how he earned a living, which surprised us. We walked to a small wooden tool shed where he showed us the glass wind chimes he made by hand. Actually, he had a crafty, circular glasscutter for making rings from beer, wine, and soda bottles of various sizes. Tree preferred certain types of bottles. Once the bottle was cut in two places he'd tap the glass from the inside with a small pivoting hammer-type tool right at the etched scribe. With a little finesse and patience the glass would break on the etch. Repeated effort on the same bottle produced glass rings of various diameter and thickness. He'd grind off the sharp edges by hand with emery cloth then finish the rings with a magic marker of differing colors on the sanded edge of each ring. By hanging them from a stick with fishing line in differing arrangements, they made a unique tinkling tone as they spun and collided in a gentle breeze.

We were amazed with the simplicity and ingenuity of their design but we could see his was a frustrating means of making little money. There was broken glass everywhere as things didn't always break as planned. His hands were rough from handling so much glass. He admitted that it was actually his dad's hobby. He had taught Tree the craft to try to keep him busy, breaking the desert boredom and to keep him from the stir-crazy delirium that came with constant desert exposure.

His dad came out occasionally to check on him, to supply him with food and to gather what few mobiles Tree had finished. Most importantly his dad came out to offer him unconditional love and support. Tree finally told us he couldn't stand making them but there was absolutely nothing else for him to do. He made them mostly because his father wanted him to.

We told Tree that we braved the heat long enough to find little of interest in the desert. He asked just what we were seeking out there. I told him that neither of us had ever seen a live rattlesnake. We asked if there were any around and where we might find one. He said there were some but our chances of finding one were much better at night. He relayed that almost all life in the desert was nocturnal. He said his dad was coming over that afternoon and if he'd lend us his car that he'd take us to a place to see a live rattlesnake that evening. We got excited about the quest ahead.

Tree's dad showed up as scheduled that night and we visited briefly with him. He agreed to let Tree use his car for a few hours. A short desert drive in quest of a live rattlesnake offered Tree an escape from old Tucson, having a therapeutic quality for sure. His dad stayed behind to cut glass instead, his therapeutic escape no doubt.

The three of us blazed off into the desert night with a trailing cloud of dust in an Oldsmobile with a great big front seat. We asked Tree where we were headed and he said, "Nowhere in particular."

We may have gone five miles or so when sure enough, Tree shouted, "There's one." He slowed the car to a stop as we could see a fat snake sprawled out in the middle of the dirt road just in front of us. A cloud of dust overtook us so we waited a minute or two before getting out. The rattler was in no hurry to move on. Tree said that they kind of slowed down a bit at night because of the cooler night air. He said they liked to stretch out on the road to stay a little warmer a little longer.

We hopped out of the sedan and walked toward the snake and just being near the rattler kind of shrank our pupils and straightened our hair. Tree wasn't the least bit afraid though.

As the snake curled up we could see it was aware of our presence and assumed a coiled posture. The snake appeared to be perhaps three feet long or better.

I asked Tree if he'd strike out and Tree said, "Maybe, let's see." Tree began teasing the snake with the sole of his bare foot! We watched in absolute horror as the snake struck out at his foot.

Libby shouted, "Oh my God, Tree! Be careful!"

The snake struck at him repeatedly as Tree continued to tease him.

"There ain't no way that snake can get his fangs into me," Tree said with a laugh.

The soles and rims of his feet were so hard that the snake would easier break off a fang before penetrating his incredibly weathered hide. Tree knew it and in fearless confidence continued to pester the rattler. He kicked dirt and rocks at it as it struck out at him over and over again. We could not contain our laughter in the dusty headlights of that desert night.

We woke the next morning on the porch of the old grand hotel to the sound of carpenters slamming pickup truck doors and gathering up their tools. The foreman came over to us for our day's assignments, which began with pulling the nails out of a pile of old, weather-beaten boards. We started in on our work and about an hour later he reassigned me to a different task on the other side of town. I worked for maybe fifteen minutes stacking lumber when I realized that I, for one, had had enough of the old desert west and figured it was time to move on.

I walked over to Libby and said, "No wife of mine will be pulling old rusty nails for a living." We went up to the foreman and told him that it was time we start moving on.

"Fair enough," he said and thumbed out our pay from a huge roll of cash. We shook hands and thanked him for the work and the grub.

We gathered up our packs and strapped up. We stopped at Tree's trailer on the way out to find him still sleeping. We told him that we were on our way out. He was sad to see us go. Tree, as it turned out, was a mountain of a man with a heart as good as gold and a temperament as sweet as honey. As we headed out from town by foot on that old dirt road, we worried what might lie ahead for him and his family. His life was a hard one but infinitely better than one behind bars, we agreed. Someday, we figured, it would probably all catch up to him, when he'd begin a new sentence and end his present one.

The hike back to the interstate was a long, hot one and by the time we got there we were both beaten down. Old Tucson had been a fun stop along the road, one of life's ups among a smaller number of downs. We'd left without food and little water and the beast in my stomach was reawakened by the time we found the on ramp east. There was no on ramp traffic so once again we walked down to the interstate to thumb the traffic careening by.

We hop-scotched a few short rides to an exit for a town that was off the interstate several miles. We needed to water up our canteen, but feared the long hike back to the interstate and chose to travel on and take our chances instead. A lot of travelers in the desert carried coolers with cold beverages, usually beer. It seemed to be the norm, customary in a sense.

At high noon, a blue low-rider pickup truck, all chromed out, pulled up slowly to give us a lift. In the cab were two young, husky Mexican fellows about our age. They spoke no English and signaled us to ride in the bed of the truck. We didn't go very far with them, perhaps four or five miles when we pulled over on the side of the road to learn that their truck was overheating. That came as no surprise to us because we too were boiling from the sun. They just sat there waiting for the engine to cool as we fried in the scorching heat of midday. Perhaps a half hour later they fired up the rig and we headed back out to brave the blistering asphalt one more time. We went perhaps another five miles where they shut her down to cool again. That went on and on and by mid-afternoon we were baked to a golden, dry, crispy brown. At that pace we figured it would take years for us to reach El Paso.

We limped into a rest area that had no water. My stomach was on fire and I found relief behind a yucca plant a short walk from the truck. Libby stayed with our packs and the Mexicans who had the hood up trying to figure out the problem. I returned to them and we all huddled in the shade of the hood of their truck to face an even hotter engine. We learned that they just had the water pump replaced.

Me, in my infinite wisdom of everything at the age of twenty, surveyed the water pump and such. I could see fresh gasket sealer oozing out where the new water pump met the face of the engine block. We checked the water coolant level and it looked fine. Had we known then what we'd learn later in life removing the thermostat would've been a very easy fix on the spot, but I had an insatiable capacity to learn things the hard way.

In my expert assessment, I relayed to the two Mexican gents it appeared the mechanic, who recently put in the new water pump, had inadvertently reinstalled the fan backwards. I told them the fan's blades were blowing air against the engine instead of the radiator. They both smiled with delight as they followed in mind my rationale. The driver had a toolbox and started to remove and reverse the fan. Great, we all thought, as we would soon be racing for cold drinking water in minutes.

When he reversed the fan, however, the blades retained the exact same orientation and pitch. It was kind of like how your left glove will only fit your left hand, even if you turn it around. They looked to me for further advice. I scratched my head and explained that the new pump probably didn't fit the old fan. The new fan was just backwards of what they needed, I explained. I told them that unless the fan blew air against the radiator to cool it, we weren't going to go anywhere.

The driver was a pretty husky fellow and wore a white muscle tee shirt. He asked if I thought it would work if he could reverse the pitch of the fan blades so that they would blow air against the radiator instead of blowing air against the engine.

I said, *Sí, pero como lo harías?*" as I nodded my head questionably up and down. The driver proceeded to the tailgate of his truck. He then placed the tip of each fan blade in the body seam between the tailgate and the bed. With flexing, brute strength he began twisting each blade to the reverse of its manufactured and balanced pitch.

Interesting, we thought as he tried so hard to field form one of the most vital components of his engine. He started to bolt the bent and sadly warped fan back onto the water pump. At that instant I realized that the fan blades were originally designed, not to blow air, but to suck air through the radiator and shroud. There was nothing wrong with the fan's original shape at all. But its newly-distorted, eccentric, warped, backward and unbalanced disfiguration certainly assured that the little blue truck, its two Mexican owners, and we, wouldn't be going anywhere, not one inch.

I told Libby in plain English, "Oh shit. This sumbitch ain't goin' nowhere." Fortunately, they couldn't understand my English summary of the problem. We decided it better to gather our packs and head for the interstate. Those poor fellows stood there in the blistering, afternoon sun as we caught a ride straight away east in another pickup truck. So much for mechanical aptitude but it was a lesson learned by all, the hard way.

Scorched, hot, burned, and I again sick, we stood roadside in the middle of a blistering desert. It wasn't really an exit and the traffic, which had become occasional, was moving by fast. The chance of someone stopping was damn near zero. The landscape had flattened and the only sight of contour on the horizon was a mirage. We could see how easily you could be fooled into thinking it was actually a lake, especially when parched. It was a hopeless place completely devoid of shade. The desert was so hot and dry that cactus couldn't even grow. There was some kind of thorny, skinny bushes of sorts and even they grew few and far between. The sun hurt my face and lips, which were blistering, and we were still without water.

Over the course of weeks in the desert sun, Libby's skin had turned a gorgeous dark brown. As sad as I looked, she just got more beautiful day-by-day. Her transformation into

womanhood was exquisite. I sat all hunched over and my
stomach growled as it twisted with pain.

Libby said, "Hey, we might have better luck if I hitch alone.
What do ya think?" I knew she was right and we were getting
desperate for a ride to water. My stomach cramps stretched out
as I stood and headed off into the desert with my pack draped
over one shoulder. I found one of those scraggly, old bushes
and flopped down to the ground. I had to get low and out of
sight. Libby was our bait and we had to use that technique only
on rare occasion.

As I lay flat on the burning desert dirt I could feel it scorch
the skin of my back. *This God forbidding heat,* I thought. The
overhead sun just would not go away. It persisted so, even
burning the palm of my hand as I tried to shade my blistering
face and eyes. In total exhaustion my hand fell back to the
dirt. I thought back to those two poor Mexican fellows we left
roadside a ways back. It made me feel bad; after all, they had
stopped to help us. I in my stupidity I had done an outstanding
job of wrecking their whole day and guilt overcame me as I lay
flat in the dirt on my back in the searing sun. I felt again like a
worthless piece of shit, a dumb-ass know-it-all piece of shit.

What on earth will ever become of me and my worthlessness? I
thought. In that moment of resignation, I thought back to the
night we'd spent trapped roadside in the cold Oregon rain. I
remembered how cold and wet we were. I recalled the pain of
getting sick and how I prayed for the heat of the morning sun
in the cold, wet dark of that night. My body shivered with the
memory. And there I was, months later, my prayer had been
granted as an almost absurd reward. *Surely someone is looking
down on me right now, not with pity nor in sorrow, but in delight and
laughter at my plight and humility. Be careful what you ask for,* a
little voice said aloud in the corner of my mind.

I was brought back by the long sound of screeching rubber
and Libby's loving voice in the distance. "Hey, let's go," she
yelled to me.

I gathered up myself and as I walked back to the interstate
I could see that she'd thumbed over a white pickup truck and

was already talking with a guy in the passenger seat. The closer I got the better I could see that he was a cowboy and so was the driver. Libby told me that they wanted her to ride up front with them and that they said it was okay if I hopped in the back.

She told them, "Thanks for the offer, but we'll both ride in the back." She was a little blushed with embarrassment or perhaps she was more flattered than anything. I could see they were just a couple of good old boys out to have a good time. What a disappointment for them to see me lumbering through the mesquite brush all dilapidated, burnt, sad, beat, and bumming a ride in tow. I threw both our packs in the bed of their truck then we hopped in.

No sooner did we start rolling out when the sliding window of the back of their cab opened and one of them struck up a go with Libby. She eventually popped her head right into the cab through the little window to visit a spell, much to their delight. As I looked about, I couldn't help but notice that in the bed of their truck were four, maybe five, cases of beer. Our canteen was empty and we were bone dry. My lips savored for one of those beers but they weren't mine to have. I reached over to run my hand across a couple of cans. They must have been in the bed of the truck all day long in the sun because they were hot to the touch. I knew that in Europe they preferred their beer warm but I couldn't ever remember anyone favoring to drink hot beer.

Libby would from time to time turn around and relay the details of her flirting conversation with her new cowboy friends. She said they'd been to the dog races the night before and were on their way back. They'd apparently asked her what was wrong with me. We looked like quite a mismatch, me in my poor state and she so full and vivacious.

She said they knew a sure-fire cure for my stomach woes as she handed me a small green pepper just a little longer than my thumb. "They said to eat a half-dozen of these whole. Don't chew 'em 'cause they're real hot," she relayed with an excited and optimistic smile.

I wasn't real sure about it and looked into the cab to see the passenger cowboy pop one right on down the hatch like it was a piece of candy. He snapped off the stem and said, "Go ahead, they'll fix ya right up. Might help if you wash 'em down wif bair," he added. "You just drink as much a dat bair as you want," he generously offered.

Libby and I looked at each other. We each licked the waxy surface of a pepper. It had no taste and wasn't the least bit hot. We kind of smirked and did just as the cowboy showed us. We snapped open a couple of hot beers to wash it down and just like that, one away.

Libby said, "He says you should eat several. He's certain it'll fix you up." The cowboy handed her a small brown paper bag full of those little green peppers. "He calls them 'hello peenya' peppers," Libby explained.

Fair enough, I went on and downed perhaps a half-dozen of them with little trouble. I was willing to try just about anything by then and with renewed hope I thanked the cowboy for his help.

"Now the last one you should chew up like dis hair." He took a pepper and just chomped it right up and down. "That'll get things goin'," he said. "You guys drink as much a dat bair as you want," he again said.

Well, we each did just as he instructed. We chose the largest peppers because we hadn't eaten a thing all day. We chomped and chewed and ground them to a pulp with our molars before swallowing. At first it had a good, tangy, green pepper taste. Within a minute or so it felt like Satan himself was brandishing a flamethrower inside our mouths. We'd eaten hot peppers before, but never, not ever, had we an experience like that. In the course of five minutes we each had downed about a six-pack of hot beer to quench the fires in our mouths. There was no way of getting relief. The beer reacted with the hello peenya juice to make a bursting foam. The only way it would go down was with heads tilted straight back and by pouring it right on down the gullet to the stomach. We were both frothing at the mouth. Between beers we had to hang over the side of the truck with open mouths in the wind as we blared down the highway. But that only worked for so long so we had to crack another hot beer and slam it down. We never knew that hot beer could taste so damn good. The cowboys roared with knee slapping laughter in the cab. We laughed occasionally too but constantly downed hot beer between chuckles.

Dark settled in on us as the burn slowed to a hot bed of coals in my stomach. We asked them cowboys to pull over so we could bag up for the night. We got out between exits somewhere near the southernmost border of Arizona or New Mexico. We bid them farewell and as they drove off we hopped over the range fence and rolled out our bags on the dirt behind a small, scant bush. We'd gotten accustomed to sleeping on our bags rather than in them for the desert heat.

I slept little that night from the whirr of woes in my stomach. My only consolation was the thought that those peppers might do the trick and kill whatever was eating my insides. Libby, as always, fell fast asleep like a baby.

The coming of morning light was soon about and I hadn't slept a wink at all. My stomach had wrenched and turned all night. I'd sweated all night too and my clothes were wringing wet. We hadn't laundered in many weeks and so I was, in a word, filthy. Before sun up the pain in my stomach was so intense that I had to walk about to find a bush for relief of diarrhea. Now let me tell you that nothing could've prepared me for the "after burn" so to speak from the passing of those peppers. I had a downright spiritual transcendence. I went into a hypnotic, almost catatonic state from the indescribable pain. I saw an apparition of Montezuma himself laughing loud across the barren and worthless Arizona/New Mexican desert dawn. When I regained consciousness, I cleaned myself up as best I could and returned to Libby who was still peacefully snoring. I didn't want to wake her but, with the break of day and the first touch of sun on my blistered face, I knew that we had to get up and find some shade and water.

Libby wanted to sleep on but she knew well that we had to get going. By the time we got rolled up and on the asphalt the sun was already slanting in hot from the horizon. We had that puffy, crusty, sleep deprived feel about us. I had bags under my eyes and we both had incurable cottonmouth as we stood side by side with thumbs out staring west.

Our first ride of the day was a huge dump truck. The driver had only a bucket seat for one passenger so we climbed into the dump bed. He was headed for El Paso several hours east and offered us a long ride. The dump bed was full of scrap iron that looked like the remains of enormous pistons from some type of large, internal combustion engine. Each piston was twelve, maybe fourteen inches in diameter. *This must be scrap from a large power plant generator or locomotive,* I thought.

We found it difficult to get comfortable but could recline somewhat on our backpacks. The open-air breeze of morning was soothing as we traveled east in that old dump truck. We talked out loud over the rumble of the truck and agreed that our biggest problem of late was our latitude. Continental travel east meant Texas, west was worthless and south meant certain death. Our only option was north but we'd have to wait until Las Cruces to catch that route. As I bounced around in the back of that old truck, I thought long about our situation. I'd admittedly grown out of faith through my teen years, but perhaps my being so sick and an abrupt need for maturity had led me back to the comfort and peace of mind that comes with a rebirth of spirit.

How had we come to this, riding on a pile of junk? Maybe this whole journey was a bad idea. Maybe we'd be better off to make a cross-country run for Pennsylvania, back home. I remembered my mother; how understanding she was. The day after our wedding she learned that we were headed out for parts unknown. As only a mother could she told us that if we got into trouble or life got too troubling, we could just "come right on home," as she put it. I remembered how we were resolute in mind, that under no circumstances would we allow that to happen. My mom's offer then was precisely what we needed to hear, to give us the courage and confidence that comes with unconditional love. At the same time I also knew that there would be no chance of any Dorothy and Toto welcoming home with Libby's folks in New Hampshire. No, ours was a one-way ticket out west.

I wondered how Libby would feel about retreating back east in failure. I started hearing a song from my youth in my head and began to hum along. I sang to myself as Libby slept. *The alkali desert was barren and bare, and Johnny's soul shrank from the death that lurked there. Dear old Pennsylvania, I'll come back to you, said Libby, you'll go by yourself if you do.*

Somehow we'd strayed too far south on our journey to nowhere. We'd all but abandoned the search for our mountain. I recalled how we both loved to fish and that passion had no bearing on our daily travels because there wasn't any water, anywhere. *How could there possibly be any fish in any direction for days from here,* I thought. No, we had to get back on track. The thought came as almost a revelation, as though my life's giver and creator had again put His great hand down before us. Our path was not through Mexico, Texas, or Pennsylvania but it was north.

Then why the grand detour and pain? There must be some sort of timing component to all this. Maybe He has us on some type of wild goose chase so that we'll be at the right place at the right time. Something great will come of all of this if we can sustain a blind faith, a resignation that at each turn and choice in the road we believe in His guidance. Without it, there is no hope. This it must be. But then again, maybe we are just hopeless.

Minutes later we were both asleep on a pile of junk steel in that old dump truck.

We were awakened by the heat of day that slowly changed the passing breeze into a blast furnace. By the location of the sun and the greenery of the river west, we could see that we'd slept right straight through El Paso and were headed further south on the Rio Grande River. We asked the dump truck driver to let us out. We had to back-track to El Paso, then Las Cruces to get somewhere north of hell. We made it back to

El Paso in the dead heat of midday struggling to get through the sprawl and chose to keep pushing for the interstate north despite a desperate thirst.

Short ride after another we finally found ourselves at a lonesome, slow section of interstate. There was no shade to be had and we were genuinely worried about our dehydration. We found an old piece of cardboard and rather than write a destination on it we wrote, "No Water," instead. We took our empty canteen and hung it upside down on a reflector post with the cap dangling free from the chain. Any and all passers by could easily see that we desperately needed water.

No one stopped. No one seemed to care. We could see them look straight at us as they passed only to look away to avoid eye contact. The blisters on my cheeks, nose, and brow had burst. Libby was faring much better and stood on the solid white line to thumb for help. I sat on my pack in the background of her efforts.

Lo and behold a New Mexico state trooper approached and at long last we'd be rescued, or so we thought. The trooper slowed then pulled his patrol car right up to us. As Libby approached his car, he sped off. His was a deliberate refusal to lend us a helping hand or even a sip of water. She yelled at him to stop, waving her arms as he drove off. He apparently had other plans for his afternoon and stopping to help us was not as entertaining as the prospect of making an arrest or grabbing a jelly-filled we agreed. *Where are the Royal Canadian Mounted Police when you need them?*

Another hour or so passed when finally a guy in an older white van pulled up to help us. He could see that we were broiled by the sun's heat and offered us cold beer from his cooler. Hot beer, cold beer, it made no difference to us; anything to wet the whistle was a blessing. He said he lived about an hour north and that we could water up at his place. He then offered us another beer that we gratefully drank.

We pulled off the interstate several miles and eventually came to his stucco, Spanish house. He showed us to the kitchen where we drank water to our fill. He offered to let us use his bathroom, not to bathe but to freshen up a bit. He said that he'd meet us in the courtyard. I filled the canteen as Libby used the bathroom. I found him in his courtyard, which was in the center of the house. I'd never really seen anything quite like it. It had no roof or glass covering and was like being outside but inside the walls and various rooms of his house.

"What do you think?" he asked.

I was so impressed with his generosity and the layout of his home that I failed to recognize that his inquiry was regarding the lush green marijuana plants growing from his courtyard soil.

Libby joined us as we examined his plants that were just starting to flower. Our new friend told us that each day the buds would bloom fuller into profuse and potent flowers. He said that we should come back in about a month to share our pick of his crop. By then we'd lost an appetite for drugs other than something that would reset my stomach to normal function, though his offer was genuine and friendly. We told him we'd certainly come back to take him up on his offer though we knew our whereabouts a month out were anybody's guess but ours.

He offered to run us back out to the interstate. When we got to the on ramp he asked if we'd had a decent meal lately. Aside from our "hello peenya" supper the previous evening, we hadn't eaten since Old Tucson, days before. I wasn't much interested in food but Libby was hungry for us both. Our new friend drove us north another two exits to a restaurant that served what he said was some of the finest, authentic New Mexican food in the state. We thanked him so for his open caring and waved him goodbye as he drove off.

Well, he was right about the food. It was late afternoon and we were their first two patrons for the day. It was a supper club and the smell of fine food aroused my dormant hunger. We ordered fried chile relleno with rice, corn, refried beans, and sopapillas for dessert. It was fabulous and being fed and filled with water gave me renewed strength for the two-mile trek back to the highway. Libby was absolutely flushed with energy, enthusiasm and unequaled, natural beauty. By the time we reached the interstate my supper had turned in my stomach and I sought the privacy of a bush to relieve me of the intense cramps brought on from my only recent meal.

We got a ride in the back of a pickup truck with two Mexicans headed north. We rode with them for several exits until they pulled up to a bar just a short hike from the exit ramp. We figured they needed gas or something but they headed right straight into the bar and started shooting pool. We were still thirsty so Libby went in to get a glass of water.

I was in no mood for either beer or pool so I just hung out with our packs to watch the advance of evening. My stomach had settled down some and I felt worse having food in me than nothing at all. Libby headed into the bar to see what was up with our Mexican escorts. As the three of them played pool apparently they made her an offer.

She walked confidently out of the bar and told me, "We might as well head out. Those guys are losers." We strapped up and paced to the on ramp still in sight of the bar. We walked up to the merge of traffic and thumbed as we walked and talked.

"The short guy told me that they'd slit your throat if I wanted them to," she said.

"You've got to be kidding me," I replied.

"It was no problem. I could a whipped 'em both with a couple good swipes of my cue stick," she said. I could see she wasn't joking. Neither of us was the least bit afraid. We were unfettered in the face of any threats whatsoever.

A long station wagon stopped to give us a ride. There were already five riders in the car, two men and three women. All their gear was piled up on the luggage rack on top of the car. We threw our gear on top as well. They were German students touring the United States and let us have the little seat clear in the back of the station wagon all to ourselves. They really liked having us in the car because it gave them non-stop practice with their English. Libby did most of the talking as I soon fell asleep with the approach of night. The station wagon came to a stop on a rural dirt road beneath a cluster of short, scrubby trees as we all hopped out and rolled out bags for the night. Libby said that we could travel with them to Colorado the following day. I expressed a tired sigh of relief as we settled for a hopeful night's rest.

We'd slept inside our bags as the night and morning air had a slight chill. I woke up tired the next day and everyone was anxious to get going except me. Libby helped me roll up my bag because I couldn't find the energy to talk, let alone work. One of the other guys in the group helped her throw my pack onto the luggage rack as I found gastric relief behind a bush before moving on. My stomach was on fire. My entire abdomen was on fire and I truly felt it consuming the life within me. Going to the bathroom always brought me temporary relief of cramps and pain, but not that time. All were waiting for me to climb into the station wagon when I returned. I said nothing and just got into the car so that we could all move on without worry.

By the gist of conversation going about the car in German, somehow I gathered that they were talking about me. Finally, one of the women started in English with Libby. They were worried about me, because I didn't talk and I looked awful, or so she said. They suggested that we go to a doctor even though we'd known them for just a few hours. Libby asked me if I needed a doctor. We had very little money, certainly not enough to see and pay a doctor so I pushed back the pain and put a smile on my face and told her that I was feeling pretty darn good. I told her not to worry because I was on the way back up. It was a lie and I knew it but she kind of believed me more on trust than truth of the moment.

The car stopped at a McDonald's restaurant for breakfast. Everyone else ordered food and drink but I passed and never got out of the back seat. Libby offered me a bite of hers but I passed on her offer. I told her that having a full canteen would do me well for the day. I had no interest in food or drink though I sipped her coffee to ease her concerns.

After our short breakfast stop, we chipped in for gas then headed north on the interstate. Hour by hour the landscape changed to distant, hilly canyons, prairies, and such. The trees became more abundant and the desert gave way to a land more livable. Shortly after noon we pulled into an historic site, a Spanish mission dating well back to the 1800s.

I worked up enough strength to walk into the old church and was met with a familiar smell though I'd never been there before. I could see in the mission though, the fight to live that was so arduous for the early settlers of the American West. Had they traveled another half-day south of there they'd have certainly perished in the desert, we knew. We returned to the cruiser though some wanted to stay longer than others and were disappointed to leave so soon.

We traveled off interstate from there and it was a welcome relief to be on two lanes instead of four. It'd been almost a month since we'd last traveled over two-lane roads. Two-lane travel had a completely different feel to it. It was slower and indirect. There were more turns, curves, and stops. It was dynamic and comforting giving me another chance to doze off in the far back seat of the station wagon. At one point Libby shook me awake to see some tremendous mountains in the distance. I was relieved at once to know that we'd soon be nestled in the valleys and grassy meadows tucked into the folds of those great, shelving peaks.

The group stopped for a late lunch of burgers and ice cream at a roadside grill. I again passed on all food and drink. Libby had an ice cream cone; she always loved ice cream; it was one of her most favorite treats. But even its sweetness couldn't remove the frown from her brow when she sat and talked with me in worry about my complete loss of appetite. I'd had very little to eat or drink since Old Tucson and she knew it. But I had no hunger or thirst, just an endless and painful growling in my stomach.

We all piled back into the station wagon and headed for the great sand dunes of the San Luis Valley. The dunes were backed right up to a technically difficult and impressive range of mountains called the Sangre De Cristo. As we drove further remote to the dunes I got to wondering if there really wasn't something more wrong with me than a case of Montezuma's revenge. I'd been sick on and off almost all summer with fever, nausea, diarrhea, chills, shakes, fainting spells...you name it. I didn't care to either eat or drink when I knew that I was badly dehydrated and should've been hungry. I didn't feel as weak as I truly was and everything in mind was strong. My body had definitely hit a bump in the road but perhaps there was more to me being sick than I really knew.

Maybe I should go to a doctor. But then again, we had so little money and I really didn't want to go. In my thoughts I had a growing impatience for riding in the back seat of the car. I'd had enough German too but the complacency and convenience of a longer ride overruled any thought of self-driven initiative or adventure. It had gotten away from being Libby and me, just us two. For an entire day we'd become part of a group and I had a growing distaste for it.

We pulled to a stop at a parking lot for day visitors at the Great Sand Dunes National Monument. It was far off the beaten path and no place for hitchhikers, we agreed. Our ride as passengers in the station wagon was our only way to get back out of there and we knew it. Libby was joyful in the moment though and as we walked toward the dunes we came upon a piece of bread on the sand.

She jokingly said, "Hey, look. A sandwich." She was always on the lighter side and could find joy in any situation; there was always a silver lining in any black cloud of her life. She raced off to catch up to the others to climb and play on the dunes.

I tried to go too but couldn't walk fifty yards before fatigue got the best of me. I told her to go on and that I'd stay behind to keep an eye on our stuff even though there were no other visitors around. I could see concern and genuine curiosity about the dunes in her eyes. She smiled and turned to run and join the others already playing, laughing, and rolling in the sand.

I returned to the parking lot and sat beneath a large cottonwood tree. I watched the group as they hiked up the dunes, eventually disappearing from sight. I wanted to be among them and felt somewhat left behind and lonely. The setting was so peaceful, though, and it was the first chance for me to be alone in a long time. I thought back on our travels and how far we'd come, recalling the good times and the bad. I started thinking about the night we spent in Vail playing piano and partying. Then I thought back to Gordon and Sharon and whatever they'd be up to about then. I wanted to talk with Randall and Marilyn to share with them so many fun stories. Then I thought of Mack and shuddered with nervous fear at just how close to the edge we may have come in meeting him. I thought about big Gene and how he'd roar with laughter at all the twists and turns of our honeymoon affairs. I thought about my mom and Dood and how glad I was that they knew nothing of our travels. It wouldn't matter much to Dood but I knew that my mother would worry so.

Late afternoon turned into evening and Libby's approaching laughter awakened me. I couldn't wait to see her beautiful, smiling face as she and the others walked a small trail through the brush back to the car. It was clear they'd had an outrageous time of it on the dunes. They watered up as they laughed and prepared to head out. I passed on a drink from our canteen; minutes later we climbed into the station wagon and headed back out from the monument. We took a round heading and in a half-hour or so, I could see a big, full moon rising over the sand dunes and the Sangre de Cristo Mountains in the distant east. At the same time the sun was setting in the western sky. I asked the male driver to please stop the car, perhaps as an acknowledgment of faith and timing.

"What is wrong?" he and others asked.

"Nothing," I said. "Just please, stop the car."

Libby had a confused look as well. "What's the matter, John?" she asked as I started to remove our packs from the roof of the car.

"Nothing, honey," I said. "It's just time for us to stop, right here, right now, just us, to feel this moment."

I can't really explain what came over me except to say that when their rented car pulled away, we stood alone on a very straight, long, and flat two-lane road running north and south. The light of the end of day wouldn't relinquish and the reflection of an opposed, brilliant moon would intensify throughout the night.

Libby immediately joined me in the moment. The sun and moon, the dunes, the Sangre de Cristo Mountains, and the San Luis Valley could never have been more beautiful. In that moment we knew and felt that God did not always reward those who followed the ways of man, but rather those who followed their hearts. It was a spirited moment that had inexplicably called me out of that car. In blind faith it had something to do with being in the right place at the right time. I tried to explain all this to Libby who shared the beauty of the evening with me.

"Yeah, it sure is beautiful," she said. "But the very first car that stops in the morning, you're going to see a doctor, first thing tomorrow morning."

I reluctantly and sorrowfully agreed to it as well. We rolled out our bags right then and there on the side of the road.

COMING HOME

The Sangre De Cristos spanned the eastern horizon making the sunrise a little later the next morning. We got up before the sun and as we rolled up, Libby reconfirmed the day's mission, to seek medical attention. She was serious and for the first time had a determined look about her. The cramps and pains had left me overnight but were replaced by a tightness.

From the moment I awoke, I had a strange new sensation, sort of like I had a basketball lodged in my stomach. Not like I had overeaten, but more like a tight huge lump had settled in and seized my middle body. My entire abdomen felt almost like an appendage, almost like it was separated from me entirely. As I walked it almost felt like it was out in front of me, not leading but separate. It felt firm and hard on the inside but my stomach was normal to the touch and not the least bit distended. I was convinced that it wasn't a sensation of body but of mind. Surprisingly, I was otherwise in little gastric pain and though we'd slept a full night, I was still very tired.

Our first ride of the day was an old flatbed pickup truck. We threw our packs on the bed and stumbled into the cab. It had a musty, old, classic smell. No sooner did we start to roll when our Native American driver asked Libby what was wrong with me though neither of us had yet spoken a word. She looked to him as I stared straight ahead and down somewhat at the passing road. Libby told him that I'd gotten sick real bad in old Mexico. She told him that I'd stopped eating and drinking and that I had real bad stomach pain.

He goes, "I know the cure for it. It grows off the road up here. Do you mind if I pull off the road a ways to get it? It's a plant called 'artemisa.' My mother and grandmother used it on us any time we had stomach problems. It works well. Do you want to give it a try?"

Libby looked to me. I'd heard their conversation but he hadn't spoken a word to me. I was still fixed on the road ahead. I could hear in her voice a need for my compliance. She had great respect for Native Americans, their understanding of nature and the medicinal properties of so many plants. I was slightly embarrassed, but was willing to try almost anything, even going to a doctor as a last resort. I said nothing but nodded my head up and down.

"That'd be great," Libby told the driver.

We hadn't moved more than a couple of miles from our camp the previous night when he pulled just off the asphalt onto a dirt road heading west. He immediately stopped, hopped out of the truck, and started picking weeds. We looked on in absolute and curious fascination. In less than a minute, he walked around the front of the truck to my window with a handful of weeds.

"Eat as much of this as you can and you'll be fine by this afternoon," he said as he handed me the small fistful of pungent, medicinal plants that he'd just gathered. I already knew their smell. Libby wanted to smell them too and also recognized the familiar aroma.

He then asked, "Do you have any water?"

"Yes," I said.

"It's a lot easier to take with water," he advised.

I took a single, small leaf and started to chew on it. I immediately appreciated his suggestion about water, as it was bitterly awful. I looked at him to weigh whether or not he was sincere, but I could see in the pupil of his eye that he not only wanted to help us, but more, that he was confident in his remedy. I stepped out and grabbed the canteen from my pack.

He asked, "When did you eat last?"

"Two nights ago," I answered.

"That's good. You should always do this on an empty stomach and don't eat anything for several hours after you've taken the medicine. If you can, start by eating yogurt. The plant will kill everything in your digestive system, including the bacteria you need to digest food. That you can get back from yogurt, but wait until the medicine has finished working, sometime this afternoon," he prescribed.

We got back in the cab and started down a perfectly straight and long road again. He told us that it always worked on anything wrong with your digestive system whether it was nausea or diarrhea. He said that it was likely I had some sort of parasite that had gained control of me and had to be killed entirely.

I chomped down a good bite of it and started to chew and my impulse was to spit it right back out. It was absolutely revolting in taste.

"Wow," I said. "I'm not going to be able to eat very much of this."

He explained, "Sometimes it's better to roll up a small wad of it and gulp it down like a big pill rather than chew it. The main thing is to eat as much as you can, to the point of gagging, just before vomiting. When you can't take one more bite, then you've had enough. But you must take it to the edge."

I wadded up another clump and put it down tough with another gulp of water. Not quite as bad but it still made me gag and my eyes water. He told us that at home his mother would brew it into a tea and serve it with honey, but it was still hardly palatable and was only used to cure gastric illnesses. As I wadded up a larger clump I realized that it looked just like sagebrush. I asked if it was indeed.

"Yes. It's the small, tender growth with the softer green leaves, not the woody stem part," he said.

I choked down another wad of it as Libby took a small taste of leaf too. Libby asked him if it would work on chest colds or flu.

"No. It's only good for gastrointestinal problems," he answered. "There are other herbs for respiratory and sinus problems," he said but did not detail.

I swallowed as much as he said I should, to the point of teary-eyed gagging. Then I took one more mouthful and chewed it whole and forced it down while suppressing the urge to vomit.

"That's it," I said. "I can't take any more." The after taste would not go away. I suppose like cough medicine, there was something therapeutic about eating something repulsive, to reinstate a healthy state of body and mind.

Though we were hopeful, Libby wasn't about to take any chances and still asked him where we'd have to go to see a doctor. He said there was a medical clinic in an alternate direction. He gave us a ride to a crossroad and directed us to travel west.

"The clinic is in the town en route, it's real obvious. Just ask for the clinic when you get there," he said.

We thanked him for his caring he then drove north as we paced west.

We came to the small town and found our way to the clinic. Their only physician was out of the office but was scheduled to be in around eleven o'clock so we filled out some papers and waited for his arrival. The doctor was on time and I was promptly seated in a waiting room and prepared for a physical examination.

When the doctor stepped in, I could see that he was a professional for sure. He wore glasses and had dark hair. He took one look at me and exclaimed, "What on earth is wrong with you?"

I gave him the short course on my illness.

"We've got to get more fluids in you immediately," he said as he took my temperature, pulse, and blood pressure. He asked a lot of questions. He said that he was going to prescribe an intravenous drip to get me hydrated. He asked if I could give him a stool sample. I told him that I hadn't eaten in a couple of days but that I would give it a try.

He said a sample would likely confirm his suspicion that I had an advanced case of what he called "amoebic dysentery." He said it was a potentially life threatening illness but that drugs were readily available to help me get over it. There was no doubt in his mind that the first course of treatment was to get some fluids in me and to regain my ability to take solid food. It sounded like one way or another, I was hospital bound.

Fair enough, I figured. He gave me a small bottle and I was led to a bathroom to try to get a stool sample. Nothing could've prepared me for what I saw in myself when I turned on the light and gazed into the mirror. I hadn't seen myself in a mirror in many weeks and many thousands of desert miles and I wore the look of its wear and tear. I was gaunt, hairy, and filthy. I could see the bones of my face, my cheeks, and around my eyes for the first time ever. The bridge of my nose, brow and cheeks had hard black scabs. I'd become but a weak shell of a man. I looked like an old, old man and my reflection scared me. I washed my face and drank water from the sink by cupping the palms of my hands. I then sat on the toilet and pushed hard to try to get a stool sample as I'd been instructed. There was nothing, not one drop.

But wait. What's this? Low and behold, I squeezed off one tiny, perfectly oblong, hard, little turd, my first hard number two since Mazatlán. It wasn't much of a turd, but it was hard and just a little bigger than a grape. It brought a smile to my face and with that I felt hungry. I washed up a bit more and thought things through. I knew that the medical routine would be a costly one in both money and time and that the minute they did a lab sample or an intravenous drip, the meter would start running. I thought maybe my encounter with the Native American that morning might have been more than a coincidence. Almost like I had to believe in it more than be afraid.

Enough, I thought as I flushed that little turd right on down the toilet. I came out of the bathroom and told the nurse I had no luck with the stool sample and handed her back the empty bottle. When I rejoined Libby in the waiting area I told her, "Come on. Let's go."

She asked a lot of questions but could see that I was finished with the clinic and the doctor. There was a sort of rural assistance program in place at the clinic and so my visit with the doctor only cost fifteen dollars, which we paid in cash.

As we walked out of the clinic I told Libby not to worry because I had just passed a small, solid stool and that I was hungry.

We walked a few blocks to a grocery store where we bought some dried fruit and such. We had cold yogurt with some granola and watered up our canteen. I convinced Libby that I was doing pretty well and that we should continue on in search of a better meal that evening somewhere.

We pulled out the atlas and chose a route west. Ride by ride, we found our way up a grand valley braced by rim rock mountains to the little town of Creede. It was an old, hard rock mining town that kind of sat at the end of a great, box canyon. It had all the makings of the old West and we surely felt at home. It was evening when we arrived and minute-by-minute, hour-by-hour, I was recovering well. I had forgotten how good it felt to feel good and I was beginning to feel great. I eased into the dried fruit in our pack and drank water like a mule.

We found in Creede a small sign that said, "BINGO" and learned that the weekly game was to occur that evening. *What the heck, let's play some BINGO and meet some of the locals.* We did just that but learned that BINGO in Creede was serious business, more of a highly competitive, low stakes game. People went to BINGO to win money, not to socialize. We imagined that table poker from the old days had given way to BINGO and to perhaps the very same type of gambling crowd. It was dark when the games wrapped up and we got out of there having only lost five bucks. We walked uphill through town to the nose of the box canyon and rolled out our bags on the hard, rocky ground.

We woke hungry the next day and headed for the only town cafe. We walked in to find a very local crowd including the town sheriff, who sported a cowboy hat, badge, and a hog leg. It was great to see some of the old western flair still alive. We each ate a full breakfast of bacon and eggs with toast, juice, and coffee that went down the hatch without a moment's trouble. We visited with a few folks to learn that the only real local employment was remnant gold mining and the chances at that were slim to none. In asking around we learned that a local jeweler could probably let us know about our jar of opals we'd bought in old Mexico. Any chance to turn some cash we needed and so we headed for the gem guy's house. Besides, we weren't ready to give up on Creede just yet. It was such a quaint, small town.

The jeweler lived in a singlewide trailer and turned out to be a real friendly, hippie-type guy with a beard, long hair, and one long earring. He offered us each a cup of tea as he surveyed our jar of rocks.

"Not worth much, really," he said. "The opal is embedded in the matrix. It'll just keep on cracking."

We told him that we could've bought a jar full of finished, polished opals for a hundred bucks.

"That would have been a real bargain," he said. "These are fairly worthless, though, because there's a lot that goes into finishing them," he stated as a matter of fact. He obviously had no interest in them so our jar of gems was more like a bottle of dud firecrackers rather than the investment we'd hoped they'd be. Libby cheerfully said that they made a wonderful souvenir from old Mexico though and were a heck of a lot cheaper than diamonds.

We talked on about Creede and its history. Mining was dying out as an occupation throughout the West. He said the only real mining jobs left were in the coal mines.

"Coal mining is just downright dangerous," he said. He pretty much assured us that Creede was a no man's town that had already seen its better days. We left the jeweler around noon and headed back down the rim rock valley and eventually started heading west again.

A suped-up blue pickup truck stopped to give us a lift. The driver had to get out and help us with our packs because he had one of those vinyl snap-on bed covers. Somehow we piled into his front seat, all four of us. He was an honest, road-worn man and his girlfriend was a pure Navajo. She and Libby crammed in side by side in the center and hit it right off. We shared as couples that our relationships with family had gotten off to equally, rocky starts. His parents weren't so sure about his girlfriend and neither were her parents about him. We kind of knew how troubling that could be. They were on their way back to the reservation from his home in Kentucky. They were drinking home-stilled white lightening and offered us some. It was mixed with cola in a small thermos and though I took a small sip, I realized my stomach wasn't in need of such. I thanked them for their generous sharing. Libby and the Navajo gal got along like long lost friends and imbibed well into the afternoon as we drove.

As we topped out on Wolf Creek Pass, Libby recognized that she'd been there before. She'd driven through there the previous January after her stint teaching Navajo kids on the res at Chinle. She said it looked a lot different because back then the snow was ten feet high on each side of the highway. Her communion with the young Navajo continued as the beautiful young woman removed a ring from her finger and gave it to Libby explaining that her grandmother had given it to her. She went on that it had been in her family for many distant generations. It was shaped like a large exclamation point. Its centerpiece was a dark green mineral, kind of like turquoise but much, much darker. The stones were large and were held in place by pure silver that eventually rounded about a finger setting. Embedded in the silver work were four distinct buttons. The young Navajo explained that each button was actually a teardrop. They signified courage, strength, kindness. and understanding. She said the ring bearer would find all these characteristics, but that the last, understanding, was the hardest to achieve.

Given all that her people had endured through centuries of persecution we could well appreciate why "understanding" would be the most difficult attribute to attain. We saw her gift as a priceless one.

A short ride west of Wolf Creek they turned south for the reservation so we bid them a thankful farewell on our continued direction west.

Evening came upon us and we settled to camp alongside a gentle, flowing stream beneath a stand of cottonwood trees. It had been another great day and my stomach and I were again finally at peace with each other, just as I'd been told would happen by our Native American friend at dawn of the previous morning.

The San Juan Mountains of the southern Rockies offered few opportunities at passage and by midmorning the next day we found ourselves back in Durango to have completed an enormous, long, painful, and strange loop in our travel. Libby was playing the flute, practicing a beautiful rendition of "Greensleeves" as I rolled up our gear. The mountains in their sheer magnificence also offered protection, endless clear waters, and a strengthening of the soul. We had little choice but to retreat north to their heart. All directions were known and so, just as the wind can blow the faithful at heart, we let faith carry us north.

By noon we'd reached the old mining town of Silverton. A newer, light-duty pickup pulled to a stop as we headed deeper into the mountains. Our driver was a young man just a few years older than us. He knew a lot about the mountains and as we drove we fell privy to his wealth of knowledge. He worked for a government-funded wildlife type of agency of sorts. He said that he was a researcher and that he was paid to drive all around the mountains and hike and fish and camp and stuff like that. We couldn't believe our ears. He said he had to spend a lot of time above "timberline" as he called it, where the trees stop growing because the air was too thin. He knew a lot about bighorn sheep and had to follow them and study them a lot.

We were shocked to learn from him that there was a disease that he and others were afraid might cause their extinction. He called it "lung worm disease" or something like that. The more he spoke the more we respected him and his efforts to save the bighorn sheep from what sounded like certain fate. We learned that the government provided all of his expenses, meals, gas, and even his little pickup truck. When we learned those details we immediately asked him where and how we could sign up for the same paycheck. He tried his best to explain but it sounded incredibly complicated and without an education, it was clear that we had no chance.

As we drove on with him we were in complete awe at every unfolding vista around each turn. We stared off into the distant valleys and crags and wondered what it must be like to be so far back in there, away from all, the roads, and the people. We knew it had to be spectacular but we also knew that an arduous mountain trek to get there wasn't really possible. Our cash was almost gone and soon we'd be looking for work out of necessity and though I was again well, I was still very weak from our desert loop.

Someday we'll come back here, though, and hike way back into those mountains, I thought.

The mountains finally gave way to a great valley, as did the day give way to afternoon and then evening. At dark we made our way to Delta and at a crossroads we decided to hole up for the night. We planned to head east the following morning into some new country and we really preferred traveling by day so as not to miss a single inch of the ever-changing landscapes. We found an old rodeo arena just north of town within an easy walk from the highway to spend the night and rolled out our bags beneath the cottonwoods.

As we were falling asleep we heard a commotion on the steel bridge several hundred yards to the east. A car had screeched to a stop right on the bridge. Then we heard a car door slam followed by a woman's blood-curdling scream. We could see the shadows of moving bodies going to and fro in the headlights as she screamed on and on. We stood up out of our bags and thought to run over to the bridge, but were afraid because the woman sounded desperate for help. We recalled our first pass through Delta when Libby rode in the cab with the woman that had huge knife scars across her face and arms. We watched and listened carefully as shadows spun about in the night to her screams.

In less than a minute another car, then another pulled to a stop on the bridge. Car doors opened and more shadows scurried about in the night. Then as quickly as they appeared we heard car doors slam and they all sped off at racing speed. In a moment, it was again quiet and we sat back down on our packs. We never really learned what the ruckus was all about, but hoped it was just a domestic flare by those that had perhaps had a little too much to drink. We hugged each other and vowed to never even imagine that discourse in our future. We turned in again and were soon asleep.

It was a short walk the next morning to the main street cafe from the old rodeo grounds and we were feeling a little guilty about being bystanders to the screams of someone in desperate need the night before. When sitting down to a breakfast of eggs and coffee, we asked our waitress about the commotion on the bridge the previous evening to learn that the news had already gone through town. Apparently a woman known about town for being a regular bar patron had gone out of control again. Our waitress and another knew her by name. They made it sound as though it was another normal night out for her as they laughingly each drew on their cigarettes. We were relieved to know that all had ended well the night before.

We finished our breakfast and returned to the two-lane highway east. As we walked, we passed a motorcycle shop. *How fun would it be to own a bike or two? It would kind of have the adventure of hitchhiking but without the wait to constantly test one's patience.* We really enjoyed the unpredictability of our travels, but knew well that soon the lack of money and the coming of fall would narrow our choices. The dream of traveling by motorcycle would have to wait.

Our day's travel was led by curiosity because the road east headed toward some new mountains. We'd gotten a few short rides back to back and around noon we found ourselves walking across a small coal mining town called Somerset. In the heart of town was a small, one-room post office and a kind of bar. We ducked into the bar to get the local read on job prospects.

The bar was dark and had a dank, musty smell masked by that old fragrance of rotting beer and cigarette smoke. I ended up in conversation with the owner as Libby shot a rack of pool. Midway through our conversation another patron joined in with an attentive ear. We talked much about the local area. As it turned out mining was the be all and end all of the tiny town. There was no other employment. We learned too that the hills were teaming with game. Elk and deer mostly but ample bear, sheep, and even goats could be had within a short drive from town. The land didn't seem typical of what I always figured elk and deer habitat would be but the bar owner and the other guy were enthusiastic about the abundance of local game.

It sounded like getting a mining job wasn't easy and you almost had to know somebody to get your foot in the door. A short, pudgy fellow listening in on my conversation with the bar owner turned out to be a coal miner. He said that the money was good as a miner but it was a tough lifestyle. I could see in his eye that he had undisclosed intention as he invited us to his house to learn more about Somerset. Libby had finished her game of pool and so the three of us walked less than a block to his little coal house. His was a cookie cutter Victorian house, cute in all respects except that it was less than ten feet from the two-lane highway that cut straight through the heart of the little town. Everything in Somerset, including his house, was covered with a light dusting of fine, black coal.

He sat us down in his living room and offered us a beer. He was a friendly fellow we could tell but he soon changed the subject from coal mining to another means of making wealth. We listened with full, undivided attention as he rambled on and on about a side business he was starting called "Amway." We watched in utter fascination as he drew circles then more circles on a piece of paper.

We both really struggled to follow his rationale but we were hooked the moment he drew a circle, pointed to it with his pen and said, "This is you!" Then he said, "Once you go direct you'll have a monthly paycheck for the rest of your life." Then he started to show us pictures of folks that had gone direct, some in as little as a few weeks.

We looked at each other dumbfounded. We had no clue just where the money would come from but he said it was completely legal and that we could do "it" too. We struggled so hard to understand just exactly what "it" was. We learned that "it" had something to do with soap. Time and time again he explained how "it" worked. But "it" made absolutely no sense whatsoever to either of us. After an hour or so of presentation the coal miner made a phone call to his Amway boss. Minutes later we were in his car headed once again for Grand Junction, the opposite direction of our day's intended path.

Grand Junction was a two-hour drive from Somerset and the coal miner had changed into his Sunday best before we left his house. As we drove there was no chance of changing the subject, as he was clearly obsessed with his Amway business. He talked on and on and I started feeling stupid because I couldn't understand "it" despite his persistent efforts. Except for knowing that within a few days we'd be raking in money hand over fist, we'd have walked away right then and there. Our stupidity was so obvious. I felt almost like I was back in trigonometry class. We had talked about it before and Libby and I both swore that trig was a conspiracy. Even though we studied trig in high school several states apart, we remembered how the teacher and the two kids clear in the back of the class understood it completely. To them it all made perfect sense. But everybody else in the class looked at each other scratching their heads wondering just how it was that the teacher and two pupils in the back of class had cooked up such an elaborate scheme. We really wanted to understand but the more we learned the more befuddled we got.

As we drove on I started to daydream back to when I was a kid and my mom got into something similar back east. Back then they called it Shaklee instead of Amway. I knew little about it back then but it had all the makings of the same kind of ordeal. I remembered how they advertised that you could drink their brand name. Now why you or anybody else would want to drink a glass of basic H is beyond me except to say that you could drink it. Maybe it was the same kind of motivation that drove the goofy neighbor kids to down night crawlers on the school bus.

Then I remembered how Shaklee had branched out to a more diversified product line. One time the sales rep, who was dealing to my mom, got busted by the cops for handing out some kind of protein pills to the other little kids on our block. Apparently, one of the parents in the neighborhood was afraid he was peddling LSD or something to the kids on their bikes and tricycles. He spent the night in jail I remembered.

Yeah, maybe we'd better be a little careful, I thought as we pulled into a residential community in Grand Junction. I could see our new friend was desperate to get something going that would get him out of the mine once and for all. Perhaps the motivation was the same for my mom, to feed five hungry mouths. *Yeah, these are all good folks trying to find another way,* I concluded.

We climbed up a staircase to a condominium to meet our coal miner's dealer who too wore spiffy Sunday clothes. We sat down in his living room to talk about money and dreams and such. Then he started in again with those damned circles on paper and promises of never-ending, monthly income. When he finished the first segment of his spiel we walked outside to view the setting western sky from the balcony. That Amway thing had taken up an entire day and we were no closer to understanding "it" then than we were at two o'clock. There was another young man there who was a bit further into his indoctrination. I asked him if he got "it." He kind of looked at me with a smile.

"I guess so. My weekend plans fell through anyway," he explained.

I asked him what else he had planned. He said that he and some friends were originally going to the Telluride Jazz Festival for the weekend but it didn't work out. He said that if we wanted his tickets, we could have them for free. He opened his wallet and handed me two concert tickets.

"Are you sure?" I said as I took the two tickets in hand.

"No, you guys go right ahead," he said. "Chic Corea is playing tomorrow night. It should be one heck of a show," he added with a smile.

We immediately walked over to our new, pudgy, coal miner friend and told him that we'd think his offer over for a few days, but that we were going to head back up to Telluride for the jazz festival. His subtle disappointment was broken with a grin and moments later we were strapping on our packs headed south for Telluride, just we two. Well into the night we hopped out of a truck somewhere between Delta and Montrose to sleep just off-road a stretch.

The next morning was a sunny one. The crisp air and blue skies gave way to the San Juan and San Miguel mountains to the south. They were our destination for the day. We'd never been to Telluride, which was a refurbished old mining town. The ski industry had settled into Telluride and was doing well. We were excited about the day's events and perhaps again being among a large crowd was enticing, though we'd long ago resigned to ever again seeing a single familiar face.

The previous day's business affairs and the whole Amway deal kind of took us out of Gene's plan and our honeymoon mode. We'd let the need for money and its temptation lead us astray. But somehow on that morning we got right back on track in a round about way. We'd done a lot of double back traveling in the previous couple of days, especially since completing the great desert loop. In a way it seemed that something was there for us that either we'd not yet found or perhaps hadn't yet found us. We had a sense of closing in on something and running out of money perhaps heightened the senses.

The light changed in the Rockies in late August. The skies turned an even deeper blue. The clouds took on a different light and the light of day itself was different. The color of landscape and sky became much more pronounced in anticipation of the glory of fall which was just weeks away. Even the wildlife changed in hue and character. The deer started rubbing out and changed from red to buckskin, seemingly overnight. The light changed the character of the mountains too. They seemed to get even taller and their valleys, deeper and greener. The San Juan and San Miguel mountains were not so inviting and as we got closer we could see they warned of their unrelenting might as snow from the previous winter was still captured in their secluded, north-facing recesses. We could see that it'd soon be winter up there and new snows were due at any time.

The hitchhiking slowed at a crossroad. We decided that our packs were somewhat intimidating so we ditched them for the day in a willow thicket just off-road on our way. That gave the day a known measure of completion; that we'd have to return to our packs before the day was over, so we agreed. Telluride was yet an hour's drive so we rustled up a few things from our packs and hit the two-lane to catch a ride.

As only fate would have it, our ride to the jazz festival came in the way of a long, black Packard hearse. Its driver was a Dead Head hippie-throwback guy who laughingly let us ride clear in the back where countless corpses had been escorted to their graves. In all its creepiness, it seemed right. Our would-be undertaker drove us right to the concert grounds where we hopped out to join the mass assemblage of others. Music was already playing in the background and from our vantage we could hear a great echoing as the sound bounced off mountains in all directions. As we neared the stage the sound became more direct as did our attention. It was an entire day of music in the mountains. A number of bands were slated to play through the day. Stan Getz was to warm up the stage at dusk and Chic Corea with Gary Burton were set to close. There was no way that we were going to leave before the music ended that entire day.

By mid-afternoon, we were pretty darn hungry. The town of Telluride was just a hitchhike from the concert grounds but we didn't want to miss any of the music. We found a hot dog vendor at the concert. His little two-wheeled hot dog cart was the only concession among the ten thousand or so concert goers so we bought two hot dogs for a buck each. Then in sheer amazement, we watched that single hot dog guy with his little hot dog cart plop a dog in a bun, one after another, as fast as he could to an endless congregation of hungry patrons, each for a buck. He had almost a stressed and concerned look on his face because he was making money. He was making a lot of money. As fast as he could drop a dog in a bun, he was turning a buck. He didn't even mess with ketchup or mustard; that was the buyer's problem. We started to do the math and figured out that in five minutes, that guy's bottom line would be limited only by the number of hot dogs he could wheel around in his little cart. He'd clear enough money in one weekend from folks like us to travel for many, many months by thumb. Just the thought of his simple little entrepreneurial ingenuity put a smile on our faces. We sensed that the crowd of hungry gatherers knew the same and willingly honored his cornering of the market.

Stan Getz took the stage that evening before sunset. His was a brand of jazz that neither of us had ever heard live. Stan Getz was superb. He was one with his tenor sax, which was an extension of himself, almost as if it had blood vessels. Every now and again he'd step out of the music for a piano lead or drum solo. He'd light up a smoke and look on and listen, waiting for an entry to rejoin the mix. No words can really describe his brand of music. It was really without brand entirely, all encompassing and without boundary. He played with a gifted anonymous pianist, at least so he was to us. Between the two, in fact the entire quartet presented a seamless continuum of music from origins unknown.

Then Chic Corea and Gary Burton bounced improvisations back and forth, from the piano to vibraphone under a clear, starry Rocky Mountain night sky until shortly before midnight, including several encores. We were convinced that Chic Corea's music was virtually indescribable and just simply had to be heard.

It was easy to catch a ride out of Telluride in the mass exodus that followed but we didn't find our packs again until the wee hours. We weren't accustomed to staying up so late, but were happily exhausted and rolled out our bags right there, roadside in the willow thicket for the rest of a short night.

For the first time in weeks, we overslept. We were even slow to roll up our bags. I sat on my pack for the longest time just thinking things over. The concert was so much fun and the music so inspiring. The mountains off to the east were unlike the San Juan Mountains to the west. They were rock-rimmed, flat-top mountains full of cracks, crags, and valleys of their own. I so wanted to just walk into them and disappear. All of the southern Rockies beckoned the soul to abandon the self. The thought of venturing off into them was as exciting as it was fearful.

As I pondered on, Libby started to stir and eventually her bag flipped open. She sat up and gave me a direct and tired smile. Then she flopped back down and pulled the bag back over her head. Moments later, I rolled up for us both as she brushed out her lovely, long brunette hair. It was no earlier than noon by the time we stuck out our first thumb of the day.

We settled on a path back toward Delta, which was only an hour north, but on that day we'd never make it. The first ride put us on the edge of Montrose, which meant a long hike across town. We tried to avoid hitchhiking through towns unless they were either incredibly small or metropolitan. Montrose was the size that meant a three or four mile hike just to reach the north end of town. We walked side-by-side on our way. We kind of knew Montrose because, unlike all the other towns on our journey, that day would mark the fourth time we'd passed through the quaint western town. One way or another and for one reason or another, our trek kept leading us through Montrose. We gave it little thought at the time, but life can unknowingly find one at a predestined place and time.

We came upon a Dairy Queen restaurant just a few blocks before the town's main street. We were tired and hungry so we went inside to grab a bite of food. Libby kind of lost her appetite and nothing really grabbed my fancy on the menu so we headed right back out having had nothing to eat. We were tired from the walk and had another mile or two to get out of town. The traffic was slow and we were tired so we chose to try to hitchhike across town. We dropped our packs and talked on with our thumbs out in abandon to the scant traffic passing by. Our conversation was broken by the sound of a voice coming from a small green sedan that had just pulled up in front of us. The voice was masculine, recognizable, and the driver spoke directly to us in a clearly familiar, sarcastic, and almost rude tone.

"Hey, you dirty hippies! Wanna ride?'

Libby and I looked to each other with mirrored, astonished frowns. No one had ever spoken to us like that before. With thumbs still out we turned our heads and looked down to see the grand smiling face of Mack, the bank robber guy we first met in Montana almost three months earlier! He was at first only faintly recognizable through mirrored sunglasses and a red bandana. His hair was longer and not recently barbered. But make no mistake it was Mack James in full flesh and blood.

Libby and I looked back to each other in absolute disbelief with our thumbs still out in frozen suspension. Time stood still in that moment.

Now mind you that until that day we'd seen few faces twice, that of Moon Bear and C.J. McMurphy on the coast. And of all the folks that we'd met on the road, Mack's face was, without question, the one face that we'd hoped we'd never, ever see again. But there he was, half smiling at a full stop, engine idling with his windows down just a few feet from us. We could not believe our eyes. We were so delighted to finally see a face, any face of anyone that we once knew that any notion of fear vanished into thin air on the spot. We realized that he was someone from our past, someone we could talk to that already knew us, someone with whom we could share our stories, someone familiar.

"Well, don't just stand there, get in the car," he said.

We never even gave it a single moment's thought. We immediately ran over to the passenger side, threw our packs in the back seat, and jumped right in the front seat. Libby hugged him in full embrace and we laughed uncontrollably, we three. I slapped my knees and dashboard as Mack squealed the car around in an illegal U-turn. We weren't real sure what we were in for and didn't really care much because finally sharing all of our experiences with someone from our past was so joyously liberating. It was a grand reunion.

We raced a few blocks south when Mack pulled up to a small mobile home. As Mack walked into the trailer he said out loud to others who were already inside, "Hey, you guys? Remember me telling you about Libby and John, the guys I met up with in Montana a while back? Well here they are!" he said in a grand introduction. We walked into the trailer to an exciting and warm reception from folks who already knew a whole lot about us. It was like coming home.

There were three other people in the trailer, two women and one other man. All stood up and came walking over to us with handshakes and smiles that soon turned into hugs and laughter. Mack made a few introductions. The shorter of the two women was Mack's wife, Claire. She was all of a sudden like a kid sister to us. The other woman was tall, brunette, and strikingly beautiful. She was Mack's true sister, Rebecca.

The other man was in his early forties. He was a shorter, muscular man who was balding with dark hair. He wore a grand smile as he shook my hand and patted me on the back over and over again. His name was Dave. As it turned out Dave was Claire's blood father, Mack's father in-law. Dave was married to Rebecca, Mack's blood sister, despite their obvious age difference. It took us a while to make all the connections to realize that Mack's wife's father was married to his sister.

The atmosphere had the feel of a family reunion to which we were also somehow related. The girls went right for the thousand questions and they and Libby hit it off immediately. They knew all about our honeymoon and how Libby played the flute. They knew that we were both from back east where we'd dropped out of school and worked in a factory on the graveyard shift. The amount of detail they knew was startling.

It was clear to us that not only had Mack made an unforgettable first impression on us, but so had we on him.

In no time, we were invited to stay the night to share warmth and joy as company. The afternoon turned into evening and Dave prepared a barbecue while the women made side dishes and dessert. All the while, Mack basically listened in curious fascination. He was clearly unlike his relatives in that he was a quiet man of few words. His wife, sister, and father-in-law/brother-in-law all knew well of Mack's ways but were complacently accepting of them. The three all had jobs and were law-abiding folks in every respect though Mack's affairs were his and no one really seemed at all concerned about them. And so we just left it at that and enjoyed their invitation to eat, laugh, and embrace the night at their trailer. Mack's affairs aside, they were a completely normal, fun, and richly connected family.

We slept late the next morning and everything was hunky dory. As we sat there on our bags on the living room floor we talked in pure amazement as to where we'd landed for the night's rest. Mack soon came in the front door and found us stirring to wake. He offered us some hot coffee, which we gladly sipped right on the floor of their living room. He joined us on the floor and we sat and talked. We asked him what had ever become of his white Dodge tradesman van. He gave it away to a guy in a hurry. He said that he'd found himself in a situation that had gotten "tight" as he put it. He just gave it to an acquaintance, as he had to quickly get out of town.

The more we talked, the more we learned that Mack's life was a strange one. He spared us most of the specifics and stayed in the broader field of his conversation. How he'd picked up his green car and motorcycle was unclear except that they were both stolen vehicles. Mack was an admitted thief and showed no remorse whatsoever. We talked long about life and people. We were so glad for him, that he had loved ones around him. Claire, Rebecca, and Dave had all left for work. They'd not lived in Montrose very long and it wasn't clear that they had intentions of staying there. Amazingly, they functioned well as a family, setting aside, of course, Mack's ways.

As we talked on, Libby and I shared the sentiment that not going to the cops about Mack the first time was the right choice. We had no interest to intentionally or consciously hurt him or his family. Mack on two occasions, separated by many months and perhaps ten thousand miles, had stopped to help us. In a distorted conscientious rationale of mind, to rat him out would've been an act of pure betrayal. He not once ever caused us any harm.

Besides, we were certain that going to the cops would surely mean that we'd go to jail as well. We'd become more afraid of cops than of Mack. The thought of his incarceration would be so devastating to his family. No, Mack and his ways we knew, but his secret was safe with us. We willingly made repeated, subtle attempts to change him because we were worried about him. We couldn't bear the thought of him behind bars, which seemed inevitable to us and in a sense it more enabled his defiant determination. It almost seemed like our heartfelt interest was alluring to him. Make no mistake, we were worried about Mack and feared for him and anyone who would accidentally or intentionally stand in his path.

Mack clearly enjoyed our company and talked us into spending some time with him. He said that Claire had the next couple of days off and invited us to join them, to go camping at a very beautiful and remote valley in the mountains. We wouldn't decline his offer a second time as we had let fear prevail before. After all, we'd been yearning to get off road and see the heart of the mountains for quite some time. *Fine,* we thought. *We are going to go camping with Mack and his wife. What the hell?*

We needed to stock up on food for the two days in camp and so Mack, Libby, and I went shopping at a grocery store.

We grabbed a cart and Mack said, "What are you doing?"

We said we were going to get some groceries. He said, "No, you shop like this. Watch me." He walked up one aisle then down another. When he saw something he wanted he'd just pick it off the shelf and put it in his pocket. Then he'd grab something else and put it in another. When his pockets were full he started to just stuff his coat with any and all food or merchandise he wanted. When he couldn't fit one more item, he'd just casually walk out the door to his car without paying one, red cent. If that weren't enough, he then walked right straight back in and loaded up again and again until he'd apparently gotten his fill.

Needless to say within minutes we'd completely disassociated with him as we walked around the store with our shopping cart looking for bargains that could fit our ever shrinking budget of a few dollars. Mack knew well how to take advantage of people's good will. We paid for our meager cart of groceries and met him at his little, green car.

Mack said, "You guys should never, ever pay for food. You don't have to," he said with total abandon of guilt or conscience.

We decided to go for pizza. The Pizza Hut was busy with lunch patrons. We sat down and the waitress came to take our orders. The deal was that for so much you could order a pizza and a soft drink but the salad bar was extra. We had so little money that our share of the pizza and soft drink deal was all we could afford. Mack passed on the salad bar too. The waitress finished taking our order and soon after returned with our soft drinks.

No sooner had the waitress left when Mack looked to us and said, "Now, let's go get our salads."

"But, we passed on the salad bar Mack," Libby explained.

"I know, but let's just go get one anyway," he said as he tipped his head back over his shoulder in the direction of the salad bar. He got up from the table and walked over to the salad bar nonchalant and fixed himself a heaping salad with all the fixins. He returned to our table and said, "Go ahead, they'll never know the difference."

It was obvious that given any rule, Mack was driven to break it. We shared the pizza and settled up on a bill that showed they'd not charged Mack for his salad bar portion.

Leaving the restaurant, Mack took us back to the trailer waiting for Claire's return from work. He left to pick her up. Libby and I talked in private about Mack and his family. At our first meeting in Montana, it seemed to us that Mack had entered our life for a reason unknown. The same great Hand it seemed had led us, two destitute and homeless types, once again into Mack's life. We were determined to go to the mountains to share with him our worthlessness. We felt somewhat driven to save Mack from his own ways, which we knew would only further enable him.

Mack and Claire soon returned home and started to prepare for the next two days of camping. We, of course, were packed and ready to go, as always. Rebecca and Dave came home and started to share the events of their day's affairs. Rebecca and Dave were not the camping types and so we four left for the mountains late that afternoon.

Mack said that we were headed for a mountain range called, "The Uncompahgre." None of us knew what the word actually meant though it probably had a Native American translation. We drove deeper and deeper into the mountains near a place called Owl Creek Pass. We were conscious that we'd have to rely on Mack to drive us back to the paved road, but didn't really give it a second thought because we were no longer afraid of him. Perhaps ten miles from the paved road we found a camp in a spectacular meadow beside a creek, Owl Creek. The mountains in all their majesty towered in every direction. Massive and old spruce trees surrounded our camp.

In no time at all, our tent was up and ready. Mack and Claire weren't nearly as rehearsed in pitching their tent and we looked on as they fumbled through it. Eventually, theirs was up as well and we already had a small fire started. By dusk we'd settled into our camp to enjoy the evening and each other's company. We showed them how we cooked right out of the can. Mack preferred to cook out of a skillet with utensils and the like. We talked long into dusk, then dark, and settled into our tents and bags for a peaceful night's sleep.

The next morning was glorious. We felt so much at home in our tent and waking in a camp tucked into the great shoulders of the Uncompahgre Mountains felt, well...right. Mack rekindled the fire then went fishing in the creek. Claire and Libby set out on a hike and I decided to do the same. I chose a course that went straight uphill from camp. I was surprised how fast I gained elevation and soon found myself in the midst of a steep stand of small aspen trees where a couple of well-used game trails traversed the grove. I continued uphill until the trees and slope met vertical rock that rimmed to the sky. I could see that the game had to follow my very course to the rim rock. My only possible choices were to turn north or south or to retreat downhill to camp because the rim rock posed a barrier for many miles. The view to the southwest was ominous and so I wanted to gain higher ground to achieve a three hundred-and-sixty-degree view, but the rim rock denied me. I chose to sit and rest a while, to catch my breath in the quiet and still of morning. My breathing slowed and my heart's pounding resumed a normal rate.

I sat wondering how Libby was doing on her hike. *This must surely be a welcome break from the road for her too,* I thought. I could hear the creek roaring in the deep and distant valley below me and was curious as to how Mack's fishing was going. Soon I found myself not thinking at all. My busy mind just settled for the peace and beauty of the moment itself.

Movement in the foreground caught my eye and less than twenty yards away, a doe and two fawns stepped into clear view. They'd chosen the same uphill path and were unaware of my presence. I watched motionless as they stepped and fed and sniffed and looked about. The fawns were reliant on their mother's keen and wary senses. *Just a wink of an eye would send them off in a scurry,* I thought as they came ever closer. As quickly as they'd appeared, they wandered off into the forest never aware of my being there too. I sat motionless for another ten minutes or so not wanting to spook them, as the morning was theirs. I headed back to camp straight downhill from my vantage point.

Mack had returned to camp within minutes of my return and had caught a couple of small trout on flies. The women were gone still so we sat around and talked a bit. Then he invited me to join him shooting his pistols. We stepped off to a large, flat rock and pounded away at cans we'd placed on a dirt embankment. We traded pistols back and forth and threw lead until our ears rang.

As the last shot reported a fading distant echo, Mack holstered both pieces. We sat for a moment in silence to again hear only the rush of the creek and the great silence of mountain air.

Mack broke the silence with a question. "Do you remember me telling you about that restaurant in Salt Lake?" he asked.

I squinted my eyes and looked somewhat toward him and down a bit. I drew a blank to his question but didn't want him to know. I could tell that he was referring to a heist he'd apparently divulged to us on our first encounter in Montana. I still didn't want him to know that we had been scared witless then. Though I nodded my head up and down, I had no clue whatsoever as to what he was talking about.

"Yeah, how did that go?" I asked.

"No," he said. "I'm going to pull that one off this week. I'm going in through the roof. Then I'm gonna walk straight out the front door. All you have to do is drive away when I come out," he explained. "You guys could make enough money in one night to travel for years," he offered. "There isn't gonna be any shooting at all. This one's a gimme," he assured.

I could not believe my ears. Gene's plan was all but tapped out. It would soon be winter. We had no home, no jobs, no skills, no education, and very little money. We were sick and tired of being sick and tired. We were nothing. We had nothing. We knew nothing, and Mack and I both knew it. I sat with my elbow to my knee and my fist to my chin as though considering his most generous and illegal offer. Then a smile broke my thoughtful expression. We'd traversed the Continental Divide for three months and ten thousand miles, literally by foot and by day, searching for some pipe dream at the foot of some unknown mountain. And as fate would have it, we never found the mountain. All we found was what we dreaded most, Mack.

My head started to wobble left and right, then up and down, then around and around as I raised both of my hands, palms out in resignation. My resignation was not to Mack, but to the spirits of all my ancestors who stood and hovered about in all directions of the moment in witness to my answer.

"No, Mack. There is absolutely no way in hell that I am going to do that," I said in firm and final tone as I looked straight at him.

At first he wouldn't make eye contact and continued to stare off. Then he turned to me with a confused look on his face. "What is your problem? I said there'd be no shooting. I'm offering you guys enough cash to get you to Europe if you want. You could live like kings. And all you have to do is just drive away. What is so difficult about that?" His tone was belittling, almost daring, but it wouldn't work on me.

"You know, Mack, if I ever did anything like that, my grandfather would roll over in his grave. His father, my great-grandfather, and all my ancestors would look down upon me with shame. That's just not something I'm willing to do."

Mack's tone of voice changed to one of almost caring. "Look at you," he said. "You have nothing. You are nothing. What are you going to do with yourself?" he asked without rhetoric.

"I don't know, Mack," I said. "But, I'm not gonna rob anybody. That's for sure."

"What is it that you're looking for? You can't seriously go on like this," he said.

In a strange way I could see in him that his offer was a genuine gesture to help us, but I'd broken through to gain the upper hand with him. I felt that I was on higher ground and could share with him that there was a whole lot more to life than money and material possessions. I struggled through words to explain that surely there must still be a means to a life rich beyond measure.

"You know, Mack, thanks for your offer and I may regret this choice forever, but my needs are simple. All I'm looking for is an honest job, one that can put a roof over our heads and a meal or two on the table. I don't need a lot of money. If I can get a day off once and a while, that'd be great. And if I can get a weekend off, well, that'd be even better. I'd like to have Saturday and Sunday off, just like everybody else. And if I could even get a holiday off once and a great while, well...that's what I'm looking for. I don't know if it's out there anymore. But I don't care, that's what I want. That's what I'm looking for." My voice was humble, straight, soft, and unwavering.

Mack sensed my determination and compassion. "Well, you're gonna miss out on one hell of a deal," he finished.

"Maybe so, but that's just how you and I are a little different," I closed.

Libby and Claire had returned to camp. "What was all the shooting about?" Libby asked.

"We were just target shooting," I reassured her. "How was your walk?" I asked.

"Oh, this place is so beautiful, John. I wish we could just stay here forever," she said with a sigh.

I spared her the details of my conversation with Mack for the moment and told her that it was time we rolled up and headed out. I was prepared to walk the long trek to the highway but Mack offered us a ride instead. Claire stayed behind at camp to rest.

We arrived at the paved road late that afternoon. We pulled our packs out of Mack's trunk and shook hands roadside. Libby gave him a great hug and we bid each other genuine farewells as we started our pace north again.

As we walked, we talked and I filled Libby in on the details of the day. We laughed and talked as we walked. Our reuniting with Mack was beyond our belief. He was the one person we'd hoped we would never again see. But his was the *only* path that we'd again crossed. In that was a message and we knew it. We'd never again turn from fear and forever we forgot any notion of coincidence. There was a great One watching our every move and setting before us choices. Faith in Him and in ourselves to make the right choice wasn't always easy or obvious, but we always eventually resigned to our faith.

So many spend sometimes an entire life striving for something that was not to be theirs in the first place, we figured.

We'd become well practiced at following our hearts. The "want" for something can so tempt a person to pursue something that is just on the other side of God's great hand. His hand comes down before us from time to time because that "want" is not ours for the having. The faithful recognize the denial and change course. Along the way of a new course His hand again comes down, to put you back on your path, if only you have the faith and will to do so. Time after time, that was the experience of our summer's honeymoon. God's great hand had led us to that day and that moment of choice with Mack.

We knew it and we felt fulfilled. We'd forever try to live a freely faithful life thereafter, we agreed. Each and every time His hand should come down before us we'd give way to His direction. We were forever enlightened on that day and with practice our walk of faith would become less like a segmented walk through life but more like a dandelion seed gently traveling on the wind. We went to sleep that night on a ditch bank feeling renewed and fully conscious of His love and His day's blessing.

The adobe buttes which surround the town of Delta are so unique. We'd grown accustomed to their grandeur inasmuch as we'd traversed them almost a half-dozen times en route here and there before again crossing paths with Mack. It seemed only fitting to peer out to the buttes in a sunrise blaze once more from the warmth and safety of our sleeping bags. The stretch and rise of the morning sun held promise that it'd be another wondrous day for us. Libby was slow to stir and so I found the time to reflect on things. The ditch water was moving slowly and I was surprised how clear it was for being an irrigation ditch. It made no sound as it gently flowed past. We could've stumbled right into it the night before. The traffic was occasional at best. The sound of tires on asphalt by a passing car was so familiar. Far off to the west, I could hear a back-up beeper going off, time and time again, probably from a bulldozer or loader doing earthwork.

I was anxious to move out and Libby reluctantly obliged as she rose from her bag. We rolled up and walked straight into the day. We had to walk across town to the north, which was a physical start to the day and at the north end of town we reached a familiar crossroad of decision. Again our paths were either north or east. North meant Grand Junction and west meant Somerset and Amway. We recalled that we never, ever reached the distant mountains east on our first attempt and so we decided on Somerset. Hitchhiking was slow on that day and short rides seemed to be du jour. We planned that we wouldn't take a ride to Somerset if one were offered, waiting instead for one that was destined further. We really didn't want to go the Amway route. Somerset was so small, maybe a hundred people at best, and so the odds of landing again in Somerset were slim to none anyway.

Ride by ride, we found ourselves just outside of Paonia when an older white Ford van pulled up to a stop. A middle-aged, bearded fellow and his girlfriend gave us a lift. They were headed to a town called Carbondale, which would get us through Somerset for certain. We made small talk with them both as we sat on the floor of the van, centered and just behind their bucket seats. The road started to wind and the van had a bit of rumble to it, which made talking a little awkward.

As we rounded the curves of the western shore of a reservoir, the turning landscapes out of the van's windshield soon commanded the focus of all our attention. We stood up and palmed the bucket seats for balance to take in a closer full view of the mountain ranges and their incredible scenic beauty. We'd traveled far and wide, across the Rockies, north to south, and had never seen such massive terrain. The mountains were a masterpiece of creation in all respects. The driver was somewhat familiar with the area, but we couldn't really discern his accounts from the noise. The mountains called for our focused and undivided attention.

We climbed an aspen-cloaked pass to drop over and down into another valley of breathtaking dimension. There were mountains and valleys in all directions that climbed through timber and rock to the sky. Deep below was a river that carried away a crystal clear drainage. In all of our travels we'd never seen country that was so distinctly spectacular. Some of the trees were clearly beginning to turn gold with fall color.

We were captive with a strange, ironic sense of familiarity, almost like we knew the place, but we'd never been there before. Turn after turn, we drove and around each turn was another sweeping landscape or massive geologic feature. The road eventually dropped down and paralleled the winding river. The water in the river was absolutely crystal clear.

Finally, the road unfolded to a tremendous open valley, green with fertile pastures and fat livestock. It was early afternoon when the driver let us out at a tee in the road at Carbondale. One direction went to Aspen and so we chose the alternate course to avoid the tourist crowd. We hopped out of the van fully invigorated with the great ride we'd just had. We thanked them both for their kindness and again for such a great ride.

The driver said, "Hey, no sweat and good luck to you two." I slid the cargo door of the van closed and as they drove off, it was almost as if a theatre curtain had drawn open. Before us, as we stood facing south, was the great mountain we'd been searching for all summer.

I took a gasp and with my mouth and eyes wide open, Libby asked, "What is it, John?"

"That's it!" I exclaimed. "That's the one!" I shouted while pointing at the grand mountain with my arm outstretched.

"Are you sure?" she asked.

In less than a moment I assured her that it was without a doubt the mountain I'd seen only once as a youth, from that spring photograph in a color picture book of the Rocky Mountains. Its signature skyline, avalanche chutes and bowls were unmistakable. It had unfolded behind us as we traveled down the river valley. We might have traveled right on past, missing it entirely, had we not stopped at that intersection. We could not believe our eyes. We jumped up and down in circles while holding hands, laughing, then crying, then laughing again.

"We found it, Libby! We found it! I can't believe it, but we found it," I said in exhaustion, joy, and elation.

Our happiness fell to love as we melted into each other's arms in hugs and kisses and more hugs. Our heads slumped onto our shoulders and we fell onto our packs in a seated, full embrace. We stopped traveling in that moment of closure and success.

The sound of busy traffic brought us out of our trance.

"We should try to make a go of things here, somewhere, somehow," I suggested. We were tired of the road, but just integrating back into a community was daunting. We knew that winter would soon be upon us; that alone required immediate, energetic preparation. We agreed that we'd give the grand valley a fair shot. We had no clue how to proceed or what to do but standing roadside was limited in opportunity.

A new white Chevy Blazer made a U-turn right in front of us. It was one of those great big Blazers. Two bearded guys were in each of the bucket seats.

"You guys want a ride?" the passenger asked.

"Sure nuff," Libby replied.

As we started to roll down the road, she asked them, "Where are you guys going?"

The passenger said, "Well, we don't really know. We *were* headed up to Aspen for the night but saw you two standing there. Something came over us and we decided 'Screw Aspen. Let's flip around and go give those guys a ride instead.'"

Their U-turn made me cautious. That almost always meant trouble of some sort.

"The hell you say," Libby bounced, bringing smiles to all our faces. "Then the first round's on us," she declared.

Minutes later we pulled into a modernized western town. We parked the Blazer and stumbled into an old western bar. The bar sign out front was a great big six-shooter hog leg that said, "Doc Holiday's." We took a seat in a booth that overlooked the busy main street at a bridge that crossed over a grand river. The bar had the look, feel, and smell of the old West. I bellied up to the bar and ordered a round of draft beers, as Libby wished. I opened my wallet to settle up with the bartender. We had fourteen dollars.

The End

1343946

Made in the USA